Human Dignity in the
Judaeo-Christian Tradition

Also available from Bloomsbury

Intellectual, Humanist and Religious Commitment, by Peter Forrest
Skepticism: From Antiquity to the Present,
edited by Diego Machuca and Baron Reed
The Golden Age of Philosophy of Science 1945 to 2000, by John Losee

Human Dignity in the Judaeo-Christian Tradition

Catholic, Orthodox, Anglican and Protestant Perspectives

Edited by
John Loughlin

BLOOMSBURY ACADEMIC
LONDON · NEW YORK · OXFORD · NEW DELHI · SYDNEY

BLOOMSBURY ACADEMIC
Bloomsbury Publishing Plc
50 Bedford Square, London, WC1B 3DP, UK
1385 Broadway, New York, NY 10018, USA
29 Earlsfort Terrace, Dublin 2, Ireland

BLOOMSBURY, BLOOMSBURY ACADEMIC and the Diana logo
are trademarks of Bloomsbury Publishing Plc

First published in Great Britain 2019
Paperback edition first published 2021

Cover design by Maria Rajka
Cover image © Matteo Pugliese "ZENITH", bronze, 125 x 122 x 13 cm

A catalogue record for this book is available from the British Library.

Library of Congress Cataloging-in-Publication Data

Names: Loughlin, John (Emeritus Fellow), editor.
Title: Human dignity in the Judaeo-Christian tradition: Catholic, Orthodox,
Anglican, and Protestant perspectives / edited by John Loughlin.
Description: 1 [edition]. | New York: Bloomsbury Academic, 2019. |
Includes bibliographical references and index.
Identifiers: LCCN 2019004276 (print) | LCCN 2019021826 (ebook) |
ISBN 9781350073708 (epdf) | ISBN 9781350073715 (epub) |
ISBN 9781350073692 (hardback)
Subjects: LCSH: Theological anthropology–Christianity |
Dignity–Religious aspects–Christianity.
Classification: LCC BT701.3 (ebook) | LCC BT701.3.H85 2019 (print) |
DDC 233/.5–dc23
LC record available at https://lccn.loc.gov/2019004276

ISBN: HB: 978-1-3500-7369-2
PB: 978-1-3502-3813-8
ePDF: 978-1-3500-7370-8
eBook: 978-1-3500-7371-5

Typeset by Integra Software Services Pvt. Ltd.

To find out more about our authors and books visit
www.bloomsbury.com and sign up for our newsletters.

Contents

List of Contributors

Dr Miguel Acosta is Associate Professor at CEU University San Pablo and the Institute of Humanities CEU Angel Ayala in Madrid, Spain.

Rev Dr Jonathan Arnold is Dean of Divinity at Magdalen College and teaches at the Faculty of Theology, University of Oxford.

Dr Michael Burdett is Assistant Professor of Christian Theology at the University of Nottingham and a member of the Faculty of Theology and Religion, University of Oxford.

Rev Dr Richard Conrad, OP, is Director of the Aquinas Institute, Blackfriars Hall, and a member of the Faculty of Theology and Religion, University of Oxford.

Professor John Day is Emeritus Fellow of Lady Margaret Hall and Emeritus Professor of Old Testament Studies in the University of Oxford.

Dr Vladimir Latinovic is a member of the Faculty of Catholic Theology at Eberhard Karls University in Tübingen, Germany.

Professor Josef Lössl is Professor of Historical Theology and Intellectual History at the School of History, Archaeology and Religion, Cardiff University.

Professor John Loughlin is a Fellow at Blackfriars Hall, University of Oxford, Emeritus Fellow, St Edmund's College, University of Cambridge, and Emeritus Professor of Politics, Cardiff University.

Dr Calum MacKellar is Director of Research at the Scottish Council on Human Bioethics, Edinburgh, and Visiting Lecturer in bioethics at St Mary's University, Twickenham in London.

Professor John Milbank is Emeritus Professor at the Department of Theology and Religious Studies at the University of Nottingham.

Professor Roger Trigg is Senior Research Fellow at the Ian Ramsey Centre for Science and Religion, Faculty of Theology, University of Oxford, and Emeritus Professor of Philosophy, University of Warwick.

Monsignor Timothy Verdon is Director of the Diocesan Office of Sacred Art and Church Cultural Heritage and also of the Museo dell'Opera del Duomo, Florence, Italy.

Professor John Witte Jr. is Robert W. Woodruff Professor of Law, McDonald Distinguished Professor and Director of the Center for the Study of Law and Religion at Emory University School of Law in Atlanta, Georgia, USA.

Acknowledgements

I would like to thank Niamh Baker-Loughlin for compiling an annotated bibliography on human dignity, Edward Hadas, Rev Dr Richard Finn, OP, and Dr Amy McGrath for reading drafts of parts of the manuscript. Colleen Coalter at Bloomsbury Press was of enormous help both in supporting the original proposal and in encouraging the editor to persevere to the end.

The University of Notre Dame Press has given permission to publish an updated version of John Witte Jr. (2003), 'Between Sanctity and Depravity: Human Dignity in Early Protestant Perspective', in R. P. Kraynak and G. Tinder (eds), *In Defense of Human Dignity: Essays for Our Times*, 119–137, Notre Dame: University of Notre Dame Press, which appears as Chapter 8, 'Human Dignity, Equality and Liberty in Protestant Thought', in this volume.

Introduction

John Loughlin

One of the most remarkable debates among philosophers, ethicists and theologians has been whether the concept of 'human dignity' still has any value as a principle of ethics or as a guide to law and policy. This is, at first sight, surprising, since the notion of human dignity is entrenched in documents such as the UN's Universal Declaration of Human Rights (UDHR) promulgated in 1948 and the German *Basic Law* (Constitution) of 1949, both of which regard 'human dignity' (*Menschenwürde* in German) as the foundation of all rights (McCrudden 2008). Many other conventions and state constitutions have adopted similar measures since then. This use of the dignity concept has been mainly in response to the experiences of the Second World War, that is, the horrors of Nazism, Fascism and the cruelty of the Japanese. The attempted genocide of Jews, Slavs, gypsies and other categories of human beings, particularly the sick and weak, by the Nazis created a special horror, and there was a determination by the victors in 1945 that this should never happen again. Of course, the Allies too were responsible for atrocities such as the 'carpet bombing' of German cities and the dropping of the atomic bombs in Japan. The trampling of human rights and dignity in the Soviet Union is also well known.

This was the background against which the UN Committee was established to draft the UDHR. The committee included members from different religions and philosophical persuasions: Christians of various denominations, a French Jew, a Chinese Confucian as well as atheists and agnostics. The atrocities committed by the Axis Powers and especially by Germany seemed to make it clear as to what constituted violations of human dignity. But it was less clear to the members of the committee as to how the concept of human dignity could be defined positively, that is, what it meant in practice. Therefore, the drafters of the declaration decided that they should not attempt to define 'dignity' with any precision but rather that they should adopt a very general and vague understanding, sometimes called a 'place-holder' concept. The definition of the positive content of human dignity would entail specific ways of understanding human rights. It was thought best to leave that discussion to a later date. As Jacques Maritain, the Catholic philosopher who was deeply involved with the committee, said:

> It is related that at one of the meetings of a UNESCO National Commission where human rights were being discussed, someone expressed astonishment that certain champions of violently opposed ideologies had agreed on a list of these rights. 'Yes' they said, 'we agree on the rights, but on condition that no one asks us why'. That 'why' is where the argument begins. (UNESCO 1948)

In recent years, the argument about 'why' has raged at least among academics, lawyers and human rights activists. Totally contradictory definitions of the meaning of human dignity have been advanced. Some people have dismissed the concept, as we shall see below. There have been attempts to provide greater clarity. In 2012, a conference was held by the British Academy at Rhodes House, Oxford, under the patronage of Baroness Hale, a judge who currently sits on the UK's Supreme Court, and the then Archbishop (now Cardinal) Vincent Nichols, the Archbishop of Westminster and leader of the Roman Catholic Church in England and Wales. The published proceedings of the conference entitled *Understanding Human Dignity*, edited by Professor Christopher McCrudden, comprise thirty-nine chapters in which the concept was explored from several different disciplinary perspectives – historical, theological, philosophical, judicial – as well as its practical applications (McCrudden 2013). The contributors included those who endorsed the concept as well as some of its fiercest critics. Reading through these chapters, one is left with a sense of even greater confusion, despite Professor McCrudden's excellent survey of the current debate in his introduction. Baroness Hale, who, as a judge, is accustomed to finding clear-cut answers to difficult questions, said that she had hoped the book would supply her 'with some answers' (Hale 2013: xvi). She added: 'I cannot say it did', but that, nevertheless, it supplied her with a great deal of information and gave her a lot to think about in ways she could not have imagined. An even broader set of perspectives than that of the McCrudden's volume can be found in the *Cambridge Handbook of Human Dignity*, which comprises sixty-two chapters and covers the historical, conceptual, legal, biological aspects and, usefully, discusses some non-European perspectives (Düwell et al. 2014). These two books provide excellent recent overviews of the human dignity debate but do leave the reader with a certain sense of vertigo. It was this confusion that provided the impetus for the present book which originated as a series of lectures at the Las Casas Institute at Blackfriars Hall in the University of Oxford. It was felt by the organizers of the lecture series that it would be useful to present an overview of what most protagonists in the debate recognize as a major strand within this wider debate, the Judaeo-Christian perspective (Rosen 2012: 90–100). The series sought to explore the origins and development of the concept of human dignity by this tradition. Its origins lie in the synthesis of a certain interpretation of the biblical creation stories found in Genesis and the affirmation that man was created 'in the image and likeness' of God, and certain Greek and Roman concepts which drew especially on Cicero that emphasize man's status as a rational creature and his capacity for free choice. The synthesis of these basic insights provided the foundation for the understanding of human dignity from the time of Irenaeus of Lyons in the second century AD to Pico della Mirandola in the fifteenth century and, within Catholicism, has persisted to the present day. At the same time, the notion of human dignity that emphasized human greatness, what George Kateb has called his 'stature' (2011), has also to take into account the dark and negative side of the human condition and man's capacity for evil. The lectures, and the chapters that were commissioned later, wished to show the continuing relevance of this debate to contemporary divisive issues such as religious freedom, the status of the embryo and attempts at human enhancement. Of course, although most of the authors here present will agree on certain basic stances such as the transcendental aspects of human dignity and the importance of recognizing the instrinsic dignity and equality of human beings, there are many disagreements within and across denominational lines. But before turning to the contents of the chapters, it will be useful to say a few words about the origins and development of the concept itself (for a fuller account of this, see Lebech 2009).

One classical notion of human dignity which existed in classical times and has remained with us ever since relates to one's position in a social hierarchy. Everyone has a 'dignity' but for some it means the 'dignity' to rule others and for the latter to serve their superiors. Something of this notion even exists in Christianity where offices such as the priesthood are described as 'dignities'. But the notion that all are equal because we share a common, intrinsic dignity was mostly absent. In Athens, for example, participation in democracy was confined to the small minority of men who were full citizens. Non-Athenians, women and children, and slaves were excluded. Even the highest-born women could not attain the status of citizenship. The Romans also sharply distinguished between 'citizens' and others such as slaves, although they did open citizenship to people of very diverse origins. Cicero was among the first to use, in his *De officiis*, the Stoic idea that human beings, because of their capacity to 'reason', possess an intrinsic dignity that makes them superior to all other creatures. Cicero probably did not apply this idea with complete consistency as he kept a slave and, as a member of the minor country gentry, aspired to join the ranks of the Roman nobility. Nevertheless, his notion that all people have an intrinsic dignity would be taken up later and developed by Christian authors. Cicero was particularly influential on the Latin Fathers St Ambrose of Milan and St Augustine. But neo-Platonic ideas, mainly deriving from Plotinus, also helped to formulate the biblical message of human greatness in terms relevant to the Greco-Roman society of the time. Neo-Platonism was also important in providing a conceptual framework for the 'dark' side of humanity, presenting it as a 'fall' from higher levels of spiritual existence into the world of matter. The Gnostics and some of the Greek Fathers such as Origen erred in the direction of rejecting the material world and the body, but the Church always affirmed the goodness of both while recognizing man's capacity to commit evil acts because of his possession of free will. Thus, from the early years of Christianity to the Renaissance, there developed a notion of human dignity, but also of human wretchedness, that underlay a unique anthropology that became the basis of Christendom until this was shattered by the sixteenth-century Reformation and then was undermined by the 'Rationalism' of the eighteenth-century Enlightenment.

In the context of the Enlightenment, Immanuel Kant, although a Christian believer himself, attempted to justify the notion of human dignity on purely rational grounds and without recourse to Christian revelation. He did so through his formulation of the Categorical Imperative or 'the Law of Humanity'. Kant argued that human beings should always be treated by other human beings as 'ends' and never as a 'means'. He also argued that in a market situation human beings could not be compared with each other in the way that one could decide the respective value of a sheep against a cow. Human beings are literally priceless. Both these positions relate to our capacity to reason. But Kant also emphasized freedom or 'autonomy' and thought that autonomy, based on our nature as rational creatures, was the foundation of human dignity. In effect, this was actually the formulation of human dignity that had existed since the early Fathers of the Church: reason and freedom. And although Kant was attempting a purely 'rational' justification, he did think that human beings possess a 'transcendental kernel'. Kant's original formulation has undergone profound modification by neo-Kantians such as John Rawls who emphasize 'autonomy' and reject any notion of 'transcendence'. It is this completely secularized version of Kant's argument that is one of the major positions in today's debate (see Rosen 2012).

But Kant's formula as well as the Judaeo-Christian understanding were (and are) not universally accepted. Already in the nineteenth century, the German philosopher Arthur Schopenhauer dismissed Kant's approach:

> That expression, dignity of man, once uttered by Kant, afterward became the shibboleth of all the perplexed and empty-headed moralists who concealed behind that imposing expression their lack of any real basis of morals, or, at any rate, of one that had any meaning. They cunningly counted on the fact that their readers would be glad to see themselves invested with such a dignity and would accordingly be quite satisfied with it. (Schopenhauer 1995: 100)

Friedrich Nietzsche, an admirer and disciple of Schopenhauer, despised both the Christian and Kantian notions of human dignity and thought that 'dignity' applied only to certain categories of human being – the strong – and not to others who were little more than slaves (that is, he adopted the ancient classical understanding). Karl Marx also rejected Kantian ideas of human rights and saw these simply as a facade hiding bourgeois domination of the proletariat. The mature Marx (the early Marx is a different matter) reduced individual human beings to being mere members of a social class and of no importance in themselves. The notion that human beings possessed any special place in the world was also undermined by Darwin's theory of evolution that seemed to suggest that we are no more than advanced apes. It also cast doubts on the story of creation as told in Genesis and the notion that human beings are in some sense 'like God'. Finally, Freud's psychoanalytic theory, with its emphasis on the subconscious as one of the driving forces of human behaviour, and his rejection of the notion of God as a delusion cut the ground from underneath the idea human beings have a special dignity because of our capacity to make choices based on our reason.

More recently, the medical ethicist Ruth Macklin, in a short but widely cited editorial for the *British Medical Journal*, simply dismisses human dignity as 'a useless concept' (2003), while the Harvard philosopher Steven Pinker speaks about 'the stupidity' of the concept (2008). Both authors reject the concept because it allegedly introduces 'conservative' or 'religious' views into ethical debates. For Macklin, it is a religious Trojan horse introduced into debates about abortion and a woman's right to choose, while Pinker is attacking the US President's Council on Bioethics report, *Human Dignity and Bioethics*, released in 2008. Pinker describes the report as 'conservative bioethics' latest, most dangerous ploy' and claims it is a response to the challenge posed by Macklin. He is particularly incensed by the involvement of conservative Catholics associated with the journal *First Things* in the drafting of the report. The Harvard philosopher Michael Rosen, in his book *Dignity: Its History and Meaning*, adopts a similar, albeit more nuanced and less crude, approach (2012). He provides a useful historical background to the concept, but he also attacks what he considers to be the 'Catholic' understanding which tolerates hierarchy and inequality. He also criticizes neo-Kantian understandings of dignity. The Jesuit James Hanvey has pointed out that Rosen is mistaken in his understanding of the way in which the Catholic understanding has developed (2013: 212–215).

Some authors have simply abandoned the notion of human dignity altogether, whether in its Judaeo-Christian or Kantian formulation. Peter Singer has advanced the notion of 'speciesism', the idea that to claim human specialness vis-à-vis other creatures is similar to racism, sexism and what contemporary liberals regard as 'sins'. This approach takes one side of the Judaeo-Christian understanding – humanity's evil and propensity to destroy itself and its environment – and ignores humanity's greatness. This can be seen in various movements such as environmentalism, Malthusianism, veganism and animal rights activism. Singer, as a self-proclaimed atheist, rejects the notion of the sacredness of human life and, on the basis of his 'preference utilitarianism', argues that the criterion for making moral choices should be the 'preference' and 'utility' of the adults making the choice. Thus, he and his disciples argue that not only is abortion justified but so also is 'post-birth abortion', which most of us would call 'infanticide' (for the 'pro-choice' argument in favour of this, see Giubilini and Minerva 2013).

Not all atheists agree with Singer. George Kateb, for example, strongly defends the dignity of the human being, both in individuals and as a species (pace the 'speciesism' idea of Singer). He distinguishes between the dignified *status* of human individuals and the *stature* of the human species. Each individual is unique but in his or her humanity equal to all other human individuals. It is the dignity of their uniqueness and their equality which is the basis of human rights. The stature of the human species is also unique among all species because of its accomplishments. Other species may have developed specialized niches, such as bees making hives or ants making anthills. But only humanity has been able to take control of the planet itself: 'All other species are more alike than humanity is like any of them: a chimpanzee is more like an earthworm than a human being, despite the close biological relationship of chimpanzees to human beings'

(Kateb 2011: 17). Raymond Tallis makes a similar argument in his book *Aping Mankind: Neuromania, Darwinitis, and the Misrepresentation of Humanity*. He attacks what he terms the 'neuromania' of some contemporary sciences which misrepresent humanity by reducing our most impressive characteristics such as love, art, humanities to mere neurological impulses of the brain (2011). These secular humanists, unlike the Singerian or Nietzschian pessimists, are more aware of human greatness than human misery.

Most religious believers, including Catholics, will be in complete agreement with Kateb and Tallis so far. Where they will part company is in their airy a priori dismissal of any religious or transcendent dimension of the meaning of human dignity. Kateb simply assumes that Greek and Roman polytheism and Jewish and Christian theism are 'inventions' by human beings with no basis in reality (Kateb 2011: 25), while Tallis frequently reminds his readers that he is an atheist. Both authors wish to establish and justify human dignity on the basis of their 'secular humanism'. But such a foundation is rather flimsy. If humanity is all there is to justify itself, without any reference to a transcendent framework, then our species' tendencies towards self-destruction and evil would suggest a definite lack of dignity. The religious and transcendental dimensions of human dignity, affirmed by the Judaeo-Christian tradition and even, to some extent, by Kant, far from diminishing our humanity, are actually key elements in what Kateb refers to as our 'stature'. Religious awareness and experience are part of what makes people truly human. We are *homo religiosus* just as much as *homo sapiens* or *homo faber*. Atheism could be interpreted as a regression back to a merely animal state, and the notion of atheist 'humanism' is absurd since it actually diminishes our humanity. The chapters in this book are an exploration of a fuller conception of human dignity which is provided by the Greco-Roman and Judaeo-Christian traditions at the heart of Western civilization. In a way, the attacks on human dignity and human specialness by Singer and other devout atheists are the logical conclusion of their non-belief. It is gratifying that Kateb and Tallis recognize that human beings and humanity as a whole are special, but it is also necessary to present a fuller picture of religion than the caricature which Kateb, for example, proposes. What is really at stake today is the undermining of the position of humanity itself and with it the undermining of notions such as 'human rights' and 'crimes against humanity'.

The chapters in this book attempt to bring out the full significance of the concept of human dignity as it has developed in the Judaeo-Christian tradition and led to great achievements in fields such as theology, philosophy, literature, art, music and, in modern times, human rights and democracy. Within this tradition there are, of course, lively debates about both the sources and the interpretations of human dignity.

In Chapter 1, John Day returns to the Hebrew Bible (rather than the Greek Septuagint) to analyse the phrase 'image and likeness' found in Genesis. The Fathers of the Church used the Septuagint to make a distinction between 'image' and 'likeness' to argue that human beings lost the 'likeness' at the Fall but retained the 'image'. Day argues that 'image' and 'likeness' in Hebrew are simply synonyms, and the patristic theology was based on a misunderstanding of the original text. Day outlines the different ways this text has been interpreted from ancient times to the present. He concludes that the notion of humanity being made in the 'image and likeness' of God remains the basis of human dignity.

The second primary source of human dignity is Greek and Roman philosophical thought, and this is explored in Chapter 2 by Josef Lössl. This author argues that the distinction between Early and Late Antiquity is rather artificial but during what is called the 'Late' period, a transition was already taking place in which the Judaeo-Christian understanding was beginning to replace older conceptions of dignity. Lössl gives an overview of the way in which Cicero uses the term in his *De officiis*. He responds to criticism of Cicero's use by Christians by Michael Rosen (2012) who argued that Cicero's notion of *dignitas* was mainly about position in a social hierarchy. Lössl shows the context in which Cicero used the concept and its Stoic philosophical underpinnings. He accepts that the famous definition in *De officiis* is rare within Cicero's entire oeuvre but was one to which he nevertheless held.

In Chapter 3, Vladimir Latinovic explores the concept '*imago Dei*' not from an anthropological viewpoint but from a Christological one. He challenges the Nicene Christological position which placed the '*imago Dei*' in the context of the Trinity by returning to the ways in which ante-Nicean authors such as Justin Martyr, Theopholis of Antioch, Irenaeus of Lyon, Clement of Alexandria, Tertullian, and Origen used it drawing on neo-Platonic philosophical ideas such as *mimesis*. He argues that these are alternatives to the Nicene Christology and Trinitarian theology. He claims that such a return to the ante-Nicene approach would both promote a healthier spirituality which accepts more fully the material world and the body, and help inter-religious dialogue with the other Abrahamic faiths (which of course reject the notion of God as Trinity).

But Nicene Christology and Trinitarian theology did in fact form the basis of theological reflection in the subsequent centuries. St Augustine was among the first to argue that if we are made in the 'image and likeness of God', then we must have something of the Trinity in us. Augustine's anthropology is built on this idea of Trinity. Richard Conrad, in Chapter 3, explores how St Thomas Aquinas built on this Augustinian foundation to further develop this Trinitarian dimension of human dignity. He states that Aquinas argues that the image of the Trinity is found in the human soul most of all when it acts, and it acts by knowing and loving God. Aquinas also shares Augustine's notion that man is made *capax Dei* and relates this to a deeper understanding of the human vocation which is to reinforce our 'likeness' to the Trinity through love. But Aquinas also emphasizes that the journey of one's vocation is made in the body and is not simply 'spiritual'.

In the nineteenth century, there was an effort by anticlerical historians such as Jules Michelet and Jacob Burckhardt to see a break between the 'Dark Ages' of medieval Europe and the 'rebirth' of humanity in the Renaissance. In Chapter 5, Loughlin argues that there was in fact a profound continuity between the two periods and in both the understanding of the human being was dominated by the notion of his being made 'in the image and likeness' of God. In fact, the term 'Dark Ages' had been coined by Petrarch but it is now accepted that he was a devout Catholic as was Dante. Petrarch spoke of 'darkness' in relation to literary styles and rhetoric and not Christian doctrine. Dante's epic *The Divine Comedy* is suffused with Thomistic theology, and he has the Cistercian Bernard of Clairvaux (and not Beatrice) lead him into the highest levels of Paradise. Petrarch was a devotee of St Augustine and his notion of 'rebirth' pertained primarily to humane letters and rhetoric, especially as they were exercised by Cicero. Pico della Mirandola, while remaining within this framework, did understand human dignity to mean man's capacity 'to create himself' but he simply meant by this our possibility to choose between rising up (to heaven) and descending to the level of matter. In his writings it is obvious which path he advocated. Undoubtedly, there are developments in the European Renaissance that will eventually develop into a secular humanism but Renaissance Humanism was anything but secular if this term is understood to mean atheism. Renaissance Humanism was fully aware of man's 'wretchedness' (*miseria*) but chose to emphasize instead his greatness (*gloria*).

Timothy Verdon, in Chapter 6, shows how this continuity was evident in the field of sacred art when the rather formal and rigid expressions of the previous period began to give way to a more naturalistic style. Verdon argues that this development occurred with the revival of neo-Platonic philosophy in the fourteenth and fifteenth centuries, which led to a new sensitivity to the human person which expanded the emphasis of the Scholastics on 'nature'. Christ was seen as a mirror of God and artists such as Giotto sought to express the notion of 'beauty' through representations of him. There is also the notion of 'spiritual transformation' of human beings, and this can be seen in Piero della Francesca's depiction of the *Baptism of Christ*. Using Leonardo da Vinci's *Last Supper* as a guide, Verdon demonstrates the notion of 'unwavering resolve' as Christ shares his last meal with his disciples. The fresco depicts the moment when Jesus predicts that someone there will betray him and shows the shocked reaction of the Eleven (that is except for Judas). These paintings show Christ as the perfect and beautiful man who exemplifies human dignity as *gloria*. But the Renaissance artists were also aware of his *miseria*. Verdon shows how Michelangelo, in his old age, did not finish a *Pieta* on which he was working because of his sense of decline and even failure and what theologians term *kenosis* or 'emptying'. Verdon examines the theological and spiritual dimensions of Bernini's statue of St Theresa of Avila which he says expresses the notions of surrender and reciprocity that are found in the mystical interpretation of the Song of Songs. Finally, he discusses the contemporary Florentine artist Filippo Rossi whose triptych called *Magnificat* expresses the notion of 'jubilation'. It is clear from Verdon's profound theological and spiritual analysis of these works of sacred art that there is a continuity between this period and previous periods even if techniques and styles evolve in very different ways.

Jonathan Arnold in Chapter 7 argues that all cultures at all periods of history make music and that, in fact, making music is a fundamental characteristic of our humanity. He uses McGilchrist's research to show that early humans developed the control of voice and respiration for singing even before spoken language came into existence. Furthermore, music is an activity that has always been important in the building and maintenance of human communities. The Greek philosophers Pythagorus and then Plato saw music as integral parts of nature and related it to the harmoniousness and beauty of the cosmos. Plato saw it as an aspect of what he called 'the world soul'. Neo-Platonic ideas derived from this made their way into the Christian synthesis through authors such as Plotinus who influenced St Augustine. Augustine also saw music as capable of moving us towards God but was ambivalent because he thought it could also distract us from this. But he did accept that it could be part of the Christian liturgy and in subsequent centuries, cathedrals and monasteries used music in their liturgies. It is in the Renaissance that music began to develop new forms such as polyphony although still remaining under the aegis of the Church. Arnold argues, however, that music is still relevant in post-Christian society as it continues to draw us together, and the individualism of secularism begins to give way to 'post-secularism' that is opening up a renewed awareness of the beauty and uplifting nature of sacred music.

Of course, there have also been disagreements among Christian thinkers about concepts such as 'image' and 'likeness' or about the meaning of salvation and redemption. The Reformation of Martin Luther and John Calvin was the start of a new way of thinking about the human condition. A crucial shift was that Luther abandoned the distinction between 'image' and 'likeness' (by returning to the Hebrew Bible) and taught that men lost both the image and the likeness. This was also a break from the Thomistic notion that grace builds on nature (the 'image' being man's 'nature'). This shattered the medieval Catholic synthesis. John Witte Jr., in Chapter 8, argues that Protestants retained the notion of human dignity but now it means something of a divine fulcrum between human depravity and human sanctity and keeps these dimensions of the human condition in balance. This, according to Witte, allowed Protestants to the present day to develop distinctive understandings of equality and liberty. This analysis is developed using Martin Luther's *Freedom of a Christian* with its emphasis on 'freedom'.

In Chapter 9, John Milbank wonders why we should be even having discussions about human dignity today. Some see human dignity 'a cipher for outmoded, hierarchical and essentialist dogmas that tend to dilute a recognition and extension of the rights of humanity'. For others, it is simply a superficial ornament to a discourse about rights. For Milbank, however, it should be seen as an alternative to the notion of 'rights' rather than their foundation. The secular philosophical tradition rooted in Locke and Rousseau affirmed the greatness of the human being while the Kantian legacy was a mediation between these positions and the traditional Catholic one. He argues, however, that this mediation is unstable and that (liberal) 'right' and (Catholic) 'dignity'

> stand for two radically opposed political philosophies and indeed for the two *most* opposed political philosophies: namely the politics of the moderns and the politics of the ancients. For the Catholic conception of personal dignity continues to imply that universal dignity can only be expressed by the dignity of group, rank and status, while the Kantian notion of dignity is impotent to dislodge the liberal founding of dignity or worth upon right and so upon subjective autonomy.

Miguel Acosta in Chapter 10 shows how Karel Wojtyla, Pope John Paul II, understood human dignity in the context of his Christian philosophy of 'Personalism'. This was an anthropological synthesis derived from three sources: Thomas Aquinas's metaphysics; Max Scheler's phenomenology; and twentieth-century personalism. The chapter explores some of the connections between

Aquinas's philosophy and Wojtyła's personalism, and looks at some of the implications of his synthesis. This has allowed the Pope to adopt philosophical stances against individualism and subjectivism and affirm the possibility of discovering truth against a prevailing relativism. It allowed him to integrate 'nature' and 'person' in a new way. In all, Wojtyla's philosophical synthesis represents an advanced way of developing the dignity of the human person in all its spiritual and human dimensions to the fullest extent.

The final three chapters deal with the relevance of the Christian conception of human dignity to contemporary ethical problems and disputes. In Chapter 11, Roger Trigg discusses the relationship between human dignity and religious freedom. He argues that human rights are not constructs of governments or international agencies such as the United Nations. Rather these organizations simply recognize what are intrinsic features of our humanity. But he argues against using theological arguments justifying human dignity as these may be simply ignored and, in fact, this can lead to a denial of religious freedom. Trigg draws attention to the confusion concerning facts and values and how Christian values have become the target of abuse in Western societies. He also notes the development of subjectivism and relativism that grows out of this confusion and how 'personal autonomy' now trumps 'freedom of religion'. Finally, he argues that the strong belief in individual freedom which is the basic tenet of liberalism often ends with the state controlling the exercise of religion in the name of one or other policy, such as equality.

Michael Burdett, in Chapter 12, shows how our contemporary society has become completely transformed by 'technology'. But technology is transforming not just our environment but ourselves instead. Biomedical advances have vastly improved our health but they may be further used to 'enhance' our capabilities through genetic engineering and editing our DNA structures. Burdett argues that we are at a tipping point in our evolutionary history. But this confronts us with serious ethical issues. Just because we possess the scientific know-how to do these things doesn't mean that we ought to. Choices should be made on the basis of our human dignity. Burdett examines a current fad called 'human enhancement' or 'transhumanism' which has become an ideology seeking to go further along the lines of experimentation. He argues that Christians ought to pay attention to this movement because of its potential for changing the nature of our humanity and, therefore, its impact on human dignity. He usefully lays out the impact of transhumanism on different dimensions of our humanity: on mind and rationality; on information; on freedom. Finally, he offers an evaluation of the movement from the perspective of the Christian notion that we are made in the image and likeness of God. He argues that Christianity basically diverges from transhumanism.

In the final chapter, Calum MacKellar tackles the question as to whether the concept of dignity should play a role in bioethical issues. Responding to some theorists who argue that it should not, MacKellar argues that, to the contrary, it should be central to such discussions. He goes on to discuss the different ways in which it can be understood: as (i) non-inherent (contingent) human dignity and as (ii) inherent (absolute) human dignity. The first refers to ways in which persons are perceived by others and oneself and is something that may be lost. But MacKellar suggests that this may not be a strong enough foundation for respecting human dignity in issues of bioethics. Instead, there is need for a definition where it is seen to be inherent in the human person. He then goes on to examine how this can be universally accepted by what he calls 'network inherent dignity', which means 'a secular belief in the notion of the absolute worth of all persons supported by a system whereby all individuals continually value and confer inherent dignity on everyone else while recognizing that everyone else has already conferred this dignity on all in society'. This is a kind of secular belief that cannot be fully defined, but it does demand that boundaries between what is human and what is not human be established. Otherwise, the concept itself would be undermined. This happened when the human status of particular groups has been questioned: the Amerindians by the Spanish conquistadores and various categories of people – Jews, the disabled and others – by the Nazis. The chapter goes on to discuss how the notion of inherent network human dignity relates contemporary understandings of human autonomy and considers its application in issues such as euthanasia and abortion.

Although all the authors here share a Christian perspective, they represent different theological traditions, including traditional and liberal Catholicism, Eastern Orthodoxy, Anglicanism and evangelical Protestantism. All would agree on the central importance of the dignity of the human beings, although they might differ as to the interpretation of Genesis 1.27 or the Trinitarian notion of the human being. Most would also agree that the wonder of human dignity needs to be balanced by an awareness of the tragic side of the human condition – our tendency to destroy other people and to wreck the planet. But placing the human experience in the broader transcendent framework of Christian faith, we also have grounds for hope. All the chapters show the importance of the concept of human dignity for contemporary political and social life but also how difficult it is to define the term. Nevertheless, it is hoped that they demonstrate the depth, richness and fruitfulness of the Judaeo-Christian development of the concept.

References

Düwell, M., J. Braarvig, R. Brownsword and D. Mieth, eds (2014), *The Cambridge Handbook of Human Dignity*, Cambridge: Cambridge University Press.

Giubilini, A. and F. Minerva (2013), 'After-Birth Abortion: Why Should the Baby Live?', *Journal of Medical Ethics*, 39: 261–263.

Hale, B. (2013), 'Preface', in C. McCrudden (ed.), *Understanding Human Dignity*, xv–xvii, Oxford: Oxford University Press for the British Academy.

Hanvey, J. (2013), 'Dignity, Person and Imago Trinitatis', in C. McCrudden (ed.), *Understanding Human Dignity*, 209–228, Oxford: Oxford University Press for the British Academy.

Kateb, G. (2011), *Human Dignity*, Cambridge, MA: Belknap Press of Harvard University Press.

Lebech, M. (2009), *On the Problem of Human Dignity: A Hermeneutical and Phenomenological Investigation*, Würzburg : Königshausen & Neumann.

Macklin, R. (2003), 'Dignity Is a Useless Concept', *British Medical Journal*, 327 (7429): 1419–1420.

McCrudden, C. (2008), 'Human Dignity and Judicial Interpretation of Human Rights', *European Journal of International Law*, 19 (4): 655–724.

McCrudden, C., ed. (2013), *Understanding Human Dignity*, Oxford: Oxford University Press for the British Academy.

Pinker, S. (2008), 'The Stupidity of Dignity', *The New Republic*, 28 May.

Rosen, M. (2012), *Dignity: Its History and Meaning*, Cambridge, MA: Harvard University Press.

Schopenhauer, A. (1995 [1818]), *On the Basis of Morality*, trans. E. F. J. Payne, Providence: Berghahn Books.

Tallis, R. (2011), *Aping Mankind: Neuromania, Darwinitis, and the Misrepresentation of Humanity*, Abingdon and New York: Routledge.

UNESCO (1948), *Human Rights: Comments and Interpretations*, UN Doc. UNESCO/PHS/3 (rev.), http://unesdoc.unesco.org/images/0015/001550/155042eb.pdf.

1

'So God Created Humanity in His Own Image' (Genesis 1.27). What Does the Bible Mean and What Have People Thought It Meant?

John Day

Introduction

One way in which the dignity of human beings has been grounded is in the belief that we are all created in the image of God. For example, during the Renaissance, Agrippa von Nettesheim ([1529] 1990: 49, ET 1670: 1) appealed to this belief in the very first paragraph of his book in defence of the status of women. Again, more recently, Archbishop Desmond Tutu (e.g. 2014: 19–21) frequently appealed to this notion as a basis of his opposition to apartheid and racism in South Africa. The belief has played a larger role within Christianity than in Judaism, even though it is rooted in the Hebrew Bible. But within the Hebrew Bible it is somewhat unusual, for it affirms the Godlikeness of human beings, whereas so much of the Old Testament emphasizes God's otherness over against humanity.

But in what sense exactly are human beings Godlike? What does humanity's creation in the image of God actually mean? This has been a most disputed topic and has given rise to a vast literature in Old Testament studies[1] as well as in theology more generally.[2] Over the centuries, theologians have made many suggestions which are essentially guesswork. As one Old Testament scholar put it, 'Many "orthodox" theologians right through the centuries have lifted the phrase "the image of God" (*imago dei*) right out of its context, and like Humpty-Dumpty, they have made the word mean just what they choose it to mean' (Snaith 1974: 24).[3] This is certainly true, but it also has to be admitted that working out exactly what the Bible does mean is not that simple, since it does not offer an explanation.

Curiously, in view of its later importance in Christian theology, there are only three passages alluding to the image of God in humanity in the Old Testament, though it is referred back to occasionally in the Apocrypha and New Testament. These three Old Testament passages are all from the Priestly source in the early chapters of Genesis. First and best known, in connection with God's creation of humanity, is Gen. 1.26-7:

> And God said, 'Let us make humanity[4] in our image, after our likeness; and let them have dominion over the fish of the sea and over the birds of the air, and over the cattle, and over all the earth, and over every creeping thing that creeps upon the earth.' So God created humanity in his own image; in the image of God he created them; male and female he created them.

This is later referred back to in Gen. 5.1-3, 'When God created humanity, he made them in the likeness of God. Male and female he created them, and he blessed them and called their name humanity when they were created. When Adam had lived 130 years he became the father of a son in his own likeness, after his image, and named him Seth.' Finally, the last reference is in Gen. 9.6, where, following the Flood, God declares to Noah, 'Whoever sheds the blood of a human, by a human shall their blood be shed; for God made humanity in his own image.'

The nature of the image

Spiritual views

Traditionally in Christian theology the idea of people being made in the image of God has been understood as referring to humanity's reason, soul, spirituality or suchlike: some internal aspect of the human person that sets us apart from animals and makes us resemble God. This is probably the best-known kind of interpretation for many people, even though most modern Old Testament scholars believe it to be either mistaken or only partially true. For example, Augustine of Hippo (*De Trinitate*, esp. books 7–15; see Sullivan 1963) saw an analogy between the Trinity and the threefold division of human memory, intellect and will. But this is purely fanciful, and of course the Old Testament knew nothing of the Trinity. Many like Athanasius (*De Incarnatione*, 3; see Bernard 1952) and Aquinas (*Summa Theologiae*, part 1, Question 13; *De Veritate*, 10) envisaged the image as specifically referring to human reason, whereas Ambrose (*Hexaemeron*, 6.7-8) and Calvin (*Institutes*, 1.15.3) believed it alluded to the human soul. But in suggesting these various ideas, Christian theologians were clearly simply speculating when endeavouring to calculate what it was that humanity had in common with God (in contrast to the animals), rather than relying on biblical evidence.

A further Christian reading distorting the original biblical meaning is to be found in the second-century Church Father Irenaeus (*Adversus Haereses*, 5.6.1; 5.16.1-2; see Holsinger-Friesen 2009), who made a distinction between the image and likeness of God. He thought the image referred to the permanent features of the human person, like reason, whereas the likeness of God alluded to human qualities lost at the Fall, but which could be regained through Christ. This view persisted till the Reformers rightly questioned its exegetical viability. The evidence of the Bible suggests that there is no essential difference between the image and likeness of God; the two terms are used interchangeably. Thus, whereas Gen. 1.26 declares that God made humanity in the image and likeness of God, the very next verse as well as Gen. 9.6 simply say that he made humans in the image of God, while Gen. 5.1 only says that God made humanity in the likeness of God.

Another misguided idea is found in the Protestant Reformers, who tended to speak of the image and likeness of God in humanity as something that was marred or obliterated as a result of the Fall (Luther in Pelikan 1958: 61; Calvin 1847: 94–95). However, in Gen. 9.6, we still read of humans possessing the image of God long after the Fall, in the time of Noah; similarly, the New Testament letter of James declares that we are made in the image of God (Jas 3.9). It is somewhat puzzling that the Reformers, who claimed to give priority to Scripture, adopted such a manifestly unbiblical view.

The view that the image of God in humanity refers purely to some kind of spiritual resemblance between God and human beings persisted among Old Testament scholars throughout the nineteenth century and among some even into the twentieth century (e.g. S. R. Driver, W. Eichrodt, H. H. Rowley),[5] but it now has virtually no support. However, the situation is different among systematic theologians. In addition to some modern systematic theologians who reiterate older purely spiritual views mentioned above, there have been newer suggestions such as that humans being in the image of God refers to their freedom (Seeberg 1924: 499) or self-transcendence (Niebuhr 1941: 176–178) in addition to reciprocal views to be considered below. None of these can claim support from Genesis.

Nevertheless, as we shall see later, although not the whole truth, humanity being in the image of God does *partly* imply some kind of spiritual resemblance between God and humans.

The functional view

By contrast, a very different interpretation of the meaning of human beings bearing the divine image has been dominant among Old Testament scholars since the 1960s. This is the so-called functional view. By this is meant the understanding that it alludes to humanity's position as God's viceroy, having dominion over the earth and its living creatures.

This functional view was already occasionally held among the early Church Fathers, for example by John Chrysostom (*Homilies on Genesis*, 8.3) and Theodoret of Cyrrhus (*Questions on Genesis*, 20). It was also maintained later by some early Socinians (Unitarians), who incorporated this doctrine in their Racovian Catechism of 1605 (Oederus 1739: 48), as well as by some early Remonstrants (Dutch Arminians). It was also held by the prominent tenth-century Jewish rabbi Saadia (Zucker 1984: 257–258). Additionally, a few nineteenth- and early twentieth-century scholars followed this view (e.g. Holzinger 1898: 12). All these held this position because in Gen. 1.26ff. the reference to humanity's ruling the animals and the earth follows shortly after the allusion to humanity's being made in the image of God. However, it is more natural to suppose that humanity's lordship over the animals and the earth is a consequence of its having been made in God's image, rather than what the image itself denotes. This is made clear by v. 28, where God's command to humanity to rule over animals and the earth takes place only after God's blessing of them and commanding them to be fruitful and multiply and fill the earth, whereas humanity has already been made in God's image in v. 27. This important point is often overlooked by defenders of the functional interpretation.

The conclusion that God's image in humanity refers to something other than humanity's rule over the animals and the earth is also supported by a consideration of the other Genesis passages which refer to the image of God. Thus, in Gen. 5.1-2, the statement is repeated: 'When God created humanity, he made them in the image of God. Male and female he created them, and he blessed them and called their name humanity when they were created.' Then v. 3 continues, 'When Adam had lived 130 years, he became the father of a son in his own likeness, after his image, and named him Seth.' Note that the same language is used of Seth's resemblance to Adam as is used of Adam's resemblance to God. This resemblance clearly includes a physical resemblance and cannot have anything to do with ruling over animals and the earth. Again, in Gen. 9.6 we read, 'Whoever sheds the blood of a human, by a human shall their blood be shed; for God made humanity in his own image.' These words are surely implying something about the inherent dignity and worth of human life, rather than referring to humans have dominion over the animals and the earth.

In spite of all this important counter-evidence, the most common view among Old Testament scholars since the 1960s has been that the image of God in humanity refers to humans ruling over the world.[6] Why should this be? The continued repetition of this view probably owes something to intellectual fashion. Just as someone said that history does not repeat itself, but historians repeat one another, so there is an undoubted tendency for commentators to repeat one another. But the original impetus for the popularity of this view came in the 1960s, when two Old Testament scholars, Hans Wildberger (1965, repr. 1979) and Werner H. Schmidt (1964: 127–149),[7] independently presented evidence that in ancient Egypt and Assyria the king could be spoken of as being the image of a god. They further suggested that in Genesis 1 the idea that human beings generally are created in the image and likeness of God is a democratization of this concept. As stated, this view has become very popular in Old Testament circles. There is a particularly thorough defence of it by J. Richard Middleton (2005). By contrast, only a minority of systematic theologians have taken this view (e.g. Hall 1986).

There are, however, some problems with this view. Firstly, we have no evidence that the Israelite kings themselves were ever spoken of as being in the image of a god. The assumption has to be made that the Israelites borrowed the imagery from either Egyptian or Assyrian kingship and then democratized it to refer to humanity. But with regard to Assyria, it must be noted that the imagery is rare: only six references are known (see Angerstorfer 1997), and of those four come from a single scribe about three individuals in two letters from the time of Esarhaddon (681–669 BC) and a fifth comes from the reign of his successor Ashurbanipal (668–c. 627 BC), while the other is from the time of Tukulti-Ninurta I (c. 1243–1207 BC). It does not seem very likely, therefore, that P's language was adopted from the Assyrians. What then of ancient Egypt? It is true that there are far more occurrences of the concept in Egypt, but although there are occasional allusions down to Ptolemaic times, they are overwhelmingly from the eighteenth dynasty (c. 1550–1290 BC), about 800–1050 years prior to the time of the Priestly writer. Incidentally, although the Priestly writer probably wrote in the early post-exilic period, c. 500 BC, not long after the Babylonian exile, no references to the king as the image of a god are attested in Babylonia at any period.[8]

A popular variant of the functional view maintains that it was the custom of placing actual images of foreign kings in conquered territory as representations of their authority in absence that lies behind the alleged democratized representation of humans as images of the invisible God in Genesis (e.g. Brueggemann 1982: 32). However, as noted earlier, the fundamental objection to any functional understanding of the image of God is that it does not fit any of the three passages in Genesis very well. Even in Gen. 1.26ff. humanity's rule over the earth is more naturally a consequence of its being in the divine image, not what the image itself is.

Finally, those who adopt the functional view tend to argue that human beings are not said to be made in (or after) the image and likeness of God but rather as an image and likeness of God. This involves taking the preposition *beth*, 'in', in *b^etselem* as what is called *beth essentiae*, 'as' (Clines 1968: 75–80, repr. 1998: 470–475; Gross 1993: 35, 37; Janowski 2000: 1159, ET 2009: 414). However, as J. Maxwell Miller (1972: 296) aptly pointed out, this is improbable here, since the preposition *beth* is used here interchangeably with the preposition *kaph*, 'after/ according to', but there is no *kaph essentiae* in biblical Hebrew. We thus have to conclude that humans are said to be made in (i.e. according to) the image of God (cf. Septuagint *kata*, Vulgate *ad*), not merely as an image of God.

Karl Barth and the reciprocal view

We shall now consider what might be called the reciprocal view of the nature of the divine image in humans. It was made famous by Karl Barth (1945: 205–226, ET 1958: 183–201), who argued that the key to understanding the meaning of humanity's being made in the image of God is to be found in Gen. 1.27, which declares, 'So God created humanity in his own image, in the image of God he created them; male and female he created them.' From this he deduced that the image of God consists of the reciprocal relationship of male and female. In this he sees a reflection of God himself, who says 'Let us make humanity', implying (he supposes) a plurality within the Deity himself (though not explicitly the Trinity, as the Church Fathers and some later Christians supposed). But Old Testament scholars generally find this unconvincing. Thus, firstly, 'Let us make humanity' is generally understood as God addressing the heavenly beings or angels around him (cf. Gen. 3.22; 11.7; Isa. 6.8), rather than implying a plurality within God himself. We can rule out a royal plural or a plural of exhortation here, as these are unattested elsewhere with verbs in biblical Hebrew.[9] We may assume that God includes the heavenly court in the momentous decision to create humanity, even though it is God alone who finally enacts it (Gen. 1.27). Secondly, it is much more natural to suppose that male and female both bear the divine image individually, rather than that the image consists in their reciprocal relationship. Thirdly, animals too consist of both male and female, but we should expect humanity's being in the image of God to be something distinguishing them from the animals, which would not be so on Barth's interpretation. Fourthly, it is difficult for Barth's understanding to make sense of Gen. 5.3, where Seth is said to be made in the likeness and image of his father Adam, implying a resemblance in appearance, so the same logically ought to be the case with Adam's likeness in the image of God mentioned only two verses earlier (Gen. 5.1). Fifthly, Barth's understanding also does not fit Gen. 9.6, where God's making humanity in his own image is cited as the reason for forbidding the murder of a human being. The mutuality of the sexes seems quite irrelevant here. Rather, the words seem to be highlighting the value and dignity of human life which its Godlikeness betokens.

Karl Barth was neither the first nor the last scholar to put forward a relational view of the image of God. He appears to have been dependent on Dietrich Bonhoeffer ([1933] 1989: 58–60, ET 1988: 52–57), who asserted that part of being in God's image was the freedom to exist in relationship with other human beings, including between men and women. A number of other scholars who understood the image of God in relational terms are (prior to Barth) the systematic theologian Emil Brunner (1937: 92–96, ET 1939: 102–105) and the Old Testament scholars W. Riedel (1902) and (subsequent to Barth) F. Horst (1950), J. J. Stamm (1959) and C. Westermann (1974: 217, ET 1984: 157). However, these scholars understood the mutuality not to be that between a man and a woman but the fact that God and humans can speak to each other. But it is difficult to find anything in Genesis that implies this as the meaning.

Physical likeness

We now have to consider the idea that humanity's being in the image of God refers to a physical resemblance between God and humans. Though this might seem rather crude to the modern sophisticated person, there is good evidence that this is at least part of what Genesis envisaged, even if finally we conclude that both a physical and a spiritual likeness are intended.

Firstly, it should be noted that the word used for image, Hebrew *tselem*, is regularly employed elsewhere in the Old Testament to denote the physical representation of something, most frequently images of pagan gods (Num. 33.52; 2 Kgs 11.18; 2 Chron. 23.17; Ezek. 7.20; 16.17; Amos 5.26). The only other examples are images of the Chaldeans (Ezek. 23.14) and of tumours and mice

(1 Sam. 6.5 [twice]; 6.11).[10] Furthermore, the biblical Aramaic cognate *ts^elem*, *tsalma'* is used eleven times in Dan. 3.1-8 of the statue of a pagan god that the people are commanded to worship by Nebuchadrezzar, and the same Aramaic word occurs several times in Dan. 2.31-5 of the statue symbolizing the four world empires in Nebuchadrezzar's dream. It may seem surprising that a word which is used overwhelmingly of pagan images should be employed in Genesis of humanity's high dignity. However, the fact that its meaning was not confined to idols but could refer to an image generally meant that it was acceptable.

The word 'likeness' (Hebrew *d^emut*) tends to be more abstract in meaning. Sometimes it means 'appearance, form', though on occasion it is used in the comparison of two things. Most frequently it is used in Ezekiel's visions, where it sometimes seems to make the comparison more approximate and less definite (e.g. Ezek. 1.5, 26; 8.2; 10.1). So some think that in Genesis it is used to make humanity's physical resemblance to God a bit more approximate and less definite. However, there are three places in the Old Testament where the word *d^emut* is not abstract but a physical depiction of some kind; cf. 2 Kgs 16.10, 'a model (*d^emut*) of the altar', 2 Chron. 4.3, 'figures (*d^emut*) of oxen' and Ezek. 23.15, 'a picture (*d^emut*) of Babylonians'. (Note that in Ezek. 23.14 *tselem*, 'image', is likewise used of the Chaldeans [Babylonians].) Interestingly, in a bilingual Aramaic-Akkadian inscription on a ninth-century statue of Hadad-yis'i, king of Gozan, discovered at Tell Fekheriyeh in Syria,[11] the Aramaic cognates *ts^elem* and *d^emuta'* are both employed to render the Akkadian word *tsalmu*, 'image', used of the statue. Ultimately, it is likely that there is no great difference between the 'likeness' and 'image' of God in Genesis, seeing that both terms are used interchangeably, as noted earlier.

Secondly, very tellingly, in Gen. 5.3 we read that 'Adam … became the father of a son in his likeness, after his image, and named him Seth'. It will be noted that the identical terminology of Gen. 1.26f. about humanity being made in the image and likeness of God is employed here. Moreover, just two verses before Gen. 5.3 in v. 1, we read that 'When God created humanity, he made them in the likeness of God'. Since Seth's likeness to Adam undoubtedly implies a physical resemblance, the natural conclusion is that there is similarly a physical likeness between God and human beings.

Thirdly, in addition to frequent references to Yahweh's body parts,[12] it ought to be noted that the Old Testament sometimes envisages God as appearing in human form (cf. Gen. 18.1-2; 32.24-5, 30). Perhaps the most well-known example is Isaiah's famous call vision in Isaiah 6, where the prophet 'saw the Lord sitting upon a throne, high and lifted up; and his train filled the temple'. But most relevant for our present purpose is Ezek. 1.26, where the prophet states that in his vision of God he 'saw a likeness as the appearance of a human being'.[13] It is significant that Ezekiel was a priest, not so long before the Priestly account of creation in Genesis 1 was written. Moreover, the word 'likeness' (Hebrew d^emut) which Ezekiel uses in Ezek. 1.26 (cf. 8.2) is the same word that the Priestly source employs in Gen. 1.26 to denote humanity's likeness to God. Ezekiel's statement that God had 'a likeness as the appearance of human being/man' and Genesis's statement that humanity was in the likeness of God sound like the obverse and reverse of each other.[14]

Fourthly, it should be noted that God says, 'Let us make humanity in our image.' There is general agreement among Old Testament scholars that God is here addressing his heavenly court, the angels, since as already noted, in Hebrew the verb has no royal plural, and there is no evidence for a plural of exhortation. Accordingly, a point often overlooked, humanity is made in the image of the angels, and not merely of God. Now there is good evidence that angels were envisaged as being in human form. Compare, for example, the angel Gabriel, who is described in Dan. 8.15 and 10.18 as 'one having the appearance of a man' and in Dan. 10.16 as 'one in the likeness of the sons of men'. Again, in Genesis 19, those referred to as angels in v. 1 are called men in v. 5.

So it seems likely that human beings were thought to have a similar physical appearance to God and that this is at least part of what the image of God in humanity includes. To the objection that men and women do not have an identical appearance, L. Koehler (1948)[15] argued that we could think more generally of human beings sharing upright form as what constitutes their resemblance to God. He compares Ovid's *Metamorphoses*, 1.85-6, which alludes to 'upright man we made in the image of commanding gods'.

Conclusion: Both a physical and spiritual likeness

But though a physical likeness seems to be clearly implied when humans are spoken of as being in the image of God, it seems likely that it is not confined to that. It must be recalled that the ancient Hebrews did not envisage humans in terms of a body–soul dualism, but rather as a psychophysical totality. So it is humans as a whole who are created in the image of God, not simply their body, but also including the spiritual reality within, the human psyche. And of course this is precisely what Gen. 1.26-7 states – humans are made in God's image – not just the physical or spiritual part of them. This view of the image has previously been proposed by a number of scholars, some emphasizing more the physical and some the spiritual element.[16]

That a spiritual element was included is implied by Gen. 9.6, where the reason given for prohibiting murder of a human being is that 'God made humanity in his own image'. It would seem ridiculous to suppose that this simply meant that humans had the same upright form as God. The inviolability of human life must surely have to do with the innate dignity and worth of human beings in their inner being.

Again, humans being made in the image of God in Gen. 1.26ff. provides the foundation for humanity having lordship over the animals and the world. It would again seem ridiculous to think that this exalted position was simply because of humanity's upright form or physical appearance. True, humans' physical strength doubtless played a role, but it was surely above all their superior intelligence and creative power that enabled humans to take charge of the world. So this must also be a part of what is implied in humanity's being in God's image.

Later biblical references to the image (real and alleged)

Alleged echoes of Genesis 1.26ff. in the Old Testament

It has often been supposed that Ps. 8.3ff. (Heb. 4ff.) is dependent on Gen. 1.26ff. The text reads as follows:

> When I look at your heavens, the work of your fingers,
> The moon and the stars which you have established,
> What is man that you are mindful of him,
> And the son of man that you care for him?
> Yet you have made him little less than the gods [or angels],
> And crown him with glory and honour.
> You have given him dominion over the works of your hands,
> You have put all things under his feet,
> All sheep and oxen,
> and also the beasts of the field,
> the birds of the air, and the fish of the sea,
> whatever passes along the paths of the sea.

There is undoubtedly a close similarity here with Gen. 1.26ff., in that both combine a confident belief in the high status of humanity with an allusion to the God-given rule of human beings over the animals. The royal language is more marked than in Gen. 1.26ff., for the psalm speaks not merely of giving humanity dominion over the works of God's hands but also of crowning humans with glory and honour. However, it is important to note that the psalm does not actually speak of humanity being made in the image or likeness of God. Rather humans are said to be little less than the gods (or angels). Elsewhere in this psalm God is referred to as Yahweh (vv. 1, 9, Heb. 2, 10), so the reference to humanity being a little less than the *elohim* more naturally refers to the gods or angels. This was already perceived in the principal ancient versions (Septuagint, Vulgate, Targum and Peshitta), which all rendered 'angels' here.[17] Rather than being dependent on Gen. 1.26ff., it is possible that Psalm 8 lies behind Gen. 1.26ff. or is at least less theologically advanced than it (Barr 1968–1969: 12, repr. 2013: 67; Anderson 1975: 43) – note, e.g., creation by Yahweh's fingers rather than divine fiat – just as I have argued elsewhere that Psalm 104 lies behind Genesis 1 (Day 1985: 51–53).

We turn now to the prophet known as Second Isaiah (Isa. 40–55). The view was first put forward by Moshe Weinfeld (1967–1968: 105–132, ET 2004: 95–117), and subsequently followed by Michael Fishbane (1985: 322–326) and Benjamin Sommer (1998: 142–145),[18] that there are various verses in Second Isaiah which reject particular points of the Priestly account of creation (Gen. 1.1–2.4a). Although superficially the various points might at first seem enticing, when carefully analysed individually we find that they do not bear out Weinfeld's position. But here we need only consider Weinfeld's arguments in so far as they concern Gen. 1.26. In this connection Weinfeld claimed that Isa. 40.18 (cf. 40.25) is a deliberate rejection of Gen. 1.26's notion that humanity was made in the image of God. In Isa. 40.18 the prophet declares, 'To whom will you liken God, or what likeness compare with him?' However, the very next verse makes clear that Second Isaiah was emphasizing Yahweh's uniqueness over against idols, rather than opposing Gen. 1.26, for he says, 'An idol? A workman casts it, and a goldsmith overlays it with gold.' Then v. 20, which is somewhat obscure, says more about idolatry. Isaiah 46.5 repeats the question, 'To whom will you liken me and make me equal, and compare me, as though we were alike?' And just like after Isa. 40.18, the prophet again goes on to speak of idolatry:

> Those who lavish gold from the purse and weigh out silver in the scales – they hire a goldsmith, who makes it into a god; then they fall down and worship. They lift it to their shoulders, they carry it, they set it in its place, and it stands there, it cannot move from its place. If one cries out to it, it does not answer, or save anyone from trouble. (Isa. 46.6-7)

Furthermore, Isa. 46.1ff. makes it clear that Second Isaiah was thinking in terms of Babylonian idolatry (he mentions Bel [Marduk] and Nebo [Nabu] in v. 1.). So it is clear that in raising the question to whom one might compare God, Second

Isaiah is rejecting the view that other gods, such as the Babylonian ones, can compete with Yahweh in power or importance. He is not alluding to Gen. 1.26's implication that there is a certain physical or spiritual resemblance between Yahweh and humans in appearance or inner psyche, a text which in any case is probably later than Second Isaiah.

But there is another verse of Second Isaiah which Weinfeld thinks is also countering Gen. 1.26. We have already seen that the words 'Let us make humanity' imply that God addressed his heavenly court, the angels, when creating humanity. Weinfeld thinks that this idea is being countered in Isa. 40.13-14, 'Who has directed the spirit of the Lord, or as his counsellor instructed him?' He also points to Isa. 44.24, 'I am the Lord, who made all things, who alone stretched out the heavens, and spread out the earth. Who was with me?' However, this last verse is speaking of the creation of heaven and earth, not of humanity, and as for Isa. 40.13-14 it is not clear that the prophet is speaking of creation at all. It sounds rather as if he is speaking generally of Yahweh's not needing anyone to instruct him in wisdom (cf. Isa. 40.14, 'Who taught him the path of justice?').

The Apocrypha

Before we come to the New Testament there are three references in the Apocrypha that we need to consider. The earliest of these is in Ecclus 17.3-4, which declares, 'He [God] endowed them [humans] with a strength like his own, and made them in his own image. He put the fear of him in all living beings, and gave them dominance over beasts and birds.' So on the one hand humans being in God's image is taken to imply that they are strong, and on the other hand it is associated with humanity's domination over the beasts. But this is not the peaceful, harmonious rule over the animals to which Genesis 1 refers, but rather the fear-ridden rule of Genesis 9, after humanity has been given permission to eat meat following the Flood.

Another apocryphal reference is in Wis. 2.23, where we read, 'for God created us for incorruption, and made us in the image of his own eternity'. The book of Wisdom was much influenced by Middle Platonism and continually emphasizes human immortality, so it is in keeping with this that the image of God in humans is taken to refer to their immortal spirit. Somewhat similarly, another Alexandrian Jew, Philo, explains the image of God in humans as 'the most important part of the soul, the mind' (*Op. Mund.*, 69), thereby anticipating some later Christian ideas.

Finally, 2 Esd. 8.44 refers to 'people who have been formed by your [God's] hands and are called your own image because they are made like you, and for whose sake you have formed all things'. This both emphasizes humanity's resemblance to God and refers to the consequent human domination of the earth.

The New Testament

What is said about humanity being in the image of God in the New Testament? First, we should note the letter of James, where the writer says of the tongue, 'With it we bless the Lord and Father, and with it we curse those who are made in the image of God' (Jas 3.9).

But the most interesting passage is in one of Paul's letters, in 1 Cor. 11.7, where in the course of a discussion of what headdress is appropriate when praying or prophesying in Church, Paul declares, 'For a man ought not to have his head veiled, since he is the image and glory of God, but woman is the glory of man.' This is explained by the continuation in v. 8, where Paul says, 'Indeed, man was not made from woman, but woman from man.' For those of us who are accustomed to the view expressed in Gen. 1.26 that both men and women are made in the image of God, Paul's words here will come as a shock. The explanation for what he says lies in the fact that whereas we read Gen. 1.1–2.4a and 2.4b–3.24 as two separate stories (from the P and J sources, respectively), Paul read them as a unity. In addition, he understood ha'adam in Gen. 1.26-7 to mean '(an individual) man' rather than 'humanity', a meaning which it has in Genesis 2–3. Accordingly, the words 'male and female he created them' at the end of Gen. 1.27 are understood to be partly proleptic, i.e. 'male (and later) female he created them', corresponding to the Garden of Eden story in Genesis 2, where the woman is made from the side (traditionally rib) of the man. Woman would thus be in the image of God but only indirectly so for Paul, via the man.[19]

But there are also other Pauline references to the image of God of a different character, and these are probably not dependent on Gen. 1.26ff. In particular, Col. 1.15 refers to Christ as 'the image of the invisible God' and 2 Cor. 4.4 speaks of Christ as 'the image of God'. Although it is true that Paul calls Christ 'the last Adam' (1 Cor. 14.45), there is probably no direct connection with Gen. 1.26ff. when Christ is called the image of God. Rather, as is the case with Heb. 1.3 stating that Christ 'reflects the glory of God and bears the very stamp of his nature', it seems more natural to detect Wisdom influence here. Compare Wis. 7.26, 'For she (Wisdom) is a reflection of eternal light, a spotless mirror of the working of God, and an *image* of his goodness.' The role of Christ in the creation of the world in Col. 1.15ff. also supports this background, since Wisdom was active in creation, the phrase 'the first-born of creation' that follows on after 'the image of the invisible God' being taken from Prov. 8.22, where it refers to pre-existent Wisdom.

Furthermore, Pauline passages refer to Christians being transformed into Christ's image or likeness; for example, they are 'to be conformed to the image of his Son' (Rom. 8.29). Again, 'we all … are being changed into his likeness from one degree of glory to another' (2 Cor. 3.18), and 'you have put on the new nature, which is being renewed in knowledge after the image of its creator' (Col. 3.10).[20] For Paul, unlike the later Reformers, this transformation into the likeness of Christ is not to be understood as a restoration of the image of God in Gen. 1.26f., since as we have seen above, for Paul all men (and by extension women) are already in the image of God referred to there (1 Cor. 11.7).

Theological consequences of humanity being made in the image and likeness of God

What theological consequences might one draw from the fact that human beings are described as being made in the image and likeness of God? Firstly, it clearly indicates that humans have enormous dignity, since there is something Godlike about them. Psalm 8 puts it in a different way when it declares that humans are a little lower than the angels or gods. Because of humanity's Godlikeness Gen. 9.6 deems it inappropriate to murder a human being. However, many nowadays would expand the biblical writer's vision and argue that the judicial murder of the murderer should also be outlawed. This is in line with the New Testament's reversal of the book of Exodus's doctrine of an 'eye for an eye and tooth for a tooth', which follows on 'a life for a life' (Exod. 21.23-4; cf. Mt. 5.38-42). The idea of the Godlike dignity of human beings is expressed elsewhere in Prov. 17.5, which declares, 'He who mocks the poor mocks his maker.' Somewhat comparable are Jesus's words at the last judgement, 'Truly, I say to you, as you did it to one of the least of these my brethren, you did it to me' (Mt. 25.40, cf. v. 45).

Interestingly, both men and women are said to be created in the image of God. This seems undeniable from Gen. 1.27 and 5.1-2. Gen. 1.27 states, 'So God created humanity in his own image, in the image of God he created them, male and female he created them', and Gen. 5.1-2 declares, 'When God created humanity, he made them in the likeness of God. Male and female he created them.' From this we should draw the conclusion that men and women are deemed equal in the sight of God, something generally accepted throughout the history of Judaism and Christianity (see Horowitz 1979, who also notes a minority of dissenters). Men and women are thus subsequently both given dominion over the earth and the animals (Gen. 1.26, 1.28). While this is generally accepted, it has curiously been denied by one feminist scholar, Phyllis Bird (1981: 151, repr. 1997: 145), who maintains that the dominion is confined to men. However, it is explicitly stated in v. 28 that the command to rule over the animals and the earth was given by God 'to them', which can only mean to both male and female just referred to. But this does not mean that the Priestly writer had thought through the full implications of this in terms of social equality. For example, the Priestly writer of Genesis 1 later on tends to list almost entirely men in his genealogies, and he has only men, not women, performing a priestly role within the cult. We may compare the fact that St Paul in Gal. 3.28 declares that 'there is neither Jew nor Greek, there is neither slave nor free, there is neither male nor female; for you are all one in Christ Jesus', but it took hundreds of years for slavery to be abolished, and there are still some branches of the Christian church which exclude women from the priesthood.

In Genesis 1 humans being made in the image of God is something that distinguishes them from the animals. Subsequently, humans are commanded to have lordship over the earth, including the animals. Lynn White (1967) famously declared that that the modern environmental crisis can be blamed on this passage. However, this is not the case. First, if one goes on to read the next few verses one discovers that at the end of Genesis 1 the food of human beings is limited to a vegetarian diet (Gen. 1.29). Accordingly, the lordship over the world implied here can only be meant in a benign sense, more akin to stewardship.[21] We are reminded of the lovely biblical image of the king as a shepherd (Isa. 44.28; Jer. 23.4; Ezek. 34.23; 37.24; Mic. 5.4 [Heb. 3]). Secondly, there is little evidence that this passage was later misunderstood to justify the ruthless exploitation of nature (Barr 1972: 23–24, repr. 2013: 354–355). The allusion to having dominion over (*radah*) the animals and the earth (Gen. 1.26, 1.28) seems to appropriate royal terminology (cf. Ps. 72.8; 110.2; 1 Kgs 4.24, Heb. 5.4; Isa. 14.6; Ezek. 34.4), though this language is not exclusively royal. But in the current context it lacks all harshness. Furthermore, the reference to subduing (*kabash*) the earth (not animals!) in v. 28 is probably basically the same as having dominion over the earth. It most likely refers to humanity establishing territorial authority over the earth, as later implied in the table of the nations in Genesis 10. This coheres with the usage of the verb *kabash* in a number of other

Old Testament passages, including some others from the Priestly writer (Num. 32:22, 29; Josh. 18.1), as well as elsewhere (2 Sam. 8.11; 1 Chron. 22.18), though unlike these the initial settling down would not have been understood violently. It is also possible that the establishment of agricultural order on the world, tilling the soil, might be included, as James Barr proposed (Barr 1972: 22, repr. 2013: 353). This is not to deny that since the Flood a harsher regime is regarded as having been in operation, with humans being given permission to eat meat (Gen. 9.1-7).[22] But with Paradise restored the ultimate biblical eschatological hope is for the restoration of harmony in nature, including between humans and animals (Isa. 11.6-9).

Notes

1   In addition to the many works cited below, see Jervell (1960), Loretz (1967), Mettinger (1974), Jónsson (1988), Garr (2003), Crouch (2010), Schellenberg (2011).

2   For works by modern systematic theologians, see Berkouwer (1962), Cairns (1973), Hoekema (1986), McFarland (2005).

3   Not that Snaith's own view – that it refers to humanity's dominion over the earth – is right either. See below.

4   Here the Hebrew word *'adam* means 'humanity' rather than an individual person. This is shown by the plural verb that follows on afterwards, 'and let *them* have dominion'. Furthermore, v. 27 makes clear that *ha'adam* includes both male and female. Again, Gen. 5.2 states, 'Male and female he created them, and blessed them and called *their* name humanity (*'adam*)'.

5   Driver (1904: 14–15), 'self-conscious reason'; Eichrodt (1961: 60–65, ET 1967: 122–131), originally a physical likeness but P has spiritualized the concept; Rowley (1956: 78–79), 'man's spiritual nature'.

6   Apart from scholars listed below, see, e.g., Davidson (1973: 25); Brueggemann (1982: 32); Levenson (1988: 111–116); Amos (2004: 11); Arnold (2009: 45).

7   However, this subject was first raised by J. Hehn (1915), primarily citing Mesopotamian sources. Specifically on Egyptian kingship and its alleged relationship with Gen. 1.26-7, see B. Ockinga (1984).

8   Merely of one Neo-Babylonian priest do we read this (Angerstorfer 1997: 54).

9   A majority of scholars today see a reference to the heavenly court here. For a defence of this view, see especially Patrick D. Miller (1978: 9–20). This view follows in the train of an ancient and medieval Jewish interpretation attested in Philo, Targum Pseudo-Jonathan, Rashi and Ibn Ezra. Interestingly, early Jewish rabbinic sources seem more concerned in Gen. 1.26 with the interpretation of 'Let *us* make humanity' than with the precise nature of the divine image borne by humans.

10   The occurrences of *tselem* in Ps. 39.6 (Heb. 7) and 73.20 probably mean something like 'shadow' or 'phantom' and appear to be an extension in meaning of *tselem*, 'image', i.e. *mere* images as opposed to reality. One recalls the shadowy images in Plato's famous allegory of the cave. This is more likely than that *tselem* here means 'darkness'.

11   Abou-Assaf, Bordreuil and Millard (1982: 23–25), lines 1, 12, 15, 16 of the inscription.

12   E.g., note references to Yahweh's face (Exod. 33.11, 20, 23), back (Exod. 33.23), loins (Ezek. 1.27; 8.2) and eyes (Prov. 15.3; 2 Chron. 16.9).

13   Similarly, in Ezek. 8.2, referring to God, the prophet says he saw 'the likeness (*dᵉmut*) as the appearance of a man'. It is generally accepted that the Septuagint preserves the original reading, 'man', and that the last word in the Hebrew text, '*esh*, 'fire', should be emended to '*ish*, 'man'. The parallel description in Ezek. 1.27 confines the fire to the lower part of the divine body, which supports this emendation in Ezek. 8.2, as does the personal possessive in 'his loins', later in the verse. The occurrence of 'fire' later in Ezek. 8.2 could well have given rise to the confusion. Alternatively, Geiger (1928: 343) and Zimmerli (1969: 191, ET 1979: 216) held that the original Hebrew text was changed out of reverence for the divine appearance.

14   Incidentally, Benjamin Sommer (2009: 225 n. 72) notes that apart from the Hellenistically influenced Philo, the Jews tended to envision God as having a body right up till the time of Saadia in the tenth century.

15   The case for the physical nature of the divine image was made most forcefully by Humbert (1940).

16   E.g., with varying degrees of emphasis, Dillmann (1886: 31, ET 1897: 81–82); Skinner (1910: 32); Simpson (1952: 484); von Rad (1958: 45–46, ET 1963: 56–57).

17   Though Aquila, Symmachus and Theodotion altered the Septuagint to read 'God'.

18   I previously followed this view in Day (1985: 54–55), but am no longer convinced.

19   See Barr (1993: 165–167). We should also note Barr's conclusion (167) regarding the nature of the image in Paul here: 'It seems to side with a *physical* understanding of the image in Genesis more than with any other. The image is a sort of luminosity which radiates from the man.'

20   Similarly, the Deutero-Pauline Eph. 4.24 has, 'put on the new nature, created after the likeness of God in true righteousness and holiness'.

21   This is rightly emphasized by Barr (1972, repr. 2013); Rogerson (2010). Other important studies are Rütersworden (1993: 81–130) and Neumann-Gersolke (2004).

22   Schellenberg (2009: 102) curiously maintains that after the Flood humanity is no longer God's viceroy, deputed to rule the world. She emphasizes that Gen. 9.1-7, which recapitulates much of what God says to the first humans in Gen. 1.26ff., fails to employ the verb *radah*, 'to have dominion over', in connection with humanity's

role. However, it is stated that God delivers the animals into human hands and that the fear of humanity will be upon them (Gen. 9.2). This surely betokens divinely sanctioned human rule, albeit on a harsher level than previously, as a concession to human weakness. The absence of the verb *radah* is not significant, any more than the absence of the verb *kabash* with reference to subduing the earth. Furthermore, the table of the nations in Genesis 10 reflects human territorial authority over the earth, which fulfils an aspect of the human dominion over the world commanded by God in Genesis 1. If Schellenberg is right that humans no longer exercise God-given authority over the world following the Flood, this point would surely be expressed clearly in Gen. 9.1-7, which is not the case.

References

Abou-Assaf, A., P. Bordreuil and A. R. Millard (1982), *La statue de Tell Fekherye et son inscription assyro-araméenne*, Etudes assyriologiques, 7, Paris: Editions Recherche sur les civilisations.

Agrippa von Nettesheim, H. C. ([1529] 1990), *De nobilitate et praecellentia foeminei sexus*, Geneva: Droz, ET (1670), *Female Pre-eminence: Or the Dignity and Excellency of that Sex, above the Male*, London: Million.

Amos, C. (2004), *The Book of Genesis*, Epworth Commentaries, Werrington: Epworth Press.

Anderson, B. W. (1975), 'Human Dominion over Nature', in M. Ward (ed.), *Biblical Studies in Contemporary Thought*, 27–45, Burlington, VT: Trinity College Bible Institute.

Angerstorfer, A. (1997), 'Ebenbild eines Gottes in babylonischen und assyrischen Keilschrifttexten', *BN*, 88: 47–58

Arnold, B. T. (2009), *Genesis*. NCBC, Cambridge: Cambridge University Press.

Barr, J. (1968–1999), 'The Image of God in the Book of Genesis: A Study in Terminology', *BJRL*, 51: 11–26, repr. in J. Barton, ed. (2013), *Bible and Interpretation: The Collected Essays of James Barr*, vol. 2: 55–67, Oxford: Oxford University Press.

Barr, J. (1972), 'Man and Nature – The Ecological Controversy and the Old Testament', *BJRL*, 55: 9–32, repr. in J. Barton, ed. (2013), *Bible and Interpretation: The Collected Essays of James Barr*, vol. 2: 344–360, Oxford: Oxford University Press.

Barr, J. (1993), *Biblical Faith and Natural Theology*, Oxford: Clarendon Press.

Barth, K. (1945), *Kirchliche Dogmatik* 3.1, Zollikon: Evangelischer Verlag, ET (1958) *Church Dogmatics* 3.1, Edinburgh: T&T Clark.

Berkouwer, C. G. (1962), *Man: The Image of God*, Grand Rapids, MI: Eerdmans.

Bernard, R. (1952), *L'image de Dieu d'après St Athanase*, Paris: Aubier.

Bird, P. A. (1981), '"Male and Female He Created Them": Gen 1:27b in the Context of the Priestly Account of Creation', *HTR* 74: 129–159, repr. in Bird (1997), *Missing*

Persons and Mistaken Identities: Women and Gender in Ancient Israel, 123–154, Minneapolis, MN: Fortress Press.

Bonhoeffer, D. ([1933] 1989), *Schöpfung und Fall*, Dietrich Bonhoeffer Werke, 3, Munich: Chr. Kaiser, ET (1988), *Creation and Fall: A Theological Exposition of Genesis 1-3*, Dietrich Bonhoeffer Works, 3; Minneapolis, MN: Fortress Press.

Brueggemann, W. (1982), *Genesis, Interpretation*, Atlanta, GA: John Knox Press.

Brunner, E. (1937), *Der Mensch im Widerspruch*, Berlin: Furche-Verlag, ET (1939), *Man in Revolt*, London: Lutterworth Press.

Cairns, D. (1973), *The Image of God in Man*, rev. edn., London: Collins.

Calvin, J., *Commentaries on the First Book of Moses*, vol. 1, 1847, Edinburgh: Calvin Translation Society.

Clines, D. J. A. (1968), 'The Image of God in Man', *TynBul*, 19: 53–103, repr. as 'Humanity as the Image of God', in Clines (1998), *On the Way to the Postmodern: Old Testament Essays 1967–1998*, vol. 2, 447–497, JSOTSup, 293, Sheffield: Sheffield Academic Press.

Crouch, C. L. (2010), 'Genesis 1: 26-7 as a Statement of Humanity's Divine Parentage', *Journal of Theological Studies*, 61: 1–15.

Davidson, R. (1973), *Genesis 1–11*, CBC, Cambridge: Cambridge University Press.

Day, J. (1985), *God's Conflict with the Dragon and the Sea: Echoes of a Canaanite Myth in the Old Testament*, Cambridge: Cambridge University Press.

Dillmann, A. (1886), *Die Genesis*, KEHAT, 5th edn, Leipzig: S. Hirzel, ET (1897), *Genesis Critically and Exegetically Expounded*, Edinburgh: T&T Clark.

Driver, S. R. (1904), *The Book of Genesis*, Westminster Commentaries, London: Methuen.

Eichrodt, W. (1961), *Theologie des Alten Testaments*, vol. 2, Stuttgart: Klotz, ET (1967), *Theology of the Old Testament*, vol. 2, London: SCM.

Fishbane, M. A. (1985), *Biblical Interpretation in Ancient Israel*, Oxford: Clarendon Press.

Garr, W. R. (2003), *In His Own Image and Likeness: Humanity, Divinity, and Monotheism*, CHANE, 15, Leiden: Brill.

Geiger, A. (1928), *Urschrift und Übersetzungen der Bibel*, 2nd edn, Frankfurt: Madda.

Gross, W. (1993), 'Die Gottebenbildlichkeit des Menschen nach Gen 1,26.27 in der Diskussion des letzten Jahrzehnts', *BN*, 68: 35–48.

Hall, D. J. (1986), *Imaging God: Dominion as Stewardship*, Grand Rapids, MI: Eerdmans.

Hehn, J. (1915), 'Zum Terminus ‚Bild Gottes', in G. Weil (ed.), *Festschrift Eduard Sachau zum siebzigsten Geburtstage*, 36–52, Berlin: Georg Reimer.

Hoekema, A. (1986), *Created in God's Image*, Grand Rapids, MI: Eerdmans.

Holsinger-Friesen, T. (2009), *Irenaeus and Genesis*, Journal of Theological Interpretation, Supplements 1, Winona Lake, IN: Eisenbrauns.

Holzinger, H. (1898), *Genesis*, KHAT, 1, Freiburg: Mohr Siebeck.

Horowitz, M. C. (1979), 'The Image of God in Man – Is Woman Included?', *HTR*, 72: 175–206.

Horst, F. (1950), 'Face to Face. The Biblical Doctrine of the Image of God', *Interp*, 4: 259–270.

Humbert, P. (1940), 'L' «Imago Dei» dans l'Ancien Testament', in *Etudes sur le récit de Paradis et de la chute dans la Genèse*, 153–175, Neuchâtel: University of Neuchâtel.

Janowski, B. (2000), 'Gottebenbildlichkeit', in *RGG*, vol. 3, 4th edn, Tübingen: Mohr Siebeck: 1159, ET (2009), 'Image of God', *Religion Past & Present*, vol. 6, Leiden: Brill, 414–415.

Jervell, J. (1960), *Imago Dei: Gen 1, 26f im Spätjudentum, in der Gnosis und in den paulinischen Briefen*, FRLANT, NF 58, Göttingen: Vandenhoeck & Ruprecht.

Jónsson, G. A. (1988), *The Image of God: Genesis 1: 26-28 in a Century of Old Testament Research*, ConBOT, 26, Lund: Almqvist & Wiksell.

Koehler, L. (1948), 'Die Grundstelle der Imago-Dei-Lehre', *TZ*, 4: 16–22.

Levenson, J. D. (1988), *Creation and the Persistence of Evil*, San Francisco, CA: Harper & Row.

Loretz, O. (1967), *Die Gottebenbildlichkeit des Menschen*, Munich: Kösel-Verlag.

McFarland, I. A. (2005), *The Divine Image: Envisioning the Invisible God*, Minneapolis, MN: Fortress Press.

Mettinger, T. N. D. (1974), 'Abbild oder Urbild? »Imago Dei« in traditionsgeschichtlicher Sicht', *ZAW*, 86: 403–424.

Middleton, J. R. (2005), *The Liberating Image: The Imago Dei in Genesis I*, Grand Rapids, MI: Brazos Press.

Miller, J. M. (1972), 'In the "Image" and "Likeness" of God', *JBL*, 91: 289–304.

Miller, P. D. (1978), *Genesis 1-11: Studies in Structure & Theme*, JSOTSup, 8, Sheffield: JSOT.

Neumann-Gersolke, U. (2004), *Herrschen in den Grenzen der Schöpfung: ein Beitrag zur alttestamentlichen Anthropologie am Beispiel von Psalm 8, Genesis 1 und verwandten Texten*, WMANT, 101, Neukirchen-Vluyn: Neukirchener Verlag.

Niebuhr, R., *The Nature and Destiny of Man*, vol. 1, London: Nisbet, 1941.

Ockinga, B. (1984), *Die Gottebenbildlichkeit im alten Ägypten und im Alten Testament*, Ägypten und Altes Testament, 7, Wiesbaden: Harrassowitz.

Oederus, G. L., ed. (1739), *Catechismus Racoviensis*, Frankfurt: J. A. Schmidt.

Pelikan, J., ed. (1958), *Luther's Works*, vol. 1: *Lectures on Genesis Chapters 1–5*, St Louis, MO: Concordia.

Rad, G. von (1958), *Das erste Buch Mose: Genesis*, ATD, 2.4, Göttingen: Vandenhoeck & Ruprecht, ET 1963, *Genesis*, OT Library, 2nd edn, London: SCM.

Riedel, W. (1902), 'Die Gottesebenbildlichkeit des Menschen', *Alttestamentliche Untersuchungen*, vol. 1, 42–47, Leipzig: A. Deichert.

Rogerson, J. (2010), 'The Creation Stories: Their Ecological Potential and Problems', in D. G. Horrell, C. Hunt, C. Southgate and F. Stavrakopoulou (eds), *Ecological Hermeneutics: Biblical, Theological Perspectives*, 21–31, London: T&T Clark.

Rowley, H. H. (1956), *The Faith of Israel*, London: SCM.

Rütersworden, U. (1993), *Dominium Terrae: Studien zur Genese einer alttestamentlichen Vorstellung*, BZAW, 215, Berlin: W. de Gruyter.

Schellenberg, A. (2009), 'Humankind as «Image of God»', *TZ*, 97: 87–111.

Schellenberg (2011), *Der Mensch das Bild Gottes*, ATANT, 101, Zurich: Theologischer Verlag.

Schmidt, W. H. (1964), *Die Schöpfungsgeschichte der Priesterschrift*, WMANT, 17, Neukirchen-Vluyn: Neukirchener Verlag.

Seeberg, R. (1924), *Christliche Dogmatik*, vol. 1, Erlangen; A. Deichert.

Simpson, C. A. (1952), 'Genesis', *Interpreter's Bible*, vol. 1, 437–829, New York: Abingdon-Cokesbury Press.

Skinner, J. (1910), *A Critical and Exegetical Commentary on Genesis*, ICC, Edinburgh: T&T Clark.

Snaith, N. H. (1974), 'The Image of God', *ExpTim*, 86: 24.

Sommer, B. D. (1998), *A Prophet Reads Scripture: Allusion in Isaiah 40-66*, Stanford, CA: Stanford University Press.

Sommer, B. D. (2009), *The Bodies of God and the World of Ancient Israel*, New York: Cambridge University Press.

Stamm, J. J. (1959), *Die Gottebenbildlichkeit des Menschen im Alten Testament*, Theologische Studien, 54, Zollikon: Evangelischer Verlag.

Sullivan, J. E. (1963), *The Image of God: The Doctrine of St. Augustine and Its Influence*, Dubuque, IA: Priory.

Tutu, D. (2014), *In God's Hands*, London: Bloomsbury.

Weinfeld, M. (1967–1968), 'God the Creator in the Priestly Source and Deutero-Isaiah' (Hebrew), *Tarbiz*, 37: 105–32, ET (2004), *The Place of the Law in the Religion of Ancient Israel*, VTSup 100, 95–117, Leiden: Brill.

Westermann, C. (1974), *Genesis 1-11*, BKAT, 1.1, Neukirchen-Vluyn: Neukirchener Verlag, ET (1984), *Genesis 1-11*, London: SPCK.

White, L. (1967), 'The Historical Roots of Our Ecologic Crisis', *Science*, 155 (3767): 1203–1207.

Wildberger, H. (1965), 'Das Abbild Gottes. Gen. 1,26-30', *TZ*, 21: 245–259, 481–501, repr. in Wildberger (1979), *Jahwe und sein Volk: Gesammelte Aufsätze zum Alten Testament*, ed. H. H. Schmid and O. H. Steck, T. Bü, 66, Munich: Chr. Kaiser, 110–145.

Zimmerli, W. (1969), *Ezechiel*, vol. 1, BKAT, 13.1, Neukirchen-Vluyn: Neukirchener Verlag, ET (1979), *Ezekiel*, vol. 1, Hermeneia, Philadelphia, PA: Fortress Press.

Zucker, M., ed. (1984), *Saadya's Commentary on Genesis* (Hebrew), New York: Jewish Theological Seminary of America.

2

The Pre-Christian Concept of Human Dignity in Greek and Roman Antiquity

Josef Lössl

Introduction

The focus of this chapter is on Classical (Greek and Roman) Antiquity, comprising the period between the sixth century BC and the first century AD. In 'Late Antiquity' (from the second to eighth century AD) Greco-Roman culture was already beginning to be shaped by early Christianity and its concept of the human being as created in God's image (Gen. 1:27) and an understanding of human dignity emerging from that concept.

The separation between 'Early' and 'Late' Antiquity is somewhat artificial. Late Antiquity is part of Antiquity. However, it is also a transitional period. Traditionally, Classics and Ancient History have tended to exclude the biblical and early Christian traditions, and the modern reception of the concept of human dignity tends to reach back directly to Classical notions, especially to Cicero's concept of *dignitas humana*, to which much of this chapter will be dedicated. Now Roman *dignitas* cannot simply be equated with the English word 'dignity' in its present-day meaning, let alone with the phrase 'human dignity'. Moreover, there are significant differences between the Roman notion of *dignitas* and similar ancient Greek concepts such as *axíōma, semnótēs, timé* or *ógkos* (see more on these expressions in the relevant section below). The present chapter is therefore about 'Greek' and 'Roman' (and not about 'Greco-Roman') concepts of human dignity. By contrast, it may be justified to refer to the post-Classical culture of Late Antiquity as 'Greco-Roman'. But this is beyond the scope of this chapter.

The main questions addressed in the chapter are to what extent are the pre-Christian Greek and Roman notions of human dignity different from later understandings and to what extent have they nevertheless influenced and continue to influence the latter? The chapter will attempt to answer these questions indirectly by tracing a number of Greek and Roman notions of human dignity outlining their contexts and developments. It will consider cultural and literary aspects from all sections of the period but focus especially on later philosophical developments, in particular Cicero's concept of *dignitas humana* as developed in *On Duties* (*De officiis* 1.30.105–6).

Human dignity, in the way it is generally understood today, originated only in the eighteenth century in the context of the struggle for political freedom and equality, which resulted in the formulation of universal human rights; and it was only after the Second World War that the concept was included in legal and constitutional documents such as the United Nations' Universal Declaration of Human Rights of 1948 or the *Grundgesetz* or 'Basic Law' of the Federal Republic of Germany of 1949 (Rosen 2012: 1–2). The fact that since then it has often been used in 'faith-based ethical discourse' (Rosen 2012: 3), for example in controversial discussions about ethical borderline issues such as abortion or euthanasia, has led to a widespread belief that 'human dignity', understood as 'dignity of human life' or 'dignity of the (individual) human being,' is a faith-based concept and as such 'redundant' (Rosen 2012: 5–6), at least as far as philosophical discourse is concerned. However, this perspective overlooks its connection to the eighteenth-century Enlightenment idea of human emancipation and to the concept of an 'unconditional, intrinsic value' of each individual human being due to the inalienable 'human nature' constituting it and endowing it with a specific set of inalienable 'human rights' (Rosen 2012: 10). It was this 'natural law'–based understanding of humanity, developed by legal theorists in the 1930s and 1940s, that motivated lawmakers in the immediate post-war period to include human dignity elements in basic legislation (most recently perhaps in Article 1 of the *EU Charter of Fundamental Rights*, dating from 18 December 2000 [Volp 2006: 3]). It is this development which is also at the source of further legislation and legal decisions relating to equality and human rights, a development that might benefit from an accompanying philosophical (and not just faith-based) discourse on the concepts of equality, human rights, and the value and dignity of human life.

The importance of the Classical (Greek and Roman) contributions and of Cicero in particular

The Enlightenment interest in the concept of human dignity – the most significant contribution during that period was made by Immanuel Kant (Rosen

2012: 19–30) – was itself influenced by an interest in a universalist, pre-Christian, non-religious, but philosophically grounded concept of the human being. The locus classicus of such a concept was found in a text from Classical Antiquity, Cicero's work *On Duties* (*De officiis* 1.30.106), written about 44 BC, where Cicero not only understands *dignitas* as a 'conventional status term' (Rosen 2012: 12), best translated perhaps as 'prestige', but refers to human 'dignity' in connection with the high ethical demands that are placed on human beings on account of their ontological status (above the other animals and only slightly below the gods): 'It is necessary … that we keep before our eyes how far superior human beings are by their nature to cattle and other beasts', Cicero writes. If we do that, 'we can see that sensual pleasure is quite unworthy of the outstanding excellence of man (*non satis esse dignam hominis praestantia*) … If we will only bear in mind the superiority and dignity of our (human) nature (*quae sit in natura [nostra/humana] excellentia et dignitas*), we shall realise how wrong it is to abandon ourselves to excess' (1.30.105–106).

Commentators have pointed out that this reference by Cicero to human dignity as a marker of human ontological uniqueness and moral excellence is highly exceptional. As Hubert Cancik remarks (2005: 557): 'The word *dignitas* appears frequently in Cicero, the term "dignity of (human) nature" only once.' We will return to this question (specifically on Cicero) later in the chapter. Generally, writers of Classical Antiquity are seen as primarily concerned with their own social status and conventional behaviour. It seems to be widely accepted that a more profound understanding of human dignity as a metaphysically and anthropologically grounded moral principle developed only later in the Christian era. Michael Rosen, for example, after briefly discussing Cicero on pages 11–13 of his book *Dignity* (Rosen 2012), quickly moves on to Christianity pointing out that Christianity had a fundamental problem with the notion of status (*dignitas*) because of its doctrine of reversal of status: 'the last shall be first and the first shall be last' (Matt. 20:16) (Rosen 2012: 14). This tendency in Christianity, according to Rosen, led to a rejection of the value of dignity (understood as worldly status) in favour of spiritual values. Only in the Renaissance, 'most famously in Pico della Mirandola's oration known as *De Dignitate Hominis*,' he concludes, Cicero's more extensive notion of dignity as pertaining 'to the place occupied by human beings within the wider order of reality' is taken up again (Rosen 2012: 14).

Rosen's aim in the relevant section of his book is to point to the inconsistency of the Roman notion of *dignitas*. But one can ask whether this inconsistency really lies in the notion of *dignitas* itself or whether it does not rather originate from Rosen's account. Rosen begins by pointing out that Cicero's philosophical notion of an intrinsic human dignity is an exception not only in Greek and Roman Antiquity generally but also in Cicero's own oeuvre. The predominant notion of dignity in ancient Rome was that of social status. Early Christians felt uncomfortable with that more widespread and conventional 'worldly' understanding of *dignitas* which put them at odds with the dominant culture of their day, not however with the universal concept of human dignity which Cicero had put forward in *On Duties* and to some extent also in the *Republic*. In what sense, then, was the Renaissance concept of human dignity a rediscovery of a more authentic Cicero (if, as Rosen seems to suggest, Cicero generally did not rise above Greek and Roman Antiquity) and a rejection of early and medieval Christianity (if, as Rosen also seems to suggest, the latter did rise above the conventions of that culture)?

The inconsistency in Rosen's account is caused by a certain vagueness on his part about both Cicero's and the early Christian position: If Cicero really formulated an unequivocal universal concept of human dignity, why would the early Christians have rejected that? Would it be because of their principle of 'first comes last and last comes first'? But was that really the basis of their ethical thinking or was that principle not based on the even more fundamental and universal principle of 'treat others as you wish to be treated yourself', the so-called Golden Rule (Dihle 1962)? Is it not more plausible to assume that Cicero did develop that universal concept of human dignity and that the Christians did not reject it but included it in their teaching without perhaps explicit acknowledgement until it was 'rediscovered', as Classical ('Greco-Roman'), in the Renaissance? In fact, Cicero remained a key reference for Christian thinkers throughout the Middle Ages from Ambrose and Augustine to the twelfth-century Cistercians and Scholastics. For example, Aelred of Rievaulx wrote his *De amicitia spirituale* inspired by Cicero's work. The present chapter is less interested in the latter aspects of this story, but rather in aspects that can already be traced in Cicero and in other Greek and Roman sources, which are considerable and not necessarily accredited by modern authors to ancient Greek and Roman culture as such, mainly because of preconceived notions about the differences between Classical and Christian cultures. Closer scrutiny might, however, suggest instead that Classical Greek and Roman culture is closer to early Christian culture – at least in this particular area of anthropology and social ethics – than is often assumed as has been acknowledged in a number of recent studies (see, e.g., Thorsteinsson 2010 on Stoic ethics).

For example, versions of both 'early Christian' principles ('first comes last ... ' and the 'Golden Rule', a principle known in many ancient cultures (Dihle 1962)) can also be found in Cicero's *On Duties*: In 3.6.26, Cicero says that in all actions the aim has to be that the advantage is the same for each individual and for humanity as a whole (*ut eadem sit utilitas uniuscuiusque et universorum*). Earlier, in 2.19.65, he had applied this principle to the justice system and the workings of the legal profession. He had argued that benefits (*beneficia*) are generated both for the 'Republic as a whole' and for individual citizens (*tum in universam rem publicam, tum in singulos cives*) through the delivery of personal service rather than through gifts of money (*opera, non largitione*). In the present deplorable state of affairs, however, he had continued, the link between legal professionalism and social status – the word *dignitas* is also used in this context – had been destroyed (*ut honores, ut omnes dignitatis gradus, sic huius scientiae splendor deletus est*), the relationship has been reversed: now, the lawyer who is serving justice does not receive honour and recognition for his efforts but is persecuted, even murdered, by the prevailing powers.[1] The term *dignitatis gradus* is here understood as 'ranks of public office', ranks that are held with a view to public service, including self-sacrifice, not for self-serving ends.

Thus, ancient Greek and Roman and early Christian ethical culture had perhaps more in common than Rosen's account suggests. Although – or perhaps precisely because – he had a traditional notion of *dignitas*, Cicero genuinely deplored the severance of the link between contribution to society (*opus*) and status (*dignitas*). He understood that under the circumstances in which he wrote – the collapse of the Republican rule of law and the establishment of despotic rule under the Empire – restoration of legal order could, if at all, only be achieved through personal sacrifice. Similarly, the early Christians did not abandon traditional Roman *gradus dignitatis* for some other-wordly 'spiritual values'; they redefined ('Christianized') them (Mathisen 2002). Early Christianity was in many respects a development from Classical Greek and Roman (and especially Roman) Antiquity, not its antagonistic opposite. In *De re publica* (*Republic*) Cicero had once argued that ancient Greek democracy had failed because it lacked the institution of *gradus dignitatis* (1.43). Most early and medieval Christians would have agreed. *Gradus dignitatis* also existed in their social order, while *dignitas humana* was more to them than mere social privilege and prestige based on rank. Rather, rank ought to be based on merit, but the basis of merit was an intrinsic aspect of human nature, its dignity, that is its openness to ethical perfection. Crucially, Cicero had already thought along similar lines, as will be shown in more detail towards the end of this chapter.

Thus, pre-Christian Greek and Roman notions of human dignity such as the one expressed by Cicero were also more than merely imperfect precursors (*Vorläufer*) of Christian and modern concepts (Volp 2006: 4). Rather, they are constitutive for the make-up of the latter. Obviously, they need to be critically examined and must not be used (or rather, abused) for propaganda purposes, to support or reject particular political ideologies. Ulrich Volp, in his study *Die Würde des Menschen: Ein Beitrag zur Anthropologie in der Alten Kirche*, relates an instructive and warning example in this regard. He points out that the 'human dignity' debate in Germany around the 1949 *Grundgesetz* was in part a continuation of debates on the Classical (Ciceronian) concept of *dignitas* carried over from the Nazi era, conducted in part by the same people. In 1934, for example, Max Pohlenz, professor of Classics at Göttingen, had published an internationally acclaimed study on the dependence of Cicero's *On Duties* on the teachings of the Stoic Panaitios, entitled *Antikes Führertum* (Pohlenz 1934). In 1943, Hans Drexler, professor of Latin and then rector of the University of Göttingen, held his inaugural speech (*Rektoratsrede*) on the very same topic (leadership, *Führertum*, in Classical Antiquity) under the title '*dignitas*' (Volp 2006: 2 n. 5). While at the time not considered to be a supporter of the regime, Pohlenz was loyal and continued lecturing even after his retirement in 1937. A teaching ban imposed on him was quickly lifted again. After the war he soon took up lecturing again in 1947 and continued throughout the 1950s. Drexler was closer to the regime. But although banned from holding University and Academy posts, after the war he continued to research and to publish. For example, he contributed to a volume on Roman concepts of the state edited by Richard Klein in 1966 (Volp 2006: 59 n. 283).

At one level Pohlenz and Drexler merely issued pleas to uphold traditional Classical Humanist values and not to abandon Classical Humanist education. However, they did so within – and in Drexler's case at least as supporters of – the regime and its ideology, which they saw as at least partially compatible with ancient Roman values (in this case *dignitas* as a mark of elite leadership). This discredited their contributions, though they still had a limited voice in the post-war debate.

The big difference in the post-war debate, which also led to the legal enshrinement of human rights and the concept of human dignity in the United Nations' Declaration and in the West German *Grundgesetz*, was the insight, drawn from the experiences of the Nazi era, that it is not enough to develop a philosophical understanding of these concepts but that one also has to implement structures and build institutions that enforce and defend them against their enemies (Volp 2006: 2). On the other hand, as the reference above to Cicero's *On Duties* 2.19.65 may also underline, institutions depend for their strength on the commitment of individuals trained to maintain them. In principle, the link drawn between *dignitas* and exemplary leadership is valid. Pohlenz's plea for a continuation of Classical Humanist values may still have some degree of relevance today. The historical context, however, needs to be taken into account. The Classical Greek and Roman legacy held a potential for both extreme right-wing notions such as leadership by an autocratic elite without regard for the rights of the individual and democratic liberal values such as tolerance and the legal protection of the rights of the individual. Significantly, the same ideas as proposed by Pohlenz and Drexler were also proposed by members of the resistance. A document issued by the so-called *Kreisauer Kreis* (*Kreisau Circle*), a group concerned with the democratic reorganization of Germany after the fall of the Third Reich and the reconstruction of democratic institutions, frequently contains the formula 'freedom and human dignity' with implicit references to Classical models (Cancik 2005: 558).

It would therefore be wrong to think that contributions like Pohlenz's and Drexler's belong to an ancient past and are without relevance for today. Even some more recent studies such as Viktor Pöschl's monograph *Der Begriff der Würde im antiken Rom und später* from the late 1980s (Pöschl 1989) are still influenced by a similar ethos (of duty and commitment to the state and to state authority). Pöschl incidentally began his career in the 1930s with studies on the Greek background of Cicero's concept of the state and on the concept of commitment to the state in Sallust (Pöschl 1936, 1939). Readings of Cicero's *On Duties* and the Classical concept of human dignity as those presented by Pohlenz, Drexler and Pöschl remained influential throughout the 1950s to 1980s. Only very recently, in the late 1990s and early 2000s, a tendency developed to study ancient social values less directly as philosophical concepts with immediate relevance for today but more with a view to their literary-historical contexts, which are very different from the settings and challenges of the present time (Volp 2006: 2 n. 5). The present chapter recognizes this recent trend, would, however, reiterate the point that Classical concepts should not just be seen in a tendentially antiquarian fashion as 'pre-modern', 'archaic' or mere 'precursor' concepts, but as concepts that can, within limits, be used to cast a light on current debates and critique certain aspects of present-day concepts.

Lines of development of a concept of human dignity throughout Greek and Roman Antiquity

Terminology, anthropology and legal theory

We have already mentioned that across Greek and Roman Antiquity as a whole we find a diversity of concepts of human dignity that developed over a long period and in different contexts. In order to trace these, we must look not only at obvious vocabulary but at notions for which a variety of different expressions are used. Thus, a conventional notion of dignity understood as 'honourable social status' could be expressed by words such as *axíōma* (value, worthiness) or *timé* (honour), or, at a higher level and at a level of political power, *semnótēs* (grandeur), *schéma* (magnificence) or *ógkos* (weight). At the level of citizens' privileges we have also words like *atéleia* (exemption from duties), *aspháleia* (freedom from danger, protection, security, also *ádeia*) and *exousía* (power to act, freedom of action). None of these concepts were perceived as intrinsic and inviolable rights that could be claimed in any court. They were bestowed on individuals by their community and could be withdrawn for various reasons (the committing of crimes, the running up of debts, the support of an enemy state or simply out of envy and spite). Furthermore, they only applied to fellow citizens, not universally to all human beings. However, this does not mean that there was no notion of an intrinsic dignity of the human person or of human life when we look, for example, at concepts of inviolability and sanctity (*asylía, ádeia, sebâs*). At this level, of course, the concept is linked to religion and shares with the modern, 'faith-based' concept its strengths and weaknesses, i.e. its universality and ontological depth but also its generality and lack of enforceability.

In *Annals* 3.60–63 for the year AD 22 Tacitus relates that the mighty Roman Empire under Tiberius had become increasingly concerned about the degree to which some Greek cities practised their ancient right (based on the presence of significant religious shrines) to grant asylum to criminals and absconded slaves. Temples were heaving with crowds of them, Tacitus writes, and were potentially becoming hotbeds of sedition. Tiberius did not want to act like a despot but asked the Roman Senate to conduct an inquiry into which cities should be allowed to keep their right and from which cities it should be removed. The cities were asked to send embassies. It was an impressive sight, Tacitus writes, not without irony (since only Tiberius held real power), to see so many senators brooding over the ancient documents to reach an informed decision. In the end, some cities were allowed to retain their privilege, while others were told to stop the practice of granting asylum to condemned criminals and fugitive slaves.

This story dates rather late to the first years of the Roman Empire. But it illustrates a number of relevant aspects that were valid throughout Antiquity: the practice of granting asylum to the most rejected elements of humanity beyond the boundaries of a single community was rooted in religion but also had legal status, which was even respected (at least to some degree) by a despotic power like the Roman Empire.

From the sixth century BC, philosophically based concepts of humanity and of dignity were developed as well. They differed according to the relevant philosophical schools. Examples of all of these types will be outlined further below in this section.

In many respects, there are similarities here to the modern debate. For example, there were two very different areas of potential debate, one anthropological, the other legal-constitutional. The anthropological question was: Is there something to 'being human' that makes human beings essentially different from all other beings? Is that 'something' of a higher 'quality', or 'value' (Greek *axía, axíoma, timé*, Latin *valor, qualis, honos*), so that it constitutes a distinct 'human dignity' (*axía, dignitas*)? That would imply that, on the one hand, there is a fundamental discontinuity between all human beings and all other beings, especially living beings, animals and plants, a human 'nature' (Greek *phýsis*, Latin *natura*) that makes humanity 'distinct' and 'stand out' (in the sense of being 'excellent', i.e. of higher value). This is how Cicero understood 'human dignity' when he referred to it, uniquely, in *On Duties* 1.30.106: (... *in natura* [*nostra* or *hominis*] *excellentia et dignitas*). On the other hand, this would also imply that *all* human beings are equal in that – fundamental – regard. And this leads on to the legal question arising from this: Does a common human nature also imply an underlying 'natural law' (Greek *nómos phýseōs*, Latin *lex naturae*), which would then guarantee all human beings a set of inalienable, 'human', 'rights' ('right' = Greek *díkē, dikaíōma*, Latin *ius*), as well as impose on them certain responsibilities (i.e. 'duties', Greek *táxeis*, Latin *officia*)? For example, would equality be such a right and responsibility? The following reflections will focus more on the anthropological dimension of the debate, but keep in mind the fundamental legal implications as well. As was already mentioned above, while Greek and Roman Antiquity knew these concepts of 'law' and 'rights', there was not really a set of political institutions, 'nationally' or 'internationally', that would have allowed any person to claim such 'rights' or a notion that such a set-up was possible or desirable.

The inner connection between the recognition of rationality, freedom and, following on from this, moral responsibility of human beings, their fundamental distinctiveness in comparison with other animals, was present in Greek and Roman Antiquity, although there was less of a tendency to differentiate between 'value' and 'dignity', as there is in the modern debate (Volp 2006: 10, 53–61). Value and dignity are synonymous in Greek, and in Latin, dignity was treated as just another value besides, for example, justice, trust (*fides*), duty (*officium*), manliness (*virtus*), honour, truthfulness, authority or generosity (Volp 2006: 58). Nevertheless, there was a development towards the concept of dignity as the highest value and principle of human action, which reached its culmination, in a certain sense, in Cicero's *On Duties* (Volp 2006: 53–54). But before we draw out these aspects towards the end of this chapter, let us reflect a bit more on their philosophical and cultural-historical background.

Different philosophical interpretations and their common background

If we begin, as indicated above, from a position that situates the human being within a natural order and finds that it excels within that order, but also that that natural order extends to matters concerning humans, including politics, the economy and generally, communal living, we will face two fundamental questions: (1) In what sense and to what extent are humans different (from each other and from the rest of reality)? And (2) What, if anything, follows from this with regard to ethics? We shall see that both questions are fraught with problematic implications. Let us look at some examples: 'Kinship of all people as children of Zeus and the obligation of fraternity as members of a large family' (Siewert 2005: 564) was a broadly recognized principle, invoked by Stoics (Epictetus, *Dissertation* 1.3), by dramatists (Sophocles, *Antigone* 449–455) and by Cicero in *Republic* 3.22. Cicero referred to it as 'natural [and] ..., divine, in keeping with the rational world order' (Siewert 2005: 564), a universal law that was also, as we shall see further below, manifest in the human conscience and foundational for any positive legislation.

However, in practice, positive legislation did not need to rely on such a concept of universal law. Even some philosophers tried to develop their theories without it. For example, Aristotle, in the opening passage of his *Politics*, observes just two basic realities: (1) Humans live communally, and (2) they do so governed by rules (laws). For a philosophical explanation of such a simple reality, it was not necessary to invoke an underlying universal natural law. Some philosophers, particularly Epicurus and his followers, argued that the communal human way of life, regulated by rules and laws, might also merely be based on (human) convention (*Principal doctrines* 33 and 37). As the Epicurean Lucretius famously put it in Book 5 of *De rerum natura* (1019–1028): civilisation began in primitive times, when human beings who happened to live in proximity with one another struck agreements of friendship (*amicitiem* – the rare form *amicities* is used here; cf. Konstan 2008: 88–93) for utilitarian purposes, to maximize security and minimize harm, for themselves, for their women and children and for the weak (*imbecilli*) among them. Although unity (*concordia*) was never fully (*omnimodis*) achieved, this secured at least the survival of humankind. Without this kind of what could be called a 'social contract' (although Lucretius does not use that expression), humanity would have become extinct early on (*genus humanum iam tum foret omne peremptum*). But there is no 'deeper' explanation for why human beings should have entered into this friendship agreement other than their instinct for material survival.

But let us return to the Stoic concept of a natural law that is, as it were, 'written into' the ontological fabric of human beings (cf. St Paul in Romans 2:14-15): this was a much more optimistic view of human nature. In a passage in *Annals* 3.26, the Roman historian Tacitus describes the 'natural' life of the earliest humans (*vetustissimi mortalium*) as free of the oppressions of positive legislation. They lived without evil desires, committed no crimes and knew no punishments or sanctions (*nulla … mala libidine, sine probro, scelere … sine poena aut coercitionibus*); and since they had no desires that contravened their customs (*mos*), there was no need for prevention by fear (*nihil per metum vetabantur*). Positive law was introduced later, and then it suffered from the very start from a tendency to proliferation and corruption. Ever more legislation led to ever more corruption and transgression.

This is the observation that also lies behind the story of Sophocles's *Antigone* (449–455), who justified her resistance against the official authority of the positive law by the 'unwritten, unchangeable, eternal right of the gods' (Siewert 2005: 564). But invoking a divine law or law of nature in a context where positive law is dominant does not solve the inherent discrepancy between ideal and reality. What use was it that law books (e.g. Ulpian, *Digest* 1.1.4) stated that slavery was against the natural law (*ius naturale*)? The same law books also stipulated that it could be legitimized as an institution by the laws of the nations (*ius gentium*). What ancient societies may have recognized in principle, namely that all human beings, on account of their being human beings, were free and equal and therefore entitled to identical legal privileges, did not necessarily, or, in fact, did never really translate into social and political orders that were upheld by the force of law. In practice, lines were always drawn (even though, as we saw from the example of the asylum cities, the drawing of lines could also be subverted).

Thus Solon's laws for Athens apparently included elements that recognized human dignity. According to one possible fragment there was a law that forbade the abuse of prisoners (fragment 16/a Ruschenbusch; Leão and Rhodes 2015; Siewert 2005: 564). But it did not protect prisoners in other respects, and at any rate, as Antigone's example also shows, violations could not normally be challenged in courts. Moreover, as mentioned already, the advanced and refined privileges guaranteed by Athenian law, e.g. freedom of assembly, justification of political resistance against tyrants, equality before the law, limitations of state power, respect of privacy, freedom of information, participation in cultural life and many others, extended only to a very small and strictly defined group of citizens (usually males fit for military service), and they were not inviolable rights but 'powers and competences which (unlike rights) could be taken away at any time' (Wallace 2016). A more or less codified set of positive laws for one limited political entity that translated the principle of human dignity into entitlements for a privileged minority stands here in contrast to the lack of a universal legal theory or a programme (with some institutional backing) that would have aimed at extending these rights to the entirety of humankind. It is not that such a theory did not exist in Antiquity, but it only existed as a philosophical-anthropological theory, not as an ambitious legal programme backed by institutions with a realistic prospect of implementing it by way of an ongoing strategy or policy.

The root of the concept of human dignity in Greek and Roman Antiquity does not lie in the area of legal theory but of philosophical anthropology. The discovery of rationality as a phenomenon by the Presocratics led to the distinction between a 'common reason' (*koinós lógos*) that subsists in every human being and non-rational elements (the body and the emotions). Reason became identified with the rational mind-soul and was seen as the essence of the human being. Moreover, the essence of the soul was seen as divine or of divine origin (Volp 2006: 22–23). The idea that at its core the soul possessed a 'divine spark' preceded Plato. It originated from mythology and was held in common with ancient Near Eastern mythologies, where the creation of human beings was often seen as resulting from a mingling of the blood of the gods and the earth. But here, from the Presocratics onwards, and already to some degree in Homer and Hesiod, the idea of a divine origin of the soul, or a link between the human soul and divinity, had become philosophically informed. Divinity here meant transcendence in a philosophical sense. Plato became the main exponent of this kind of thinking. Plato saw the composite state of the human being (mind-soul – *noûs*, emotional soul – *psyché* and body – *sôma*) as transitory. For him the priority lay in the exploration of the eternal mind-soul and its world (*Phaedrus* 245C-246B). Plato did not deny the existence of physical reality but saw it as less real than the intellectual world inhabited by the mind-soul. By contrast, his pupil Aristotle attributed a higher degree of reality to the physical world and attempted to formulate a theory of unity between body and mind. He did this by introducing a mediating principle, *pneuma* (*perì zôôn genéseōs; De generatione animalium* 736B28 and 744B21-22). As a consequence, he was better able to describe the human being as a being – a 'rational animal' – inhabiting the physical world, but at the same time his ability to express the eminence of the human being and to formulate a theory which would state how this eminence is rooted in the essentially transcendent nature of that being was diminished. Hence his (compared with Plato and the Stoics) very reduced explanation of communal rule-based human life, as was briefly mentioned above.

The Stoic solution to this problem was to return to the original insight that human and divine reason are related. The latter was identical with the universal world order, the natural law, at the level of which immanence and transcendence, materiality and immateriality, were no longer divided. As far as human beings were concerned, there was now one principle of metaphysics and ethics, the rule of the rational soul over the irrational body in accordance with nature, 'nature' meaning the rational, universal and divine law of nature (Volp 2006: 26). Cicero was strongly influenced by this, as we have already seen.

In contradistinction to the Stoics, Epicurus and his followers saw in rationality no more than the way in which physical reality functioned. For them there was no reality beyond the physical. The soul therefore only existed as an aspect of the body. At the disintegration of the body (death) the soul also ceased to exist. The only function of reason while the body is alive is to 'regulate' the emotional household (Volp 2006: 26) or, on a communal level, as seen above in the case of Lucretius's explanation of communal living, to secure the survival of the species. The Epicurean 'model' is also seen by some as relevant for today's materialist worldviews (Greenblatt 2012) and some have argued that its influence in Antiquity too was stronger than has traditionally been allowed for (Whitmarsh 2015).

From religious beginnings to a philosophically reflected concept

However, this does not change the fact that generally speaking Classical Antiquity was 'a world full of gods' (Hopkins 1999). The idea that religion was not compatible with Humanism would have been considered bizarre in Antiquity (Lössl 2018: 34–35). Accordingly, throughout the period, we find humanity defined in contradistinction to divinity, both positively and negatively. For example, in Homer, *Iliad* 6.146 (*c.* 750 BC), human beings are described – in view of their mortality – quasi as 'leaves in a forest'. Hesiod (*Theogony* 535–612), writing in *c.* 700 BC, paints a miserable picture of human life, accursed, burdensome, full of suffering and ending in death. But already in Homer's *Odyssey* 9.106–115 (*c.* 725 BC) we find a philosophically more informed description of earliest humanity. The passage refers to the Cyclopes as if to a type of primitive humans. They are described as inhabiting a natural world, looked after by the gods and blessed by nature, without need of work or legislation. But this 'unconstitutional' (*athémistos*) state is not seen as preferable to the 'constitutional' (*thémistos*) state of human culture. Only the latter is instituted by Zeus (*Iliad* 11.80) and thus god-willed (*Odyssey* 16.403), and only in the latter can there be 'right' (*díkē*) – or legality – and 'rightful' ('legal'; *díkaioi*) people (*Odyssey* 3.52, 13.209 et al.; Volp 2006: 30).

This model still works without the concept of human nature (*physis*), which is first introduced in the sixth century BC by Xenophanes and Heraclitus (*Fragments* B18, 22B1 and B112; Curd and McKirahan 2011: 5, 12, 40, 42) but became widespread soon after. As it was quickly adopted by the humanistic and anthropocentric Sophists, the ambivalence about the status and role of human beings (born helpless and needy, in need of constant support by others, reliant on learning and self-improvement throughout life, and ultimately transitory and prone to illness, decay and finally, death) gave way to a rampant optimism regarding the excellent nature and superiority of human beings vis-à-vis all other living beings. While the Presocratics themselves, Xenophanes, Heraclitus, Anaximander and Anaxagoras (as above plus 12A10, 59B21, 59B21b, 59A102; Curd and McKirahan 2011: 17, 102, 105, 106), still readily acknowledged this ambivalence (Anaxagoras, for example, pointed to the weakness of the human senses and the lack of physical strength of humans compared to other animals), the poetry of Pindar focused on the positive aspects of that condition. For Pindar, the need of human beings to learn, to develop and to overcome the challenges of their disadvantage vis-à-vis other animals presented an enormous opportunity to achieve self-perfection, moral excellence, *aretĕ*, something not offered to any other animal and, crucially, not even to the gods (who are above moral judgement), but only to those possessing a human nature.

Alkmaeon and Heraclitus point to reason (*noûs*) as the decisive gift of humans that turns their disadvantage into an advantage (*Fragments* 24B1a, 22B72 et al.; Curd and McKirahan 2011: 5, 42, 44). Democritus attributes reason to other animals too (*ibid.* 68B198; Volp 2006: 31 n. 125), but he was an exception. Mostly human reason (what became the mind-soul) was distinguished from the soul as the principle of life (*psychē*) which all animals (and even plants) possessed. The human *noûs* was seen as a divine power, or as participating in a divine power, that ordered the universe (Diogenes of Apollonia, *c.* 460–390 BC, cited in Volp 2006: 32). The properties of upright posture, the use of hands, language and also the fact that humans looked upwards to the sky (the dwelling place of the gods) were perceived as external physical manifestations of the *noûs* (Xenophon, *Memorabilia* 1.4.11).

The famous opening passage of the work on the Catiline War by the Roman historian Sallust dating from around 40 BC contains all these elements:

> All human beings who strive to be superior to other animals must see that they do not spend their life in silence as the beasts do, whom nature formed, bent down and obedient to the stomach. But our strength lies in the soul and in the body. The soul we use for its power of command, the body more in view of its servile nature. The one we have in common with the gods, the other with the beasts. Therefore, it seems more appropriate (*rectius*) to me to seek glory in works of ingenuity rather than of brute force … For the glory of riches and beauty is transient and frail, moral excellence (Latin *virtus*, Greek *aretē*) however stands out and lasts in eternity. (Sallust, *Catiline War* 1.1–4)

Although Sallust uses – and instrumentalizes – philosophical concepts such as soul, body, moral excellence, liberty and dignity in view of the specific political situation in which he writes (the transitional period from the late Republic to the early Empire), he also stands in a more universal tradition of Humanist thought that can be traced back to the Sophists of the fifth to fourth century BC, who first emphasized the excellence of human nature and freedom and self-determination as the most appropriate purpose of a human life. Volp cites the Sophist Alkidamas: 'God created all men free; nature made no-one into a slave (*eleuthérous aphēke pántas theós, oudéna doûlon hē physis pepoíēken*)' (2006: 34). The Sophists challenged the above-mentioned discrepancy between positive law (*thései díkaion*) and natural law (*physei díkaion*) and accused the tyranny of the positive law which created inequality in society (Hippias of Elis, late fifth century BC, cited in Plato, *Gorgias* 484B).

It was Socrates who then, around the same time, turned this political concept into a more individual instrument of self-scrutiny and sought excellence beyond social and political reality, in himself. Plato worked this into his more systematic teaching which was already briefly outlined above. Crucially, for him, reason, *phrónēsis*, compensated for the natural shortcomings of humans and enabled them to create their own, cultural, world (*Protagoras* 321CD). Aristotle added to this a programme of practical sciences, education, politics, economics, ethics etc. He recognized that human beings would not instantly 'leap' from imperfection to perfection but could only progress gradually, and in order to be able to do this they needed structures, methods and practical programmes that enabled them to realise their potential. This division of reality into potentiality and actuality is central to Aristotle's thinking (the technical term for it is *entelecheía*). But, ironically, it led Aristotle to compromise the idea of equality and to assume that there are different grades of humanity. Thus, he notoriously considered it as evident that (in all species) females fulfilled the potential of their species to a lesser degree than males and that some human beings were naturally predisposed to being slaves and possessed reason only to a degree that enabled them to obey commands (*Politics* 1254B, 1259B).

It was the Stoics who most vigorously and effectively argued that such views could not lay any claim on universal validity. The Sophists had, as we saw, used their rhetoric to proclaim the principle of equality, but it was the Stoics who, from the fourth century BC on, were to provide the philosophical underpinning against Plato and Aristotle. Already the early Stoics are reported to have stipulated a common law (*koinòs nómos*) which was considered the right thing to follow (*aretḗ*) for all humans (Diogenes Laertius 7.87–88). This is now no longer restricted to the sphere of individual communities or *póleis*, but to the whole world (*kósmos*), i.e. the human being is here addressed as a cosmopolitan (a citizen of the world).

There were still limits, however. Since reason manifested itself in language, those who were not able to speak the language of reason [?] (namely Greek), i.e. the Barbarians (those whose foreign tongues sounded like 'brabra'), were still excluded (Epicurus as cited by Volp 2006: 46 n. 214 and 215). It should however be considered that at this time (in the late fourth and early third century BC, after the conquests of Alexander the Great) the use of the Greek language (*koinḗ*) had massively expanded. It had now become hardly imaginable that there were any parts of the world where Greek was not spoken, at least at some level. In a certain sense, therefore, seen from that perspective, Greek-speaking humanity was humanity in its entirety.

The Stoics also became more theological and explained reason or the soul as the seat where a human being reveals himself or herself as an image (*mímēma*) of God (Musonius, ed. Lutz 1947: 108.15: *toû theoû … mímēma*), granted that he or she lives according to nature. In a similar way Seneca says that philosophy holds out the promise to make him 'equal to God' (or 'to a god'), *parem deo*

(*Letter* 48.11), and that the wise man lives on a par with the gods, *sapiens ... dis ex pari vivit* (*Letter* 59.14). This tendency to put the human being centre stage and elevate him or her to the rank of a god on grounds of the mind-soul increased the dichotomy between humanity and the animal world. It was no longer considered that animals possessed reason. But it would be mistaken to assume that this created a mentality that was out to subdue, ruthlessly exploit or even destroy the natural environment. On the contrary, the turn was to the 'inner man' and to a life of intellectual and spiritual pursuits and a lifestyle that did not stand in the way of such pursuits. Musonius, famously, preached vegetarianism (Dillon 2004: 20–21).

Thus, while one dichotomy was between the human being and the rest of the natural world, the other dichotomy was between the human being as a mind-soul (the so-called inner man) and the human being as a biological, physical animal or 'outer man'. The concept of the 'inner man' originated with the Platonist emphasis on the mind-soul as the core of human identity (Markschies 1994). But it worked equally well as a focal point for Stoic and early and medieval Christian introspection (Haas 1997).

The relevance of this for the present enquiry lies in the increasing influence of this tendency towards introspection in Stoic and (Middle-)Platonic philosophy, which also affected thinkers like Cicero and later Seneca and Musonius. It was to make a massive breakthrough in the third century AD with the thought of Plotinus and Neoplatonism, but these later developments lie outside the scope of this chapter.

Conclusions

The preceding sections will hopefully have helped to understand a little bit better the context in which Cicero developed his concept of *dignitas humana* and to what extent he may have been influenced in this by Stoic anthropological thinking. When he refers, for example, to 'the human race' (*genus humanum; Laelius* 5.20; *Republic* 2.26 – and often elsewhere), and when he identifies reason (*ratio*) as the core marker of what it means to be human, he thinks along Stoic lines. In doing so he constituted at least the meaning of the definition of man as 'rational animal' (*animal rationale*), when he defines man, in stark contradistinction to beast (*belua*, the same expression that Sallust uses in *Catiline War* 1.2), as *rationis particeps* (*On Duties* 1.4.11). In *Republic* 2.26, where he speaks of *humanitas* as the decisive property that makes man human and relates it to civility and sociability, attitudes that are specifically lacking in tyrants, he implies that reason (what Aristotle would have called *phrónēsis*), too, is central to *humanitas* (Stegmann 2005).

In *Laws* 1.7.23 Cicero says that the first thing that man has in common with God – or (probably more likely) with *a* god – is reason (*prima homini cum deo rationis societas*). The reason why 'a god' is the more likely expression here is because the highest reality to which Cicero refers is reason. In *Laws* 1.6.18 he had already insisted that the highest form of reason is the law which is implanted in nature and which commands that which ought to be done and that which ought to be avoided, in other words, conscience. This is the true law (*lex vera*) and stands above any form of the positive law. Insofar as Cicero intended to say that the primary form of association man has with *the* God is reason, he was identifying reason with God. This highest form of reason, conscience, the true law, also the eternal law (*lex aeterna*), is the point, according to Cicero, at which humanity is touching divinity. In *On Duties* 1.30.106 he refers to this reality as *dignitas humana* and immediately makes clear that this reality imposes a demand on man: self-control, Greek *egkráteia* (Volp 2006: 51), which is the primary manifestation of self-determination.

In *Laws* 1.5 he further explains how this eternal true law in man is related to natural law and to positive law: 'Our aim is to explain the nature of law and to derive this from the nature of man' (*natura enim iuris explicanda nobis est eaque ab hominis repetenda natura*). Thus, what Cicero wants to explain in *Laws* is not so much the workings of the (positive) laws themselves. His question is a philosophical one: What actually are laws, and why (under what conditions) do they exist? In his view, answers to both questions can be found in man. The human being, at its deepest level, is constituted as a law. The nature of that law is self-determination, which is to be practised under the condition of self-control (*egkráteia*). The 'dignity of man' (*dignitas hominis*) for Cicero consists in this 'mechanism' being available – uniquely and specifically – to human beings and to no other beings in the entire universe.

This understanding of *dignitas* is unique to Cicero and rare even in Cicero's oeuvre, but it does guide his thought. Even where he uses *dignitas* in a more conventional way, to denote social status, he does not primarily understand it as privilege for its own sake but as duty and obligation (Volp 2006: 53–54). He is influenced in all this, of course, by Stoic thought. However, the combination of the cosmological Stoic concept of natural law and man's privileged position within nature on one hand, and of the anthropological concept of human nature and man's ethical destiny, from which the unique concept of human dignity directly emerged, on the other seems to have been Cicero's very own contribution. It was taken up 400 years later by Augustine. But that is a different story (Volp 2006: 54).

Note

1   Cicero was here perhaps thinking of himself. Proscribed because of his association with Caesar's assassins, he was probably killed not long after writing *On Duties*; see Newton (2016: 3–6) on the historical context.

References

Cancik, H. (2005), 'Human Dignity', in H. Cancik and H. Schneider (eds), *Brill's New Pauly. Encyclopedia of the Ancient World*, vol. 6, 556–558, Leiden: Brill.

Curd, P. and R. D. McKirahan (2011), *A Presocratics Reader. Selected Fragments and Testimonia*, Indianapolis, IN; Cambridge: Hackett.

Dihle, A. (1962), *Die goldene Regel. Eine Einführung in die Geschichte der antiken und frühchristlichen Vulgärethik*, Göttingen: Vandenhoeck & Ruprecht.

Dillon, J. T. (2004), *Musonius Rufus and Education in the Good Life*, Lanham, MD: University Press of America.

Dyck, A. R. (1997), *A Commentary on Cicero, De officiis*, Ann Arbor, MI: University of Michigan Press.

Greenblatt, St. (2012), *The Swerve: How the Renaissance Began*, London: Vintage.

Griffin, M. T. and E. M. Atkins (1991), *Cicero. On Duties*, Cambridge: Cambridge University Press.

Haas, Alois M. (1997), 'Innerer und äußerer Mensch. Eine tragende Unterscheidung der mittelalterlichen Seelengeschichte', *Perspektiven der Philosophie: Neues Jahrbuch*, 23: 3–17.

Hopkins, K. (1999), *A World Full of Gods: Pagans, Jews and Christians in the Roman Empire*, New York; London: Weidenfeld.

Konstan, D. (2008), *A Life Worthy of the Gods. The Materialist Psychology of Epicurus*, Las Vegas: Parmenides.

Leão, D. F. and P. J. Rhodes (2015), *The Laws of Solon: A New Edition with Introduction, Translation and Commentary*, London; New York: I. B. Tauris.

Lössl, J. (2018), 'Religion in the Hellenistic and Early Post-Hellenistic Era', in J. Lössl and N. Baker-Brian (eds), *A Companion to Religion in Late Antiquity*, 33–59, Hoboken, NJ: Wiley Blackwell.

Lutz, C. E. (1947), 'Musonius Rufus. The Roman Socrates', *Yale Classical Studies*, 10: 1–147.

Markschies, Chr. (1994), 'Die platonische Metapher vom inneren Menschen', *Zeitschrift für Kirchengeschichte*, 105: 1–17.

Mathisen, R. W. (2002), 'The Christianization of the Late Roman Senatorial Order', *International Journal of the Classical Tradition*, 9 (2): 257–278.

Newton, B. P. (2016), *Cicero. On Duties*, New Haven, CT: Cornell University Press.

Pohlenz, M. (1934), *Antikes Führertum: Cicero De officiis und das Lebensideal des Panaitios*, Leipzig & Berlin: Teubner.

Pöschl, V. (1936), *Römischer Staat und griechisches Staatsdenken bei Cicero*, Berlin: Junker & Dünnhaupt.

Pöschl, V. (1939), *Grundwerte römischer Staatsgesinnung in den Geschichtswerken des Sallust*, Berlin: De Gruyter.

Pöschl, V. (1989), *Der Begriff der Würde im antiken Rom und später*, Sitzungsberichte der Heidelberger Akademie der Wissenschaften. Philosophisch-Historische Klasse 1989.3: Heidelberg.

Rosen, M. (2012), *Dignity. Its History and Meaning*, Cambridge, MA: Harvard University Press.

Ruschenbusch, E. (1966), *Solonos nomoi. Die Fragmente des solonischen Gesetzeswerkes mit einer Text- und Überlieferungsgeschichte*, Stuttgart: Steiner.

Siewert, P. (2005), 'Human Rights', in H. Cancik and H. Schneider (eds), *Brill's New Pauly. Encyclopedia of the Ancient World*, vol. 6, 563–565, Leiden: Brill.

Stegmann, M. (2005), 'Humanitas', in H. Cancik and H. Schneider (eds), *Brill's New Pauly. Encyclopedia of the Ancient World*, vol. 6, 560–563, Leiden: Brill.

Thorsteinsson, R. M. (2010), *Roman Christianity and Roman Stoicism. A Comparative Study of Ancient Morality*, Oxford: Oxford University Press.

Volp, U. (2006), *Die Würde des Menschen. Ein Beitrag zur Anthropologie in der alten Kirche*, Leiden: Brill.

Wallace, R. W. (2016), 'Review of Leão and Rhodes (2015)', *Bryn Mawr Classical Review* 2016.03.30.

Walsh, P. G. (2001), *Cicero. On Duties*, Oxford: Oxford University Press.

Whitmarsh, T. (2015), *Battling the Gods. Atheism in the Ancient World*, London: Penguin Random House.

3

Christ as *Imago Dei* – A Missed Opportunity of Ante-Nicene Christian Theology

Vladimir Latinovic

Introduction

With its emancipation of human dignity, the *imago Dei* concept is without a doubt one of the most beautiful and valuable concepts of Old and New Testament theology. The creation of human beings in the image and likeness of their heavenly creator 'implies a special relationship between God and man, between Creator and creature' (Roos 2011: 31), gives enormous boost to their self-esteem and unlocks and promotes all of their creative potential.[1] Psalm 8 illustrates the importance of this concept by placing human beings just a tad below the heavenly creatures, with the New Testament expanding their capacity to develop and grow even beyond the glory of angels.[2] It is not a coincidence that in Gen. 1.26-7, where this concept emerged, human beings are raised above the rest of creation by entrusting to them rule over the animals.[3]

As interesting and as inspiring the anthropological significance of the *imago Dei* concept is, in this chapter I wish to explore another aspect of this concept, the Christological one.[4] The main reason for this, beside the fact that most of the authors writing about it so far (Clines 1968; Miller 1972; Hoekema 1986; Jonnson 1988; Bray 1991) have focused on the anthropological aspects, is that both the New Testament and early Christian theology use the *imago Dei* concept primarily in a Christological context. As Norman Porteous puts it:

> Nothing could make clearer the tremendous impact of the revelation of God in Christ than the fact that it has almost completely obliterated the thought of man as being in the image of God and replaced it with the thought of Christ as being the image of God. (1962: 684)

Furthermore, the *imago Dei* concept greatly impacted on the ante-Nicene Christological disputes[5] and could have served as a viable alternative to the Trinitarian and homoousian theology (the notion that the Second Person of the Trinity is of one substance with the Father and equal to him), which emerged as the winner of these disputes. I believe the *imago Dei* concept still holds great potential for modern theology, especially for interreligious dialogue – possibilities which will be discussed in the final part of the chapter. First, though, I will present an overview of the development of *imago Dei* theology up to the council of Nicaea (325).

Development of *imago Dei* theology

Before I come to my analysis of the *imago Dei* concept by the early Christian authors, we need to look briefly at its emergence in the Old and its development in the New Testament.

Biblical roots of the concept

The origins of the *imago Dei* concept are rooted in Gen. 1.26-7 (see Chapter 1). The first human beings are created in God's image (Hebrew צֶלֶם [*tsélem*], Greek εἰκών [*eikón*]) and likeness (Hebrew דְּמוּת [*d'mút*], Greek ὁμοίωσις [*homoíōsis*]).[6] There are of course no Christological implications in these verses, but later patristic authors interpreted the use of plural form in v. 26 – 'let *us* make human beings in *our* image' – to indicate a Trinitarian dimension and in some cases to see the Son as the archetypal image after which first humans are created.[7] We also find the concept of creation of man in God's image in some other canonical (Gen. 5.1; 5.3; 9.6) and apocryphal (Sir. 17.3; Wis. 2.23) Old Testament books, but these are either derived from or directly connected to Gen. 1.26-7, so they are not important to our context and can be set aside.

Regarding Gen. 1.26-7, Grenz argues that 'although the Genesis text sets forth the theme that humans are to represent God, the narrative does not indicate the precise form that this representational vocation is to take' and explains this with the notion that 'by leaving the matter open-ended and suspenseful, Genesis 1:26-7 awaits a future fulfilment of the quest of the full meaning of the imago Dei' (2004: 622). This will reach its climax in the New Testament. Interestingly, the idea that God created man and woman in his image is completely absent from the Gospels,[8] but it plays quite a significant role in the anthropology and Christology of Paul and the author of Hebrews. For Paul, Christ is the only true image of

God (Col. 1.12-16; 2 Cor. 4.4-6; Heb. 1.3), and humans, being a new creation, participate in this image (Col. 3.9-10; 1 Cor. 11.7-9; Jas. 3.9; Rom. 8.29; 2 Cor. 3.18). Christ restores the original and intended image of God in human beings.

Since our topic here is primarily Christ as *imago Dei*, let us now look at some passages where Paul talks about this. In Col. 1.12-16 he states that 'the Son is the image of the invisible God, the firstborn over all creation' and connects this to Gen. 1.26-7 by stating that through and for Christ all things were created. This will later become the cornerstone for the so-called Logos theology of the Apologists (Chadwick 1965; Barnard 1971; Lashier 2012). Paul explains that unbelievers 'cannot see the light of the gospel that displays the glory of Christ, who is the image of God' (2 Cor. 4.4-6). In this passage, Christ as the image of God is something that serves to emphasize Christ's divinity and his connection to God, but in Bray's assessment, for example, this '"image of God" becomes a phrase which sets Christ apart from us, not one which unites Him to us in Adam' (Bray 1991: 211). In his opinion we ought 'to interpret it as a statement about Christ's equality with the Father, and not about his identity with us'. As we will see, Paul's use of the concept here affected patristic theology in the sense that some later writers assumed Paul's insights identified Christ as the only true image of God.

Epistle of Barnabas

One of the oldest Christian documents, the *Epistle of Barnabas* (written between AD 70 and 132) follows the path set by the New Testament books regarding the question of who represents the true image of God. For the unknown author of this *Epistle*, 'formation and reformation of the image are carried out by the same Word, who fashions and refashions the image according to himself' (Boersma 2016: 5). The *Epistle* quotes Gen. 1.26-7 directly and explains:

> There is yet this also, my brethren; if the Lord endured to suffer for our souls, though He was Lord of the whole world, unto whom God said from the foundation of the world, let us make man after our image and likeness, how then did He endure to suffer at the hand of men? (5, 5).

This verse puts Christ in the role of Logos who at the foundation of the world participated in the creation of man according to God's image and likeness and recently endured suffering for their souls. The accent is put heavily on the *kenosis* of Christ, who being the original image according to which humanity was created, emptied himself and made the greatest sacrifice for humanity. In this relatively small *Epistle* the Genesis verse is quoted a second time:

> For the scripture saith concerning us, how He saith to the Son; Let us make man after our image and after our likeness, and let them rule over the beasts of the earth and the fowls of the heaven and the fishes of the sea. And the Lord said when He saw the fair creation of us men; Increase and multiply and fill the earth. These words refer to the Son. (6, 12)

The Son plays the role not only of creator but also as a model after which humans are sculpted, the perfect *imago Dei*. Interestingly, the Spirit is completely left out of this verse and is not mentioned anywhere in the *Epistle*. Instead, God's power is the generative source in the Old Testament sense.

In the *Epistle*, there is actually a third passage that talks about Christ as the image of God but this time in connection with Ex. 20.4: 'You shall not make for yourself an image in the form of anything in heaven above or on the earth beneath or in the waters below.' On the one hand, through Moses God gave man a commandment not to create any images of him and, on the other hand, he 'himself made one that he might show them a type of Jesus' (12, 6).

Justin Martyr

Several decades later in the writings of Justin Martyr (AD 100–65), we find 'anticipations of the language of a "common image", which will become an interpretive hallmark of Ante-Nicene interpretations of Genesis 1:26' (Boersma 2016: 5). Justin was deeply influenced by Platonic and Aristotelian concepts but at the same time goes beyond them. For example, he utilizes the Platonic concept of *mimesis*[9] and actually uses the term μιμνοθμένοις ('to imitate') itself (Presley 2014: 193–194), but at the same time he goes beyond the typical Platonic understanding of physical bodies as merely passing manifestations of the eternal forms that are the only true substances[10] by defending the true value of the human body against Gnosticism. Furthermore, Justin was influenced by Aristotle, who distinguished humans from animals through their capacity for language and rational thought (Cunningham 2009: 100–117). For Justin, 'the image of God focuses on *ratio et voluntas*, reason and the soul, two primary faculties of the soul' (Van Vliet 2009: 36). Nevertheless, he clearly states 'that man made in the image of God was of flesh' (*On the Resurrection*, 7), fully cognizant of the immense value and importance of the body (*On the Resurrection*, 10).

Regarding the question of Christ as *imago Dei*, Justin asks how the plural in Gen. 1.26-7 should be interpreted (Armstrong 1962: 39). He sees here three possibilities: either God talked to himself, like humans sometimes do, or he 'spoke to the elements, to wit, the earth and other similar substances of which we believe man was formed', or, and this is the opinion that Justin supports, he commuted with his Logos (*Dialogue with Trypho*, 62). For him, Christ 'existed as God before the ages' (*Dialogue with Trypho*, 48) and being the image of the Father and 'inseparable from him in power' (*Exhortation to the Greeks*, 38), he has restored us to the original image and likeness of God.

Theophilus of Antioch

When looking at the use of the *imago Dei* concept in the *Epistle of Barnabas* and in the writings of Justin, one could easily get the impression that there is some sort of consensus among the early Christian authors in this matter. That this was not always the case we can see from the work *Ad Autolycum* written by Theophilus of Antioch at the end of the second century AD (Döpp et al. 2002: 690). In contrast to the previous examples, he repeatedly attributes the creation of man not to the Logos but to God himself (*Ad Autolycum* 2, 4; 2, 11), thus affirming the theory of his Jewish origin (Grant 1971: xvii–xix). This is best illustrated in the following passage:

> When God said, 'Let us make man after our image and likeness' [Gen. 1:26], he first reveals the dignity of man. For after making everything else by a word, God considered all this as incidental; he regarded the making of man as the only work worthy of his own hands. Furthermore, God is found saying 'Let us make man after the image and likeness' as if he needed assistance; but he said 'Let us make' to none other than his own Logos and his own Sophia. When he had made him and had blessed him so that he would increase and fill the earth, he subordinated all other beings to him as subjects and slaves. (*Ad Autolycum* 2, 18)

We see in this passage that although God is considered to be the main creator, he made humans with the 'collaboration' of the Son (Logos) and the Spirit (Sophia). Nevertheless, this passage, especially compared to the *Epistle of Barnabas*, cannot be considered as a step backwards in the development of *imago Dei* theology but rather as a small digression from what was to become one of the key patristic concepts of Christian theology.

Irenaeus of Lyon

Irenaeus of Lyon (AD 130–202) was one of the most important proponents of *imago Dei* concept. His 'entire "systematic" recapitulatory theology of creation and recreation is undergirded by an account of the image of God' (Boersma 2016: 6).

Responding to the Gnostic threat, he 'sought to move beyond the use of the Bible as a collection of "proof texts", attempting instead to deal with Scripture as a progressive account of God's self-revelation centred in the person of Jesus Christ' (Purves 1996: 102), which led him to develop quite an original *imago Dei* theology. He diverged from his predecessors by making clear distinction between the terms 'image' and 'likeness'. 'Image' for him meant 'that Adam was a being possessed of reason and free-will' (Kelly 1968: 171) and had primarily physical dimensions. Irenaeus went so far to oppose not only Gnostic[11] but also Platonic and Aristotelian views in considering the human body as part of being made in the image of God. In his fifth book *Against Heresies*, he states:

> Now God shall be glorified in His handiwork, fitting it so as to be conformable to, and modelled after, His own Son. For by the hands of the Father, that is, by the Son and the Holy Spirit, man, and not [merely] a part of man, was made in the likeness of God. Now the soul and the spirit are certainly a part of the man, but certainly not the man; for the perfect man consists in the commingling and the union of the soul receiving the spirit of the Father, and the admixture of that fleshly nature which was moulded after the image of God (5, 6, 1).[12]

We find similar recognition of the body in another passage of this same work (5, 12, 4). One very important aspect of the image concept by Irenaeus in this passage is that this image 'cannot be lost and is equally shared by believers and unbelievers alike' (Lidimus 2004: 47). This is why the Fall had no effect whatsoever upon the image of God in men and did not destroy it (4, 4, 3). For Irenaeus, there are also direct consequences of the fact that human beings are made in the image of God. The first one is general: the superiority of human beings to both animals and angels. He asks: 'But who else is superior to, and more eminent than that man who was formed after the likeness of God, except the Son of God, after whose image man was created?' (4, 33, 4). The second consequence is particular and concerns Adam. Because he was made in the 'original' image of God, he must be saved: 'But inasmuch as man is saved, it is fitting that he who was created, the original man, should be saved' (3, 23, 2).

'Likeness' meant for him that human beings enjoy a 'supernatural endowment through the action of the Spirit' (Kelly 1968: 171). As opposed to the image, likeness is communicated through a spiritual nature which was lost through the Fall (4, 4, 3). Through it, Adam lost the 'robe of sanctity which [he] had from the Spirit' (3, 23, 5; 5, 6, 1). The effect of this loss was of course not only limited to Adam but was extended to all human beings (3, 18, 1), and this is where Christology comes into the picture. According to Burghardt (1961: 150), Irenaeus's *imago Dei* theology consists of three stages:

1. *Creation*: man's formation to God's image and likeness.
2. *Degradation*: loss of the likeness but not the image through sin.
3. *Renovation or recapitulation*: restoration of the divine likeness through Christ.

Irenaeus uses the *imago Dei* concept mainly to show the importance of the role of Christ in salvation history. Christ is the one who restores believers to the original image and likeness of God (5, 2, 1). The soteriological and Christological role of the concept becomes especially clear in the following passage:

> And then, again, this Word was manifested when the Word of God was made man, assimilating Himself to man, and man to Himself, so that by means of his resemblance to the Son, man might become precious to the Father. For in times long past, it was said that man was created after the image of God, but it was not [actually] shown; for the Word was as yet invisible, after whose image man was created, wherefore also he did easily lose the similitude. When, however, the Word of God became flesh, He confirmed both these: for He both showed forth the image truly, since He became Himself what was His image; and He re-established the similitude after a sure manner, by assimilating man to the invisible Father through means of the visible Word. (5, 16, 2)

Human beings are created according to the invisible image of God, the Word himself became a visible manifestation of this invisible image; this restored the likeness that was lost through the Fall. The fact that the Word was invisible when the original image was created contributed to the ease with which that likeness was lost (Nielsen 1968: 22). Adam never achieved the full potential of *imago Dei* – this was realized first in Christ (4, 38, 1–4). As Justo Gonzales puts it, for Irenaeus the 'human creature itself is not the image of God; that image is the Son, in whom and by whom man has been created' and 'the image of God is not something to be found in us, but is rather the direction in which we are to grow' (1975: 165). This is perhaps the most exciting part of his entire *imago Dei* anthropology – it encourages human beings to grow and 'provides a promising model to understand the mosaic evolution of human capacities' (De Smedt et al. 2014: 149).

In Irenaeus's words, man is 'making progress day by day, and ascending towards perfection' (4, 38, 3). This is for him a gradual process in which 'man should in the first instance be created; and having been created, should receive growth; and having received growth, should be strengthened; and having been strengthened, should abound; and having abounded, should recover [from the disease of sin]; and having recovered, should be glorified; and being glorified, should see his Lord' (4, 38, 3). As for the final goal of this process, Irenaeus goes as far as to see it as 'approximating to the uncreated One' (4, 38, 3), which ultimately means becoming a 'part of the divine nature' (Vorster 2011: 5).

Clement of Alexandria

Another author who had the 'assimilation to God' in mind was Clement of Alexandria (AD 150–215), through whom we enter into the *imago Dei* theology of the third century. Like Irenaeus, Clement distinguished between image and likeness,[13] although perhaps not as consistently (Fantino 1985). The main difference between them is that while Irenaeus considered human beings to be images of God, for Clement, Christ represents the only true image (*Stromata* 7, 3; *Protrepticus* 12; *Who is the Rich Man That Shall Be Saved?* 36; *The Paedagogus* 1, 2; 1, 11 and 3, 12). He writes in this regard:

> For the image of God is His Word, the genuine Son of Mind, the Divine Word, the archetypal light of light; and the image of the Word is the true man, the mind which is in man, who is therefore said to have been made in the image and likeness of God, (Gen 1:26) assimilated to the Divine Word in the affections of the soul, and therefore rational; but effigies sculptured in human form, the earthly image of that part of man which is visible and earth-born, are but a perishable impress of humanity, manifestly wide of the truth (*Protrepticus* 10).

In this short passage we can see that man is not really the image of God (he is actually the image of the Word) and that Clement locates this image in the mind of man. These two aspects should be discussed more thoroughly. When explaining Gen. 1.26-7, Clement argues that it was only God's *wish* to create human beings in his image and likeness but 'with the exception of Christ who "has become fully that what God said" (γέγονεν...τοῦτο πλῆρες, ὅπερ εἴρηκεν ὁ θεός), no human being corresponds to this definition' (Havrda 2011: 35). In Clement's own words: 'Christ became the perfect realization of what God spoke; and the rest of humanity is conceived as being created merely in His image' (*The Paedagogus* 1, 12). This needs to be accepted with some caution because Clement did not count the human body as part of that image:

> For conformity with the image and likeness is not meant of the body (for it were wrong for what is mortal to be made like what is immortal), but in mind and reason, on which fitly the Lord impresses the seal of likeness, both in respect of doing good and of exercising rule. (*Stromata* 2, 20)

There are several other works of Clement where he clearly states that it is the mind that is the image of God and not the body (*Fragment* M2431, 1335 D 5; *Stromata* 2, 19 and 5, 14). The only exception can be found in the so-called *Clementine Homilies* in which the body is identified as being a part of the image (11, 4), but these writings are no longer considered to belong to his opus but were written later (Irmscher et al. 2003: 483–493).

This rather negative view of the human body is partially corrected elsewhere by Clement with the notion that human beings are created with the goal to 'attain to a perfect man, according to the image of the Lord' (*Stromata* 6, 14). Logos is in this sense the 'Educator' who takes human beings on this path of perfection, and the true (Christian) Gnostic is only the one 'who is after the image and likeness of God, who imitates God as far as possible, deficient in none of the things which contribute to the likeness as far as compatible, practising self-restraint and endurance, living righteously, reigning over the passions, bestowing of what he has as far as possible, and doing good both by word and deed' (*Stromata* 2, 19).

The end of this process means for Clement, as already mentioned, full assimilation in God and the deification of human beings. In his own words: 'The Word of God became man, that you may learn from man how man may become God' (*Protrepticus* 1). Christ is in this sense for him 'the archetype according to which humankind is to be "corrected"' (Havrda 2011: 37), and human beings can follow his path and, in many aspects, be as perfect and as divine as he was (Yingling 2009: 95–96).

Tertullian

Tertullian (*c.* AD 155–*c.* 240) was one of the most influential Latin theologians. When analysing Gen. 1.26-7 he sets this passage directly in a Trinitarian context,[14] trying to explain the use of the plural form (*Against Marcion* 5, 8; *Against Praxeas* 12). It is because the Father 'had already His Son close at His side, as a second Person, His own Word, and a third Person also, the Spirit in the Word, that He purposely adopted the plural phrase' (*Against Praxeas* 12). Although God uses the plural form, which for Tertullian shows that the creation of humans is the joint act of the Trinity, human beings are actually created after the Son's image,[15] or more precisely, after Christ's image:

> But there was One in whose image God was making man, that is to say, Christ's image, who, being one day about to become Man (more surely and more truly so), had already caused the man to be called His image, who was

then going to be formed of clay – the image and likeness of the true and perfect Man. (*Against Praxeas* 12)

Just like Irenaeus before him, Tertullian differentiates between image and likeness. Image is given – likeness is to be achieved. God 'wishes His image – us – to become likewise His likeness; that we may be holy just as Himself is holy' (*On Exhortation to Chastity* 1). By assigning image directly to the human form (*On Baptism* 5),[16] he recognizes the importance of the human body. He goes as far as to assume that 'God both raised up the Lord, and will raise us up through His own power; on account, to wit, of the union of our body with Him' (*On Modesty* 16). This is one of the rare examples of a direct connection between soteriology and anthropology in the Church Fathers. The human body will in the centuries to come, at least until Chalcedon, be regarded rather negatively. But we can find several other passages where Tertullian shows great respect towards the human body (*Against Marcion* 2, 4; 2, 5; *The Shows* 2).

Image and likeness in human beings are for him lost through the Fall[17] and 'robbed by the devil' (*On the Flesh of Christ* 17), and this is where Christ comes in. Since the seducer 'was an angel' and since the 'victim of that seduction was free' to choose, Christ had to come as restorer of the original image (*Against Marcion* 2, 8). The starting point of this restoration is baptism through which man 'receives again that Spirit of God which he had then first received from His Breath, but had afterward lost through sin' (*On Baptism* 5; more about this topic in Wolfl 1960: 238–263). 'Spirit' plays quite an important part in Tertullian's image theology. 'Breath' is for him 'the image of the spirit', and since 'God is spirit,' man as the image of God is also an 'image of the spirit' (*Against Marcion* 2, 9). This 'spiritual' dimension of *imago Dei* theology goes hand in hand with the above-mentioned anthropology and its respect for the corporeal dimension.

For Tertullian, Christ constitutes the image of God in a different way from human beings. He makes a clear ontological difference between the two. For human beings 'image is not in any case equal to the very thing. It is one thing to be like the reality, and another thing to be the reality itself' (*Against Marcion* 2, 9). As Boersma puts it, for Tertullian, 'the human person remains radically dissimilar to the divine power; always reliant on that power in which he participates but which is not his by nature' (2016: 26). By doing so, he places Christ on a different ontological level and sets him nearer to the Father.[18] He does this also by assuming that the Son is the *invisible* image of the Father (*Against Marcion* 5, 20), thus breaking with the older Latin theological tradition which held that the Son is the *visible* image of the Father[19] much before Hilary (Boersma 2016: 25), who was considered to be the first Latin theologian to do so (Barnes 2003: 341).

Origen

This overview of the ante-Nicene development of *imago Dei* theology will end with a theologian who had at least as much influence in the Christian East as Tertullian did in the West: Origen (*c*. AD 184–*c*. 253). So far, very little research has been done about his image theology,[20] although he himself used the concept on numerous occasions. The starting point for Origen is also Gen. 1.26-7. Like Irenaeus and Clement, he makes a distinction between image and likeness; he also places 'image' in the category of something given and 'likeness' in the category of that which is yet to be achieved:

> Now the expression, 'in the image of God He created him', without any mention of the word likeness, conveys no other meaning than this, that man received the dignity of God's image at his first creation; but that the perfection of his likeness has been reserved for the consummation – namely, that he might acquire it for himself by the exercise of his own diligence in the imitation of God, the possibility of attaining to perfection being granted him at the beginning through the dignity of the divine image, and the perfect realization of the divine likeness being reached in the end by the fulfilment of the (necessary) works. (*De Principiis* 3, 6)

The fact that likeness is something that can be reached only at the end of one's journey is why Sebastian Thier identifies 'a strong eschatological dimension in his interpretation of likeness to God' (1999: 121).[21] Beside being eschatological, his image concept is deeply philosophical: God created not only humans according to his image and likeness but also 'the other creatures after the likeness of some other heavenly patterns', and there is 'correspondence between all things on earth and their celestial prototypes' (*The Song of Songs – Commentary and Homilies* 12), an almost purely Platonic conception.

In his *Homilies on Genesis and Exodus* (1, 13), Origen suggests that there are two primary questions that need to be answered to understand Gen. 1.26-7. First, we need to see 'what that image of God is' and, second, we need to 'inquire diligently in the likeness of what image man is made (*Homilies on Genesis and Exodus* 1, 13)'. The first question he answers with the assertion that when creating Adam, God 'did not place his image outside, but within him' (13, 4), and the second one with the statement that man is only made after the image of Christ the 'Saviour, who is the image of God' (*Homilies on Genesis and Exodus* 1, 13). For Origen, 'men are said to be according to the image, not to be [the actual] images of God' (*Commentary on the Gospel of John* 2, 3).[22] Origen also further identifies the part of human beings that is made in the image of God. He states clearly that the 'body does not contain the image of God' and that 'it is our inner man, invisible, incorporeal, incorruptible, and immortal which is made "according to the image of God"' (*Homilies on Genesis and Exodus* 1, 13). God entrusted his image and likeness only to the human soul (*Homilies on Genesis on Genesis and Exodus* 1, 13; *Homily 4 on Leviticus* 3; *Homily 12 on Numbers* 21:16–23, 1.5; *Contra Celsum* 4, 83; 6, 63; 6, 65) 'which He formed in His own image and likeness, incorruptible; and therefore the soul, which is immortal, is not excluded by the shortness of the present life from the divine remedies and cures' (*De Principiis* 3, 13). He actually gives a nickname to those 'who claim that the image of God is the bodily form of man' and calls them 'Anthropomorphites' (*Commentary on the Epistle to the Romans* 1, 19, 8). The fact that almost all former theologians believed that the body is created in the image of God does not seem to disturb him too much.

After limiting human application of the *imago Dei* concept in such a radical way, he goes on to emphasize that 'only the Logos in his divinity is the immediate Image of the Father' (Burghardt 1961: 150). This is best illustrated by the following passage where he calls the Logos the 'archetypal image' and connects his being the image directly to his divinity:

> The true God, then, is the God, and those who are formed after Him are gods, images, as it were, of Him the prototype. But the archetypal image, again, of all these images is the Word of God, who was in the beginning, and who by being with God is at all times God, not possessing that of Himself, but by His being with the Father, and not continuing to be God, if we should think of this, except by remaining always in uninterrupted contemplation of the depths of the Father. (*Commentary on the Gospel of John* 2)

In another passage he speaks of the 'image formed by the mirror' (*De Principiis* 1, 2, 13). The Son who 'being in all respects the image of the Father, may certainly also be called with propriety the image of His goodness [...] He is rightly termed the image, because He proceeds from no other source than that primal goodness, lest there might appear to be in the Son a different goodness from that which is in the Father. Nor is there any dissimilarity or difference of goodness in the Son' (*De Principiis* 1, 2, 13).

With these words, Origen comes quite close to the later 'homoousianism' – one just needs to replace the word 'goodness' with the word 'nature' and we would have almost fully compatible Nicene Christology. This is indeed a huge step of the Alexandrian (*imago Dei*) theology, which began with Clement and was continued with Origen. The two of them were in this sense forerunners of Alexanders and Athanasius's theology.[23]

Imago Dei as an alternative to the Nicene Christology and Trinitarian theology

Although the council of Nicaea focused mainly on defining the relationship of Christ the Son to God the Father, another question discussed in the background was the question of theological and philosophical monotheism.[24] We can recognize this from the letter of Arius to Alexander of Alexandria:

> We acknowledge One God, alone Uncreated, alone Everlasting, alone Unbegun, alone True, alone having Immortality, alone Wise, alone Good, alone Sovereign; Judge, Governor, and Providence of all, unalterable and unchangeable, just and good, God of the Law and Prophets and of the New Testament; who begat an Only-begotten Son before eternal times, through whom He has made both the ages and the universe; and begat Him, not in semblance, but in truth; and that He made Him subsist at His own will, unalterable and unchangeable; perfect creature of God, but not as one of the creatures; offspring, but not as one of things begotten. (*Letter to Alexander of Alexandria* 2)

In this example we see that preserving monotheism was crucial for Arius, but we can also see that he is ready to acknowledge the role which Christ was playing in the popular piety.[25] Theologically, Arius was more than willing to accept a variation of Christ's divinity, but he rejected the notion that Christ shared the same substance with the Father (Williams 2001; Latinovic 2018: 16ff.), probably because he was aware that such an idea would introduce a parallel deity and produce some sort of polytheism. Decades would pass between the beginning of this controversy and the development of the theological language and philosophical argumentation that could express the new homoousian theology in a way that it avoids polytheistic overtones, and centuries will pass before this Christology will manage to find some sort of balance between the divine and human in Christ. Nevertheless, Trinitarian theology remains until today logically incoherent.

How is it possible that God is at the same time one and three without division? How can the Son be begotten from the Father without introducing the concept of time in God? What happened with the Trinity while the Son was united with the human nature in Christ? How can union of two utterly different natures be possible? How can something be indivisible and inseparable at the same time? How can God suffer? What happened with Christ's human nature after his ascension to heaven? Was it incorporated in the Trinity?

To these and many other questions,[26] Christian theology in my opinion does not provide a satisfactory answer. This is why I would here like to ask the (hypothetical) question: Was this confusion avoidable and was there an alternative to the homoousian Christology and Trinitarian theology?

The first part of this question can be answered rather easily. When we look at the overview of *imago Dei* theology I offered in the first part of the chapter, it seems that the development of Christology and Trinitarian theology in the homoousian direction was indeed unavoidable. Clement and Origen already provided all of the tools necessary for Alexander and Athanasius to make the final big leap and so they did. Popular devotion to Christ is also something that was moving in this direction and even if theologians wanted to stop it, their intervention would not have held for too long. As for the second part of the question, this is where things become more complex.

Let us, for the sake of argument, imagine that Christ was *not* pronounced 'homoousios' at Nicaea and that he continued to be seen 'just' as the perfect *imago Dei*. This would indeed allow us to attribute him almost all the honour and the power that he received through homoousios, short of sharing God's divine nature. In Platonic vocabulary, he would be the *form* that perfectly reflects the heavenly *idea* – God the Father. But, would this be enough for our justification in the soteriological sense? The straight answer from most modern theologians would probably be 'no', but then again this is only due to the fact that most of our current soteriologies are based on an ontological Christology model (Rahner 1975: 760–761), which emerged with the council of Chalcedon and was not present in the New Testament (Robinson 1963; Hick 1977). Another reason is that our Western anthropology is 'poisoned' with the Augustinian notion of 'original sin' (Wiley 2002), in which human nature itself is ontologically corrupted because of the Fall. But ontological Christology is not the only Christological model, not today (Grenz 2000: 263) and certainly not in the past.

Had we indeed through all the centuries believed that the Christ was a human being who achieved perfection and became divine ('adoptionism') or that he was a pre-existent being who is above all created beings ('subordinatianism'), but still not sharing the divine nature, this would have probably helped us avoid many of the traps into which the Church and theology fell during the past two millennia due to the ontological approach. This would have in my opinion contributed to a different understanding of human dignity and worth:

1. *Emancipation of and a higher valuation of human nature.* Overemphasis on Christ's divinity eventually led to the devaluation and neglect of his and our humanity, which in the Middle Ages resulted in oppressive and unhealthy views about the body, sin, sexuality, equality and gender.

2. *Encouragement of a healthy asceticism.* Having someone fulfil the path of salvation to the extent of becoming equal to God (but still not the same as God) would have stimulated others to follow.[27] Having Christ as the intermediary between God and humanity benefits soteriology more than having him on the same level with the Father.

3. *Promotion of personal responsibility and avoidance of 'intermediarism'.* Shifting responsibility for human actions to fallen human nature and the resulting need for ontological Christology is directly connected to the Church assuming the lucrative position of mediator between sinful humanity and the divine Christ.

Finally, this would give us the tools that would help us find better solutions in contemporary interreligious dialogue, which I would like to shortly discuss in the next section. Before I come to this, allow me in the context of this entire book to mention that different theological understandings of *imago Dei* among the Fathers ultimately led to different anthropologies. The homoousian tradition, coupled with Augustinian notions of grace and sin, developed into a rather pessimistic understanding of human nature and the dignity of the human being. The putative *imago Dei* theology that could have developed would have led to a quite different anthropology that is more optimistic and aware of human possibilities as it stresses the *dynamic* notion that being made in the image and likeness of God means a continual improvement of the human condition.

Possibilities for interreligious dialogue

By way of conclusion, I would like to say something about the advantages for interreligious dialogue of having Christ as the image of God instead as having him as a part of the Trinity. I will limit myself to the Abrahamic religions because they share the same roots as Christianity, although this can to a certain degree be applied to all monotheistic religions.

One of the main objections of Islam in dialogue with Christianity is that the concept of the Trinity abandons monotheism, or at best, that a Trinitiarian theology amounts to a watered-down monotheism. Qur'ānic critiques of the Trinity present that doctrine in ways that Christians find strange,[28] but we also possess very early commentaries by Muslim scholars arguing against the Trinity with a correct understanding of what it involves.[29] Christian theologians on the other side have made great efforts (especially in our times) to persuade Muslims that we believe in the same God (which the Quran also seems to accept in *Surah Al-'Ankabut* [29:46], among other places) (Jukko 2007: 106ff.). But one may rightly ask whether this has yielded much fruit outside small circles of liberal Muslim scholars. Imagine how much easier this dialogue would be if Christians stuck to the early *imago Dei* theology and considered Jesus as the perfect human or as a celestial being who reached an exalted status. The Quran itself has a very high regard for Jesus. To offer just one of many examples:

> [And mention] when the angels said, 'O Mary, indeed Allah gives you good tidings of a word from Him, whose name will be the Messiah, Jesus, the son of Mary – distinguished in this world and the Hereafter and among those brought near [to Allah]'. (*Surah Al 'Imran* 3:45)

This passage contains resonances not only with the annunciation narratives in the Christian scriptures but also with the early Christian *imago Dei* theology already discussed. Christ is seen here both as the Messiah and as one of the beings closest to God.

As for Judaism, it is unfortunate that the religion to which Jesus himself belonged has less regard for him than does Islam. In the best case, Jesus is perceived by Judaism as a Jewish teacher (Vermes 2012). His rejection by Judaism certainly coincides with his gradual establishment as God in Christian theology (Klinghoffer 2005). Positioning Jesus below God through the use of the *imago Dei* concept would certainly impact his status in and recognition by Jewish theologians. I am sure that in that case, Judaism would be willing to accept Jesus as one of the prophets and perhaps in some cases accept him as the Messiah, thus returning to the faith of the first Judaeo-Christian community.

To avoid misunderstanding, I would like to finish this chapter with a disclaimer: I am not suggesting that we should reject or reverse centuries-long developments of Christian theology and try to artificially implement an *imago Dei* theology which promotes some non-Trinitarian God. I wrote this chapter mainly for academic purposes and to show that there was an alternative path of early Christian theology and that things could have developed differently.

This opportunity was unfortunately wasted, but not all is lost. The capacity of Trinitarian theology to situate healthy anthropological insights alongside certain developments in the last decades makes one optimistic that Christian theology will continue to develop in this direction. Strengthening the role of the *imago Dei* concept would perhaps speed up these developments and move us faster on this path.

Notes

1   One of the few human activities that truly assumes creation *ex nihilo* – poetry – comes from the Greek word ποιητής ('creator'). The aspiration to grow to the full potential of *imago Dei* and become more like our heavenly creator is one of the basic instincts of our human nature.

2   Hebrews 2.7 reflects this notion found in Ps. 8.5, but Hebrews 1.4 raises Christ above the angels thus opening a path for Christians to achieve the glory of angels.

3   This goes very much hand in hand with the results of modern neural science and genetics which show that although there are similarities between human and animal brains and although they have the same origin, there are also significant differences (Vogel et al. 1997: 607ff; Herculano-Houzel 2016).

4   There have been only few studies in the past, dealing directly with the topic of Christ as *imago Dei*. One of them worth mentioning is Grenz (2004). But even this study is incomplete because after giving a thorough overview of the biblical aspects (2004: 619–625), the author completely skips the patristic period and lands directly at modern (evangelical) theology (2004: 625–628).

5   As Marshall Johnson puts it, the early Trinitarian and Christological controversies were actually a 'Crisis of Monotheism' (2005: 51ff).

6   Regarding the philological difference between these two terms, Von Dehsen notes 'that the Hebrew word צלם ("image") literally means "that which is cut out," suggesting a plastic imitation of that which it depicts', while 'the term דמות ("likeness") proposes a more abstract association and is thought by some to ameliorate the physical association inferred by צלם' (Von Dehsen 1997: 260). The question of whether there are any theological differences between these terms was thoroughly discussed by the early Christian authors.

7   Gordon Wenham lists six ways that interpreters from the Jewish philosopher Philo (25 BC–AD 50) onwards have understood the use of the plural in Gen. 1.26: (1) as a reference to the heavenly court, i.e. the angels; (2) reference to Christ or the Trinity; (3) a polytheistic account; (4) an example of plural of majesty; (5) plural of self-deliberation or self-encouragement; and (6) a reference to plurality in the Godhead in regard to the Spirit (1987: 27–28).

8   Except perhaps in the Prologue of Gospel according to John and his notion of the Logos which could be related to this idea.

9   Nathan G. Jennings explains this concept with the following words: 'Platonic philosophy strictly distinguishes between divine (*demiourgia*) and human (*poetikai/ techne*) creation. There is, however, one mode of creation that is shared by the gods and human beings, and that is *mimesis*. *Mimesis* is the production of a *copy*. So, for example, a man may make a statue of himself, and the Demiurge creates the cosmos as an imitation of himself. In both these cases the Platonists would point out that the copy has a lower ontological status than the original. Plato employs this concept in order to explain that the sensible world is created in mimesis of the intelligible world' (2010: 53).

10   See, for example, the so-called affinity argument in Phaedo 78b4–84b8. More about this topic can be found in Elton (1997: 313–316).

11   The Gnostics taught that the material world and the human body, which belongs to this world, will dissolve in the end time. Irenaeus 'was countering this gnostic idea of disintegration by one of integration, or re-integration' (Lidums 2004: 47).

12   This and the following references are taken from *Against Heresies* unless otherwise indicated.

13   He probably also referred directly to Irenaeus when he said: 'Some of our writers have understood that man straightaway on his creation received what is according to the image, but that what is according to the likeness he will receive afterwards on his perfection' (Clement of Alexandria, *Stromata* 2, 22). Making a difference between these two concepts actually enabled him to see the possibility for salvation also of those who are not Christians. In his fourth book of the *Stromata* he writes: 'And is there not some light thrown here on the expression in the likeness and image, in the fact that some live according to the likeness of Christ, while those who stand on the left hand live according to their image' (4, 6).

14   Tertullian is the first known author to use the term 'Trinity' (*trinitas*) and the first place where he mentions it is *Against Praxeas*, where he also develops a big part of his *imago Dei* theology.

15   Tertullian actually in most cases claims that only man is created after the image of God and woman is created from man (*On the Veiling of Virgins* 10; *On the Apparel of Women* 1; *Against Marcion* 5, 8; *Against Praxeas* 12), which is why he is often labelled as 'misogynist'. This he deserves only in part because there are also some positive aspects of his view of the women (Finlay 2003: 503–525).

16   Likeness in this passage is assigned to the human spirit or soul.

17   Unlike Irenaeus, Tertullian is not always precise in differentiating between the two terms. Sometimes he says that the likeness is lost and sometimes also that the image is lost.

18   Nevertheless, we still find subordinationism in his teaching (Latinovic 2018: 29 n. 128).

19 Of which he himself was also aware for example in *Against Marcion* 5, 19.

20 To my knowledge there are only two studies and one article dealing directly with his *imago Dei* theology: Crouzel (1956); Ekstrom (1997) (which unfortunately is not publicly available) and Hobbel (1989).

21 'Eine stark eschatologische Orientierung seiner Interpretation der similitudo dei'.

22 He uses this concept in other works: *Contra Celsum* 4, 30; 4, 85; 6, 63; *Commentary on John* 2, 19–33.

23 This particularly applies to Clement who was actually the first theologian to use 'homoousios' in the context similar to the one used in Nicaea (Latinovic 2018: 32ff).

24 The first one had to do with the biblical roots of Christian theology which forbids having other Gods than Jahweh and the second one with the Greek philosophy since Pythagoreans, which saw God as μονάς – single indivisible source.

25 For non-theologians, Christ played the role of the equal to the Father long before the theology recognized this through the council of Nicaea.

26 See also Maspero et al. (2012) and McCall (2010) for these other questions.

27 It is not an accident that almost all Antiochian bishops (Chrysostom, Diodor, Nestorius) were such great ascetics. This has to do with Antiochian emulation soteriology (Latinovic 2018, 80ff, 132, 138).

28 Two such examples are that Christians say that 'God is one of three' and that Christians thought the Trinity consisted of God, Christ and Mary. *Quran, Surah Al-Mā'idah* [5:73,116] (Griffith 2007: 83–110, esp. 100–108; 2014: 1–30).

29 One of the key works comes from as early as the ninth century – Abu Isa al-Warraq's *Against the Trinity* (Al-Warraq 1992).

References

Al-Warraq, Abu Isa (auth.) and D. Thomas (ed. and transl.) (1992), *Anti-Christian Polemic in Early Islam: Abu Isa al-Warraq's Against the Trinity*, Cambridge: Cambridge University Press.

Armstrong, G. F. (1962), *Die Genesis in der alten Kirche*, Tübingen: Mohr Siebeck.

Barnard, L. W. (1971), 'The Logos Theology of St. Justin Martyr', *The Downside Review*, 89 (295): 132–141.

Barnes, M. (2003), 'The Visible Christ and the Invisible Trinity', *Modern Theology*, 19 (3): 329–355.

Boersma, G. (2016), *Augustine's Early Theology of Image: A Study in the Development of Pro-Nicene Theology*, Oxford: Oxford University Press.

Bray, G. (1991), 'The Significance of God's Image in Man', *Tyndale Bulletin*, 42 (2): 195–225.

Burghardt, W. J. (1961), 'The Image of God in Man: Alexandrian Orientations', The Catholic Society of America, Proceedings of the Sixteenth Annual Convention Ottawa, Ontario, June 19, 20, 21, 22: 147–160.

Chadwick, H. (1965), 'Justin Martyr's Defence of Christianity', *Bulletin of the John Rylands Library*, 47: 275–297.

Clines, D. J. A. (1968), 'The Image of God in Man', *Tyndale Bulletin*, 19: 53–103.

Crouzel, H. (1956), *Théologie de l 'image de Dieu chez Origène*, Paris: Aubier, Éditions Montaigne.

Cunningham, D. (2009), 'The Way of All Flesh: Rethinking the Imago Dei', in Celia Deane-Drummond and David Clough (eds), *Creaturely Theology: On God, Humans and Other Animals*, London: SCM Press: 100–118.

De Smedt, J. and H. De Cruz (2014), 'The Imago Dei as a Work in Progress: A Perspective from Paleoanthropology', *Zygon*, 49 (1): 135–156.

Döpp, S. and W. Geerlings, eds (2002), *Lexikon der antiken christlichen Literatur*, 3rd edn, Freiburg im Breisgau: Herder.

Ekstrom, R. D. (1997), 'Christ as the Image of God in Origen and Athanasius', PhD Dissertation, Asbury Theological Seminary, Wilmore (KY). Available online only to faculty members: https://place.asburyseminary.edu/trendissertations/4039/ (accessed 1 September 2018).

Elton, M. (1997), 'The Role of the Affinity Argument in the "Phaedo"', *Phronesis*, 42 (3): 313–316.

Fantino, J. (1985), *L'homme image de Dieu chez saint Irénée de Lyon*, Paris: Les Éditions du Cerf.

Finlay, B (2003), 'Was Tertullian a Misogynist? A Reconsideration', *The Journal of the Historical Society*, 3 (3–4): 503–525.

Gilbert, G. H. (1906), 'Justin Martyr on the Person of Christ', *The American Journal of Theology*, 10 (4): 663–674.

Gonzalez, J. L. (1975), *History of Christian Thought, Volume 1: From the Beginnings to the Council of Chalcedon*, Nashville: Abingdon Press.

Grant, R. M., ed. and trans. (1971), *Theophilus of Antioch: Ad Autolycum*, Oxford: University Press.

Grenz, S. J. (2000), *Theology for the Community of God*, Grand Rapids, MI: William B. Eerdmans Publishing Company.

Grenz, S. J. (2004), 'Jesus as the Imago Dei: Image-of-God Christology and the Non-Linear Linearity of Theology', *Journal of the Evangelical Theological Society*, 47 (4): 617–628.

Griffith, S. H. (2007), 'Syriacisms in the 'Arabic Qur'ān', in Meir M. Bar-Asher et al., (eds), *A Word Fitly Spoken*, Jerusalem: The Ben-Zvi Institute.

Griffith, S. H. (2014), 'The Unity and Trinity of God', in Michael Root and James J. Buckley (eds), *Christian Theology and Islam*, London: James Clarke.

Havrda, M. (2011), 'Grace and Free Will according to Clement of Alexandria', *Journal of Early Christian Studies*, 19 (1): 21–48.

Herculano-Houzel, S. (2016), *The Human Advantage: A New Understanding of How Our Brain Became Remarkable*, Cambridge, MA: MIT Press.

Hick, J., ed. (1977), *The Myth of God Incarnate*, Philadelphia, PA: Westminster.

Hobbel, A. J. (1989), 'The Imago Dei in the Writings of Origen', *Studia Patristica*, 21: 301–307.

Hoekema, A. A. (1986), *Created in God's Image*, Grand Rapids, MI: William B. Eerdmans Publishing Company.

Irmscher, J. and G. Strecker (2003), 'The Pseudo-Clementines', in W. Schneemelcher (ed.), *New Testament Apocrypha*, Volume 2: Writings Relating to the Apostles; Apocalypses and Related Subjects, Louisville, KY: Westminster John Knox Press.

Jenkins, P. (2010), *Jesus Wars: How Four Patriarchs, Three Queens, and Two Emperors Decided What Christians Would Believe for the Next 1500 Years*, New York: HarperOne.

Jennings, N. G. (2010), *Theology as Ascetic Act: Disciplining Christian Discourse*, New York: Peter Lang.

Johnson, M. D. (2005), *The Evolution of Christianity: Twelve Crises That Shaped the Church*, New York: Continuum.

Jonsson, G. A. (1988), *The Image of God: Genesis 1: 26–28 in a Century of Old Testament Research*, Lund: Almqvist & Wiksell.

Jukko, R. (2007), *Trinity in Unity in Christian-Muslim Relations: The Work of the Pontifical Council for Interreligious Dialogue*, Leiden: Brill.

Kelly, J. N. D. (1968), *Early Christian Doctrines*, London: Black.

Klinghoffer, D. (2005), *Why the Jews Rejected Jesus: The Turning Point in Western History*, New York: Doubleday.

Krausmuller, D. (2011), 'Making Sense of the Formula of Chalcedon: The Cappadocians and Aristotle in Leontius of Byzantiums Contra Nestorianos Et Eutychianos', *Vigiliae Christianae*, 65: 484–513.

Lashier, J (2012), 'Irenaeus as Logos Theologian', *Vigiliae Christianae*, 66 (4): 341–361.

Latinovic, V. (2018), *Christologie und Kommunion I: Entstehung und Verbreitung der homoousianischen Christologie*, Münster: Aschendorff-Verlag.

Lidums, G. (2004), 'The Doctrine of Imago Dei and Its Relation to Self-Transcendence in the Context of Practical Theology', PhD Dissertation, University of Helsinki.

Maspero, G. and R. J. Wozniak, eds (2012), *Rethinking Trinitarian Theology: Disputed Questions and Contemporary Issues in Trinitarian Theology*, London: T&T Clark.

McCall, T. (2010), *Which Trinity? Whose Monotheism? Philosophical and Systematic Theologians on the Metaphysics of Trinitarian Theology*, Grand Rapids, MI: William B. Eerdmans Publishing Company.

Miller, M. J. (1972), 'In the "Image" and "Likeness" of God', *Journal of Biblical Literature*, 91: 289–304.

Niehr, H. (1997), 'In Search of YHWH's Cult Statue in the First Temple', in K. Van der Toorn (ed.), *The Image and the Book: Iconic Cults, Aniconism, and the Rise of Book Religion in Israel and the Ancient Near East*, Leuven: Peeters, 73–96.

Nielsen, J. T. (1968), *Adam and Christ in the Theology of Irenaeus of Lyons: An Examination of the Function of the Adam-Christ Typology in the Adversus Haereses of Ireaneus, Against the Background of the Gnosticism of His Time*, 7th edn, Van

Gorcum's Theologische Bibliotheek, Asen, The Netherlands: Koninkliijke Van Gorcum.

Porteous, N. W. (1962), 'Image of God', in *Interpreter's Dictionary of the Bible II*, New York: Abingdon Press.

Presley, S. O. (2014), 'A Loftier Doctrine: The Use of Scripture in Justin Martyr's Second Apology', *Perichoresis*, 12 (2): 185–200.

Purves, J. G. M. (1996), 'The Spirit and the Imago Dei: Reviewing the Anthropology of Irenaeus of Lyons', *Evangelical Quarterly*, 68: 99–120.

Rahner, K. (1975), *Encyclopedia of Theology: A Concise Sacramentum Mundi*, London: A&C Black.

Robinson, J. A. T. (1963), *Honest to God*, London: SCM Press.

Roos, A. (2011), 'St Augustine's Confessiones: The Role of the Imago Dei in His Conversion to Catholic Christianity', MPhil Thesis in Ancient Cultures, University of Stellenbosch.

Thier, S. (1999), *Kirche bei Pelagius*, Göttingen-Berlin-New York: W. de Gruyter.

Van Vliet, J. (2009), *Children of God: The Imago Dei in John Calvin and His Context*, Göttingen: Vandenhoeck & Ruprecht.

Vermes, G. (2012), *Christian Beginnings: From Nazareth to Nicaea, AD 30-325*, London: Allen Lane.

Vogel, F., G. Vogel, and A. G. Motulsky (1997), *Human Genetics: Problems and Approaches*, Berlin: Springer Science & Business Media.

Von Dehsen, C. D. (1997), 'The imago Dei in Genesis 1:26–27', *Lutheran Quarterly*, 11 (3): 259–270.

Vorster, N. (2011), *Created in the Image of God: Understanding God's Relationship with Humanity*, Eugene, OR: Wipf and Stock Publishers.

Wenham, G. J. (1987), *Genesis 1–15, World Biblical Commentary I*, Waco, TX: Word Books.

Wiley, T. (2002), *Original Sin: Origins, Development, Contemporary Meanings*, New York, Paulist Press.

Williams, R. (2001), *Arius: Heresy and Tradition*, 2nd edn, Grand Rapids, MI: William B. Eerdmans.

Wolfl, K. (1960), *Das Heilswirken Gottes durch den Sohn nach Tertullian*, Rome: Libreria Editrice Dell'Università Gregoriana.

Yingling, E. (2009), 'Ye Are Gods: Clement of Alexandria's Doctrine of Deification', *Studia Antiqua*, 7 (2): 93–99.

4

The Holy Trinity as Source of Human Dignity according to St Thomas Aquinas

Richard Conrad

Introduction

St Thomas Aquinas occasionally uses the phrase 'human dignity', sometimes referring to how our nature is elevated by Christ's Incarnation and Redemption and sometimes to how human dignity is spoiled by vice and enhanced by virtue.[1] In *De Veritate* q. 25, a. 6 ad 2, he says human dignity consists in our reason; in his exposition of the Apostles' Creed he says that consideration of God as Creator leads us, among other things,

> to recognize human dignity, for God made all things for humanity's sake ... And the human being is more like God than are [other] creatures after the Angels, hence Gen. 1.26 says, 'Let us make the human being to our image and likeness.' Now he did not say this about heaven, or the stars, but about the human being. Not, however, as regards the body, but as regards the soul, which has free will and is incorruptible, and as such is more like God than other creatures. Hence we should consider the human being as of more dignity (after the Angels) than other creatures.

Aquinas concludes that we should use lower things rather than be enslaved by them and preserve our God-given dignity so as to come to enjoy God.[2]

This chapter will explore Aquinas's account of the human being as made 'to the image and likeness' of God. We will draw on Merriell's account of Aquinas's increasingly confident use of Augustine (Merriell 1990) so as to bring out the transcendence of our 'rational appetite' and its consequences for moral responsibility. We will argue that Aquinas's mature account of the image emphasizes its dynamic character: it demands that we journey from one degree of likeness to God into a greater. This accords the human being a unique place in the cosmic hierarchy.

The scriptural background

Aquinas uses Gen. 1.26 – *Faciamus hominem ad imaginem et similitudinem nostram* ('Let us make the human being to our image and likeness') – as the *sed contra*, the peg on which to hang his argument that the image of God is to be found in the human being, in *ST* 1a.93.1. He takes *imago* as a more precise word than *similitudo*: the latter refers to any kind of likeness, whereas the former only applies when three features are present: (i) there is likeness; (ii) an image is derived from its original; and (iii) the image resembles the original in some characteristically specific way.[3] An image need not be perfectly like its original; hence, as the Divine Word and co-equal Son of the Father, Christ is called 'the Image' in Col. 1.15,[4] but in Gen. 1.26-7 the human being is only said to be created *ad imaginem*. Aquinas sees the word *ad* (meaning 'to', 'towards' [often in the case of movement upwards], 'in comparison with', etc.) as implying an approach towards something at some distance, hence it indicates that God, our Exemplar, exceeds us (in fact, infinitely). It is the notion of approach that Aquinas emphasizes later in *ST* 1a.93.5 ad 4: *ad* designates the *terminus* of God's making us, reinforcing the Augustinian themes of the *purpose* of God's making humanity and of the *progress* the image is called to make as God leads it upwards by grace, which we will see are prominent in this Question. In *ST* 1a.93.5 ad 4, Aquinas adds that *ad imaginem* can also be taken as indicating the Divine Nature as our *exemplar*.[5] He has explained earlier that the exemplar cause of each creature is its respective 'idea' in God's wisdom (*ST* 1a.15.3, 44.3), and Merriell points out that if with Aquinas we also see *God in himself* as the exemplar cause of his human image, this yields an indication of human dignity (1990: 175). Of course, Aquinas relied on the Vulgate,[6] not knowing the Septuagint or Hebrew. Arguably, the Latin *ad* accurately represents the Hebrew preposition *b^e* used with the word for 'image', since *b^e* can mean 'in' or 'into'.[7]

Aquinas's detailed analysis of Gen. 1.26-7 in *ST* 1a.93.5 ad 4 includes the claim that the whole Trinity makes the human being to the image of the Trinity, not to that of the Divine Word alone, otherwise God the Father, speaking to the Son, would have said '*similitudinem tuam*'.

Thus, Aquinas carefully analyses the precise text of Gen. 1.26-7 in line with his concern to base theological argument on the *literal* sense of Scripture (*ST* 1a.1.10 ad 1).[8] Since Professor Day's chapter warns us against substituting eisegesis for exegesis and argues that the biblical authors saw the image as a 'psychophysical' likeness to God, we need briefly to suggest ways to defend the legitimacy of Aquinas's use of Gen. 1.26-7 in addition to our remarks on the preposition *ad*:

- Aquinas himself views the human being as a 'psychophysical whole' and (as we shall see) our likeness to God as involving the body.[9]
- If the whole building up the Canon of Scripture was guided by the Holy Spirit, the relevant Genesis texts may be read in conversation with texts in Wisdom and in the New Testament, i.e. in the light of the affirmation of an immortal element in the human being and of the Holy Trinity's self-communication.
- We should not deny a priori that certain striking phrases in Scripture were intended by God to provoke fruitful lines of reflection. The Classical world expected inspired phrases to be used with 'controlled agility', and Jews and Christians have 'played' with phrases plucked from Scripture to make valuable points. Aquinas's use of the *ad imaginem Dei* formula fits within the reception history of this formula.

The Augustinian background

It was Augustine whom Aquinas followed in seeing the 'highest part' of the human soul, the *mens* ('mind'),[10] as the locus of the *imago Dei* and in seeing the mind as mirroring God precisely as Trinity. It is beyond our scope here to detail which earlier theologians had seen the human mind as a 'model' for the Trinity or discuss the eastern Fathers' tendency to put the Septuagint version of Gen 1.26 alongside Col. 1:15 and conclude humanity, as rational, was made 'according to' the Logos, God the Father's co-eternal Image.[11] But we must remark that all of them sought an image or model for the Trinity in something purely *intellectual*, either *logos* alone or *logos* and *sophia* (wisdom),[12] since this puts in relief Augustine's recognition of a will on the same level as intellect.[13] In the 'heights' of the human soul he recognized *memoria, intelligentia* or *intellectus* and *voluntas*,[14] *voluntas* being a spiritual ability to *love*, well defined by Aquinas (e.g. *ST* 1a.80.2) as the 'intellectual appetite', the ability to *be attracted by* the rationally perceived good. The benefits of Augustine's breakthrough include:

- It dignified human love by grounding the claim that we are in God's image both by our ability to know and by our ability to love.
- It offered some purchase on the Holy Spirit's 'personal character' by complementing the traditional picture of the Son as Wisdom-proceeding: it became possible to picture the Holy Spirit (with all due reticence) as *Love*-proceeding (Aquinas would explore this in *ST* 1a.37.1).

- It underscored the dignity of αγαπη, *caritas* (cf. I Cor. 13) as a participation in the Holy Spirit and as 'seated' in a truly spiritual power of soul (*ST* 2a2ae.23.3 ad 3; 24.1).

When he came to review his work, Augustine recalled how in *De Trinitate* Books 1–7 (henceforth abbreviated as *DT*) he had defended true doctrine on the basis of Scripture; then he had presented the 'intellectual creature which was made to the image of God' as a 'mirror' in which, obscurely, people might glimpse 'God the Trinity in our *memoria, intelligentia, voluntas*' (*DT* 15.20.39). In fact, Augustine had first developed the claim that 'the mind itself, and its love, and its knowledge (*notitia*), are three things, and these three are one; and when perfect they are equal' (*DT* 9.4.4). Since it is difficult to see the mind and two of its activities as truly co-equal, in *DT* 10 he had discerned a clearer mirror of the Holy Trinity in memory, intellect and will (or, better, remembering, understanding and loving (Hill 1985: 126; Merriell 1990: 27 n. 45)). This 'mirror' or 'model'[15] shows how the doctrine of irreducible distinction and intense unity in the Holy Trinity is not logically self-contradictory, since even within a creature irreducible distinction and intense unity coincide.

Augustine did not simply use the human psyche so as to defend the doctrine of the Trinity. Humanity has fallen: no longer does our being in the image of the Trinity make the Trinity obvious to us, because we have lost sight of our true selves as well as of God. In *DT* 11–14 Augustine effectively took the fractured image on a journey back to wholeness/wisdom, a journey made possible by the Saviour who meets our need by coming to us in and through the flesh. Because we remain in the Trinity's image despite sin,[16] we resonate with the Triune God's self-revelation (*DT* 13.20.26); an openness to the Divine Archetype makes the journey back to God possible.[17] *De Trinitate* begins with the revealed doctrine of the Trinity because only in the light of Trinitarian faith can we recognize our nature and destiny, i.e. come to realize who we are made by, how we are made and who we are made for. Being in God's image constitutes a *vocation* for this life and the next, since the image comes to its perfection and fulfilment in communion with the God it is made by and for. Sullivan (1963: 145–148) aptly distils Augustine's theology: the human mind remembering, knowing and loving *itself* is a good *analogy* for the co-equal Trinity, but the image *comes to perfection as image* in the presence, knowledge and love of *God*. Augustine puts it thus:

> This trinity of the mind is not the image of God on the grounds that the mind remembers itself and understands and loves itself, but because it is also able to remember, understand, and love him by whom it was made. When it does this, it

becomes wise … Let it then remember its God, to whose image it was made, and understand and love him … let it worship God, who was not made, by whom it was made as *capax* of ['open to', 'capable of', 'roomy enough for'] him, and of whom it can partake. (*DT* 14.12.15)

The final Books of *De Trinitate* were written some years after Books 9 and 10 (Ayres 2014: 118–120). Merriell argues that Augustine's account of the image in Books 14 and, especially, 15 had evolved significantly, with less emphasis on triads and more on the formation of an inner word and an inner love, which respectively reflect the Son's begetting and the Spirit's procession (Merriell 1990: 30–35, cf. 120–122, 125, 215–216). Certainly, despite mentioning both his earlier triads in *DT* 15.3.5, 7.12 and 20.39, Augustine has become eloquently dubious about finding any really good analogy of the co-equal and intensely one Trinity (e.g. *DT* 15.20.39, 23.43); he explores afresh how words can proceed from the memory and even how love or will can proceed from mind or memory (*DT* 15.10.18–11.20, 12.22, 21.40–41, 23.43, 16.47, 17.50).

Sullivan (1963: 216–272) explores Augustine's influence on Aquinas; Merriell demonstrates how Aquinas's careful reading of *De Trinitate* and his realization of the importance of *DT* 15 led to developments in his teaching. Against the suspicion that Aquinas moved away from Augustine, e.g. in an Aristotelian direction, Merriell[18] argues that Aristotelian tools served an increasingly *Augustinian* account to which we now turn.

Aquinas on the human psyche as limited model for understanding the Trinity

Aquinas follows Augustine in locating the Trinity's image in the human and angelic *mind* (*ST* 1a.93.2). A sign of this dignity is the way the mind's functioning serves as a model to gain purchase on the revealed mystery of the Trinity. Mindful of Augustine's warnings about the great unlikeness between the mind and the Trinity, and of how the human mind in its complexity falls short of the divine unity (*DT* 15.20.39, 23.43), Aquinas uses the model reticently. He starts his mature treatise on the Trinity by defending the claim that 'procession', coming-from, takes place '*within*' God, on the grounds that the intellect's act remains within one who understands – a concept of the thing understood proceeds from the knowledge in the intellect – and on the grounds that a 'procession of love' takes place through the act of the will – a kind of *spiritus* or impulse[19] arises towards the thing loved (*ST* 1a.27). In *ST* 1a.34 Aquinas explores how the Father's one Word both expresses the Father and causatively expresses all creatures. It is tempting to popularize this account by drawing an analogy with a human being formulating a reasonably complete knowledge of herself and her plans, but Aquinas himself points out that in us there are *many* 'small' interior words (*ST* 1a.34.3).

In *ST* 1a.37.1, on the Holy Spirit as 'Love Proceeding', we do find a triadic phrase: 'When someone understands and loves himself, he is in himself not only by identity (*per identitatem rei*), but also as what is understood is in the one who understands, and as what is loved is in the lover.' In his *Scriptum super Sententiis*, Aquinas was happier with 'Augustinian' triads as models for the Trinity (Merriell 1990: 54–57). But such triadic expressions became rare in the mature Aquinas, who preferred to rely on the two 'comings forth' of active knowledge and love in our souls as a valid if limited model for the Processions 'within' God, those of the Word and of the Holy Spirit (Merriell 1990: 154), in line with what we have seen of *DT* 15.

Memoria: We are a mystery to ourselves and to the angels

In *ST* 1a.93.7–8 Aquinas necessarily considers Augustine's triads. Arguing that the image of the Trinity is found in the human soul most of all when it *acts*, and acts by *knowing and loving God*, he distances himself from Peter Lombard's understanding of *memoria, intelligentia* and *voluntas* as 'three natural powers (*vires*) of the soul' (*ST* 1a.93.7 obj. 3).[20] Aquinas observes that because the mind is something of a mystery to itself, Augustine moved beyond *mens, notitia* and *amor* ('love') to the triad *memoria, intelligentia* and *voluntas* (*ST* 1a.93.7 ad 2), all three of which are more obvious to us. Aquinas makes this triad match his claim that while at the sensitive level we can retain past experiences precisely as past, at the intellectual level to 'remember' a concept is exactly the same as to know it,[21] hence *memoria* and *intellectus* are not distinct powers (*ST* 1a.79.6–7). Using texts from *DT* 14, he argues that Augustine did not mean *memoria* as a distinct power, but as 'the habitual retention of *notitia* and *amor*' (*ST* 1a.79.7 ad 1; 93.7 ad 3). In *ST* 1a.93.7 ad 4, Aquinas refers to *DT* 14.6.9, where Augustine qualifies his earlier claim that 'the mind always remembers, always understands and loves itself' by making this understanding and love 'habitual'. Several points are worth exploring.

In *ST* 1a.93.7 ad 3 Aquinas speaks of the habitual retention both of knowledge and of love. If we relied only on *ST* 1a.79 we might think memory is purely intellectual; in fact, just as there is habitual knowledge in the intellect, from which an 'interior word' might emerge, so there is an habitual order of priorities, a 'structure of loves', in the will, from which an 'impulse of love' might proceed. This reaffirms the claim that the will is located at the rational level of the soul. Furthermore, even though Aquinas does not seek a co-equal threesome in the mind, the co-equality of Word and Spirit invites us to re-examine the relative ranking of knowing and loving. It is well known that Aquinas sees the intellect as 'nobler' than the will. But in *ST* 1a.82.3, having explained that, in the abstract, the will 'has a narrower remit' than the intellect, he adds that, as regards their grasp of their object, sometimes the will is nobler than the intellect. In particular, loving *God*, which lifts us up to God in his totality, is nobler than knowing God, which – even in heaven – involves a certain limitation (*ST* 2a2ae.27.5; 1a.12.7).

Intellect and will are spiritual powers, transcending here-and-now material conditions. Hence only to God are they fully open (*ST* 1a.57.4–5). But, despite the intellect's greater natural nobility, in some ways the will is even more of an 'inner sanctum'. Both angels and heavenly bodies can influence our imagination and emotions, and indirectly, through them, intellect and will (*ST* 1a.111.2–3, 115.4). Angels can present us persuasively with ideas, but not directly insert concepts into our intellect, and they can also (somehow) strengthen the human intellect; thus they have a qualified mediating role between God and the intellect (*ST* 1a.111.1). But nothing at all can intervene between God and the will. Neither good nor fallen angels can influence the human will directly (*ST* 1a.111.2). The heavenly bodies have *less* influence on our will than on our intellect, because the will can rise above the inclinations of the lower appetites – maybe there is an implicit contrast with the intellect's intimate dependence on the manifold 'material' in the imagination (*ST* 1a.115.4). The Augustinian recognition that the will is an integral part of our being in the image of the Trinity has led to a recognition of the will's transcendence, freedom and nobility, and a nuanced ranking of intellect and will.

Aquinas shares Augustine's sense that the mind is something of a mystery to itself. This is not simply a consequence of the Fall; the human psyche is not naturally geared to introspection (*ST* 1a.84.7, 87.1). We are not consciously aware of concepts we have learned until some situation calls them forth; they remain habitual. Nor can we know for certain, by introspection, the state of our will; we are not conscious of its whole 'contents'. Rather as we learn what the soul is by reflection on what we can do, so we learn of our habits as they issue in acts. We are not fully aware of our priorities, the 'habits of love' that 'structure' our will, until they result in *acts* of will (*ST* 1a.87; 1a2ae.112.5). Since willed choices, as well as concepts, emerge from 'the *habitual retention* of knowledge and love' (*ST* 1a.93.7c and ad 3), we sometimes *discover* our wants; we may *surprise* ourselves (and the angels; *ST* 1a.57.5) by what we do! Hence, examining our consciences, we review the implications of past behaviour, so that if necessary we can change our priorities – or ask God to do so, since he alone can sufficiently and efficaciously move the will (*ST* 1a.105.4) not to override but to *enlarge* our freedom.

The image as vocation

We saw Augustine claim that the human soul is created *capax Dei*; Aquinas agrees. Hence the justification of a single unrighteous person is a greater work of God than the creation of the cosmos, because grace raises a creature to share God's eternal goodness – yet in a way justification is not typically miraculous, because we are *gratiae capax* ('open to grace'), geared to become 'sharers of the Divine Nature' (*ST* 1a2ae.113.9–10, referring to I Pet. 1.4). Paradoxically, while other animals can attain their natural levels of fulfilment by means of their natural powers, we cannot be truly fulfilled by our natural powers alone, since they are not proportionate to a supernatural – a divine – bliss (*ST* 1a2ae.62.1). This extra level of dependence is in fact a sign of human *nobility*; being 'higher up the scale' means we can achieve more, yet are radically impotent to achieve it unless we welcome God's offered assistance (*ST* 1a2ae.5.5 ad 2).

So, even in this life, human beings can become sharers in the Divine Nature! *Prima Pars* 43, enlarging on *ST* 1a.8.3, associates this with becoming nothing less than temples of the Holy Trinity. *ST* 1a.43.2 introduces the *giving* to us of the Divine Persons and their being *possessed* by creatures; *ST* 1a.43.3 refers to the radically new mode of presence by which a Divine Person is in someone 'as the Known in the knower and the Beloved in the lover'. *Gratia gratum faciens*, 'the [divinising] gift that makes us gracious, [morally] graceful, and grateful',[22] empowers us to *possess and freely to enjoy* the Divine Persons! This *reciprocity* can be called *amicitia*, friendship (*ST* 2a2ae.23.1), for we who are creatively known and loved by God become ourselves able to know and love God; by our God-given powers, once they are strengthened by grace, we (unlike the other animals) are able to *reach God* (*ST* 3a.4.1 ad 2)! Hence Merriell appropriately speaks of the human being coming to reflect the Trinity not merely as a mirror 'but as an actor imitating the character he plays' (1990: 245). Rather as God himself, and not only an idea in God's mind, is our exemplar, so there is an immediacy of contact between the graced (not to mention the glorified) human being and the divine Friend. The capacity for personal communion with the infinite Creator belongs to human nature, since the mind, as image of the Trinity, is open to the true and the good.

Prima Pars 43, on the Trinity's self-giving to us, and 93, on the image of the Trinity that we are, seem correlative.[23] I see Question 43 as making the transition from the treatise on God the Trinity (*ST* 1a.2–42) to the treatises on creation and salvation, a transition that pivots on each Divine Person wanting to *give* himself and on the Father wanting to send us the Son and the Spirit. That is *why* we are made in God's image and hence *capax Dei*: we are made so that the Trinitarian God can give himself to creatures in friendship and so that we can come to fulfilment in enjoying this friendship (Conrad 2018). If so, it is pertinent that Aquinas introduces *ST* 1a.93 by saying 'we must consider the *finis* and the *terminum*[24] of [God's] production of the human being, insofar as we are said to be made to God's image and likeness', for there is an 'Augustinian dynamism' to Question 93. At its climax, in the *sed contra* of article 8, Aquinas quotes *DT* 14.12.15: 'the image of God is not in the mind on the grounds that it remembers itself, and understands and loves itself; but because it is also able to remember, understand, and love God by whom it was made', a text which I suggested expresses the image's vocation to become its true self in communion with its Archetype. Aquinas has already set out this vocation in article 4, which asks whether God's image is found in every human being. If Aquinas had seen the human psyche as a model that gains us a confident purchase on the Trinity, he might have pointed out how, by nature, we know and love ourselves. Instead, he immediately goes for the *super*natural and explores how the human being may imitate God precisely as knowing and loving God's own self. He presents this as happening in three degrees:

> The human being … is most fully to God's image insofar as an intellectual nature can most fully imitate God. Now an intellectual nature imitates God most of all in this, that God understands and loves Himself. Hence we can recognize the image of God in the human being in three ways:
>
> In the first way, on the grounds that the human being possesses a natural aptitude for understanding and loving God; and this aptitude consists in the very nature of the mind, which is common to all human beings.

In the second way, on the grounds that someone actually or habitually knows and loves God, though imperfectly; and this is an image based on the conformity of grace.

In the third way, on the grounds that someone knows and loves God perfectly; and here we recognize an image based on the likeness of glory.

Clearly, in agreement with Aquinas's earlier writings, *ST* 1a.93 teaches that *all* human beings are to God's image. But Merriell's analysis of Aquinas's increasing Augustinianism should ready us to see a shift of emphasis towards the forward-looking, vocational aspect of the image.[25] The dynamic structure of *ST* 1a.93 – within that of the whole *Summa* – is perhaps Aquinas's way of leading the image of God towards its perfection precisely as image, paralleling the journey on which Augustine takes the image into increasing communion with its Exemplar. To be in God's image is a vocation, hence a responsibility; to recognize this is to become aware of the drama of a grace that demands acceptance. A human being cannot elect in a neutral way to stay at the merely natural level, and if someone try to do so, the image is frustrated, since the likeness of glory is something towards which human beings were *always* intended to journey and something which in an important way we inescapably desire (*ST* 1a2ae.5.7–8). Once the age of reason is attained, the image cannot stay at the natural level, for if it does not love God as ultimate goal, it inevitably sins by loving something else in God's place (*ST* 1a2ae.89.6).

The dynamic structure of *ST* 1a.93 concludes in article 9[26] by relating the term 'likeness' to this vocation to grow into the dignity of being like the Holy Trinity. As explained in *ST* 1a.93.1, *similitudo* can mean something more vague than *imago*. Taken another way, it can express the image's perfection as it draws closer to its Exemplar. This connects with the Patristic idea that fallen humanity lost its likeness to God while retaining the image (if in a warped way), so that salvation involves a restoration of the likeness[27]; it also brings out how the dignity of being in God's image is a vocation to progress from one degree of God-like dignity to another and another.

We may briefly summarize some elements of the God-like dignity that perfect the image:

- Charity is a participation in, a likening to, the Holy Spirit (*ST* 1a.43.5 ad 2; 2a2ae.23.3 ad 3, 24.2); at the same time it is a created reality which ensures that it truly is the human being who loves God and neighbour (*ST* 2a2ae.23.2).
- Wisdom is a participation in, a likening to, Christ the Divine Wisdom (*ST* 1a.43.5 ad 2; 2a2ae.45.6); at the same time it is a created reality which

ensures that the human being is truly engaged in instinctively making God-like judgments by being attuned to the Holy Spirit as apprentice to Teacher (*ST* 1a2ae.68.1–3; 2a.2ae.45.1–5).

- In the life to come, about which I John 3.2 says, 'We shall be like him because we shall see him as he is', the Saints' minds are strengthened so that they can at last *know God's Essence* without intermediary. (*ST* 1a.12.1, 2, 5, 9, 10)

Thus the image of God that we are, with its powers of intellect and will that make us open to God the True and the Good, and able to image the Trinity, is increasingly conformed to its Trinitarian Exemplar by grace.[28] As Aquinas honed his theology (following Augustine's development) the importance of being in God's image by conformity seems to increase in comparison with the image's value as analogy or model for the Trinity.[29]

Lower and higher than the angels: *Prima Pars* 93 and 108

Aquinas took from Pseudo-Dionysius's *Celestial Hierarchy* a highly developed notion of the angels as purely spiritual beings, intense and powerful minds stocked by God at their creation with over-arching concepts, whose wills made a firmly determined choice (*ST* 1a.50, 54–60, 62–63).[30] By contrast, the human soul is 'the lowest in the order of spiritual substances' (*De spiritualibus creaturis* 2), needing gradually to acquire 'small' concepts through sense-experience and to organize them by developing 'larger' ones (*ST* 1a.84, 85); the human will is changeable (*ST* 1a2ae.8–10). Aquinas drew the conclusion that in the core sense angels are more in God's image than we are (*ST* 1a.93.3). Looking more closely, we see this position is qualified.

Firstly, following Augustine, Aquinas recognized *vestigia Trinitatis*, 'footprints of the Trinity', throughout creation (*ST* 1a.45.7): the being of things points to the Father, their 'forms' by which they match the divine plan point to the Word in whom the Father conceives this plan, and their 'ordered interrelationships' point to the Holy Spirit as the Divine Love.[31] *Vestigia* are found in animals, which reflect God's 'fruitfulness'; if the creation involved only spiritual beings it would not mirror every aspect of God (*ST* 1a.93.2; 44.3; 45.7; 65.2). The human being occupies a unique place in the hierarchy of things, sharing faculties with the animals and with the angels (*De spiritualibus creaturis* 2). Hence, although the image is less intense in us than in the angels, we are by nature in God's image in a *wider range* of ways: we can have offspring, and so mirror the Father's begetting of his Son; and the way the soul 'fills' the body mirrors the way God is present as Creator and Guide in each part of the universe (*ST* 1a.93.3).

Secondly, Aquinas held that by the grace that grows into glory, human beings are taken up into the orders of Angels (*ST* 1a.108.8). Among the Angels who remained faithful the order of grace exactly parallels the order of nature (*ST* 1a.62.6): those that are by nature the more powerful minds received more intense grace, hence a higher degree of glory. But grace and charity, as supernatural gifts, need not be given in proportion to natural endowments (*ST* 2a2ae.24.3), to the extent that certain human souls have been given grace more intense than some, or even *all*, the Angels. Christ in his human mind possesses (and possessed from the moment of his Conception) the Beatific Vision more intensely than any other creature (*ST* 3a.10.4). Mary is 'Queen of the Angels'; there is something unsurpassable about the glory both of Christ and of his Mother (*ST* 1a.25.6 ad 4). John the Baptist and the Apostles have a place among (if not above) the higher Angels.[32] Hence some of the human beings who are brought to glory enjoy a greater glory than anyone would have enjoyed had there been no Fall![33]

Thirdly, while Angels can mediate a kind of strength to the human intellect (*ST* 1a.111.1), only human beings can be instrumental causes of grace! Aquinas's concept of instrumental efficient causality allows him to claim that Christ's humanity was the unique 'channel' of grace to all human beings who ever receive it (*ST* 3a.7.1, 9, 10, 11; 8.1, 5). But from Christ and his Passion devolves an instrumental causality to the Sacraments (*ST* 3a.48.6, 62.3–5). And Sacraments require human ministers; Angels cannot minister them (*ST* 3a.64.7).[34] While we are no more able than the angels are to put concepts directly into other minds (*ST* 1a.117.1), human beings can have the dignity of ministering to other human beings something more precious than concepts.

Being embodied is no indignity. Aquinas rejects the Manichean idea that the material creation is evil and the Origenist idea that some rebel spirits fell into bodies, resulting in human beings (*ST* 1a.65.1 and 2); on the contrary, the cosmos as first created already provided a suitable home (the empyrean heaven) for human bodies destined to be glorified (*ST* 1a.66.3). The human body is *well* proportioned to the soul, its 'substantial form' (*ST* 1a.76.5); its awkwardnesses are a 'standard' material limitation (*ST* 1a2ae.85.6; 2a2ae.164.1) overcome in one way before the Fall and due to be overcome in the resurrection world.

It is through our bodies that we are located in space and time; this allows us to *journey* towards fulfilment, both natural and supernatural, in a way that fills out the scheme of things (*ST* 1a2ae.5.7). Furthermore, reflection on aspects of our bodily and social nature gives rise to key principles of the Natural Law

(*ST* 1a2ae.94.2). Things that we do, over time, in our bodies, can result in the acquisition of virtues.[35] And ordinary activities, as well as extraordinary feats, can be 'informed' by a Charity greater than that of many of the Angels; since the degree of glory exactly matches the degree of Charity with which a person journeys into God, certain Saints, as we have seen, enjoy a more-than-angelic glory.

Taking personal dignity seriously

One might expect Aquinas to base the dignity of being in the Trinity's image on the fact of personhood. He did of course defend, and sought to clarify, the traditional use of *persona* in Trinitarian theology and Christology (*ST* 1a.29; 3a.2.2). But, to summarize, he accorded it an *ontological* meaning: it means an individual *being*. But it *connotes* dignity because it is reserved for those beings that have a rational nature. Also, it is used analogically: each human being is a person, but in a different way from the way angels are persons and from the way each Divine Person is a person.

Aquinas's route to expressing human dignity does not rest on a 'brute' claim to 'personhood' but on our having *liberum arbitrium* ('free decision'), having dominion over our acts because we can reflect on what we should do:

> As Damascene says, the human being is said to be made to God's image in that 'image' signifies 'intellectual, free as regards decision, and having one's own authority'. Therefore ... we go on to consider [God's] image, i.e. the human being, insofar as he is source of his own acts, as having free decision and authority over his own acts. (*ST* 1a2ae prologue)[36]

A moral seriousness results from possessing intellect and will: just as the starting point of morality is 'higher' than law,[37] so its 'bottom line', the human act, is particular in a way law cannot be, for we make personal decisions of conscience in individual situations, which on occasion require us to exercise *epieikeia*, the virtue of setting aside the letter of a particular law in exceptional circumstances (*ST* 2a2ae.120). Decisions of conscience are serious: we sin if we fail responsibly to judge what we should do or to follow our judgments; for such failures are voluntary, as are *culpable* failures to make good judgments by thinking well (*ST* 1a2ae.6.3, 19.4–5). The will's openness to God alone is arguably of a piece with the responsibility to make careful acts of conscience and with our acts having merit or demerit in God's sight (*ST* 1a2ae.21.4).

In a striking passage Aquinas hints that each intellectual creature has a dignity not possessed by other creatures, including the heavenly bodies. Although in its whole sweep the cosmos is a fuller good than the intellectual creature it contains, the likeness of God's perfection is found in 'a more intense and concentrated way' (*intensive et collective*) in the intellectual creature (*ST* 1a.93.2 ad 3). This may hint that the individual person's value cannot be traded off against the good of the cosmos in any simplistic way.[38]

But Aquinas seems not to make consistent use of the concept of irreducible personal worth. His disapproval of aiming at killing people in self-defence (*ST* 2a2ae.64.7) relies on the good of human life, a basic starting point for Natural-Law reflection. But when in *ST* 2a2ae.64.2 he asks whether the state may execute a criminal, he employs the model of 'the body politic' and draws an analogy between the execution of a criminal and the amputation of a gangrenous member. While the concept of 'the common good' is of immense value in moral, political and legal reflection, likening an individual to a member of an organic body seems excessively to subordinate the person and her dignity before God to the collective and is in tension with Aquinas's conviction that a collective is not a single being in the way a single organism is. The model of the body politic remained influential even after Pius XII declared that 'the principle of totality' should not be applied to the relationship between the individual and the state (1952: 786), and §2267 in *The Catechism of the Catholic Church*, concerning capital punishment, has been revised twice, first by John Paul II, then by Pope Francis, and now says, 'the Church teaches … that "the death penalty is inadmissible because it is an attack on the inviolability and dignity of the person"'.[39] It would be interesting to explore how far the 'personalism' of John Paul II drew on, or re-balanced, Aquinas's vision of the individual's irreducible dignity and responsibility as dynamic image of the Holy Trinity.[40]

Conclusions

While aware of the development of Aquinas's teaching on the image, which seems in some ways to mirror Augustine's journey when writing *De Trinitate*, we have focused on Aquinas's mature account in *ST* 1a.93 and drawn connections with other texts. We have discovered nuance in the relative nobility of intellect and will, and in the relative place of angels and embodied humanity in the cosmic order. The human psyche has a real but limited value in leading us to an understanding of the Trinitarian faith; more importantly, the image itself is called to be led into an increasing conformity with the Holy Trinity. By nature we have a direct relationship with the Triune Exemplar, to whom alone our morally responsible wills are open. We may not rest at the level of nature: if we allow God's friendship to attract us, grace, Charity and Wisdom engage us personally in a journey that brings the image to perfection in imitating as closely as possible the Trinity with whom we commune. The journey is made in the body and with the help of a sacramental ministry. All this both enhances human dignity and ties this dignity to a divine and serious vocation.

Notes

1   *Super Sent.* lib. 3, d. 1, q. 1, a. 3 arg. 5; d. 20, q. 1, a. 1, qc. 2 ad 2; d. 34, q. 3, a. 2, qc. 1 c; *ST* 2a2ae.64.2 ad 3; 3a.1.2; *De rationibus Fidei* cap. 5; *Super I Cor.* cap. 15, l. 3. St Thomas Aquinas's *Summa Theologiae* is abbreviated as *ST*, followed by numbers of part, question and article, and, when appropriate, of reply to objection. So *Prima Pars*, Qu. 93, Art. 4, appears as *ST* 1a.93.4 if the reference is to the body of the article or whole article and as *ST* 1.93.4 ad 1 if the reference is to the reply to the first objection. *Prima Secundae* is 1a2ae, etc.

2   *Expositio in Symbolum Apostolorum*, art 1. I owe this reference to Merriell (1990: 244).

3   Aquinas explains the third in *ST* 1a.93.2, having previously set out all three features in *ST* 1a.35.1.

4   *ST* 1a.93.1 ad 2; cf. *ST* 1a.35, and Aquinas's *Commentary on Colossians* 1.15, where the three features of an image are again set out.

5   He suggests the word *imago* is sometimes used when 'exemplar' would be more accurate (cf. our use of 'model' when speaking of a prototype on which other things are modelled).

6   Augustine had used the *Vetus Latina*; the *Itala* version of the *Vetus Latina* (given at vulgate.net) also uses *ad*, but, influenced by the Septuagint, fails to use *creavit* in Gen. 1.27 to translate the Hebrew *bārā'*, using *fecit* instead (the *faciamus* in 1.26 is accurate). Thus, the Vulgate of 1.27 captures better the special creative act of God exercised when the human being – each and every human being – comes into existence.

7   *b*ᵉ has a wide range of meanings. If in Gen. 1.26-7, etc., it is the '*beth essentiae*' the translation would be 'Let us make the human being as our image.' The preposition *k*ᵉ, meaning 'like' or 'according to', is used with the word for 'likeness' in Gen. 1.26 (but *b*ᵉ is used with it in 5.1) and seems to have influenced the Septuagint which uses *kata* ('according to') with both 'image' and 'likeness' in Gen. 1.26-7, 5.1; in Gen. 9.6 the Septuagint uses *en* ('in').

8   Note that metaphor, imagery, irony, parable, etc., are all part of the *literal* meaning (cf. *ST* 1a.1.10 ad 3), since in order to interpret a text – any text – we need to work out what linguistic devices and figures of speech it employs.

9   According the human being a 'psychophysical' likeness to God does not imply that God (as God) has a human-like form; after all, God does not resemble the angels either. Aquinas maintains the apparent paradox that while creatures can be said to resemble God, God cannot be said to resemble them (*ST* 1a.4.3 ad 4). Arguably, biblical authors were well aware that, inevitably, we employ metaphors and imagery when speaking of God (cf. *ST* 1a.1.9).

10   Note that *mens* includes will as well as intellect.

11   Christ is called 'the Logos' in John 1.1, 14, I John 1.1 (arguably) and Rev. 19.13, where it is normally translated *Verbum*, 'the Word'. But the Greek *logos* in general maps onto the Latin words *verbum* and *ratio* ('reason', 'account', 'definition', etc.).

12   Presumably this was due to the influence of Plato and Aristotle, who saw *logos* as our highest power.

13   Merriell (1990: 23 n. 30) mentions some tentative precedents for this. Cary says that in Book I of *On Free Choice*, Augustine 'introduces a profound new concept of Will' and agrees with earlier scholars that Augustine 'seems to have been the first to formulate the notion of a faculty of choosing that could not be reduced to some combination of reasoning and desire' (Cary 2000: 110, and 181 n. 30).

14   *Memoria, intelligentia, intellectus* and *voluntas* are, respectively, memory, understanding, intellect and will. I use the Latin as a reminder neither to import modern perceptions of what these are into our reading of Augustine or Aquinas nor to demand precise one-to-one translations.

15   Augustine makes deft use of *speculum* and *aenigma* (I Cor. 13.12). Merriell and Sullivan speak in a 'scholastic' way of 'analogies' (Augustine does not use *analogia* in *DT*). My choice of 'model' alludes to how modern scientists use the familiar to gain limited purchase on something mysterious; often, complementary models are needed.

16   Apparently, Augustine came to this realization in 412 or thereabouts (Merriell 1990: 80 n. 106).

17   I owe this interpretation largely to unpublished lectures by Giles Hibbert, OP; a fuller exploration is beyond the scope of an essay on *Aquinas's* theology.

18   Merriell (1990: 4–7, 28, 99–110, 115–134, 157–158, 176, 190–193, 208–217, 220, 223–225, 227–230, 242–243).

19   Like the Hebrew and Greek it translates (*ruaḥ* and *pneuma*), *spiritus* can mean 'breath', 'wind', 'spirit', 'breath of life'; I suspect the meanings 'animation' and 'vivacity', of which the Hebrew is susceptible, gradually crept into theological Latin through Scriptural and Trinitarian reflection.

20   Already in *Scriptum super Sententiis*, Aquinas had taken account of the contemporary awareness that Lombard's *memoria* did not map well onto Aristotelian psychology (Merriell 1990: 59–69).

21 If I say, 'I remember learning about X', I mean my imagination retains the past event of learning it. But if I say, 'I remember what X is', I mean that I possess the (timeless) concept I learned. Active use of the concept requires close cooperation between intellect and imagination (*ST* 1a.84.7), so that ageing of the brain can render the concept useless; in that sense I *can* forget it.

22 *ST* 1a2ae.110.1 explains that *gratia* can mean God's special love or the gifts he gives us out of that love. Of these, *gratia gratum faciens* (usually translated 'sanctifying grace') is a participation in the Divine Nature that raises us up to commune with God as his children; in a fallen world it must also heal our sinfulness.

23 Merriell argues that Aquinas is not very concerned to connect the two (1990: 10–11, 230–234). However, I suspect that here, as often, he wants us to make connections he does not spell out, because he wants to keep this course for beginners succinct.

24 If *de fine sive termino* is not simply a hendiadys, the former word emphasizes the motivating goal and the latter the product as brought to perfection.

25 Merriell points out that a dynamic element of *actual imitation* is already present in Aquinas's account of the image in the *Scriptum super Sententiis* (1990: 55–57, 69–79). He brings out how Aquinas increasingly emphasized the image's developmental nature (1990: 132–133, 189). But he argues against a significant shift of emphasis in the *Summa* away from the natural aspect of the image (1990: 176–182, 224–225); maybe he overstates his case lest the overall thrust of his argument compromise a dignity common to all human beings.

26 Merriell (1990: 171) puzzles over the positioning of *ST* 1a.93.9, but it falls into place if we recognize the Question's dynamism.

27 This idea remained influential. For example, it is central to St Bernard's mystical theology (Gilson 1940: *passim*).

28 For more on our likening to God by grace, see Conrad (2015, 2018); for more on the connaturality effected by Wisdom and the other Gifts, see Conrad (2009) and Pinsent (2012).

29 Merriell (1990: 12, 154, 187, 230–231). Aquinas's initial reflections on *conformitas* seem due to the influence of the *Summa Halensis* and Bonaventure (1990: 69–72, 82).

30 Since it was assumed that 'Dionysius' was a disciple of St Paul, his writings were accorded immense authority.

31 This is neither revelation nor proof of the Holy Trinity, but something we recognize in the light of revelation (*ST* 1a.32.1).

32 This is pieced together from *ST* 1a2ae.106.4; 3a.27.6 ad 1, 38.6 obj. 1 (a premise not refuted); *De malo* 7.7 ad 8; *De veritate* 24.9 sc 2.

33 Assuming, of course, that the Incarnation would not have happened had there been no Fall; *ST* 3a.1.3.

34 Because of certain legends, Aquinas allowed for God *occasionally* commissioning an Angel as minister of a Sacrament.

35 This is attractively explored in Jordan (2017).

36 Merriell (1990: 169) draws attention to this quotation. A further study would be needed to compare Aquinas's use of the concepts of dignity and *liberum arbitrium* with his predecessors' and contemporaries'.

37 It is the innate drive to *eudaimonia, beatitudo,* with which Aristotle commences the *Nicomachean Ethics* and Aquinas the *Secunda Pars*.

38 It is tempting to associate this text with the claim that the justification of the unrighteous is a greater work of God than creation (*ST* 1a2ae.113.9).

39 Rescriptum 'ex Audientia SS.mi', *Bolletino sala stampa della Santa Sede* 02.08.2018.

40 It would be a further project to explore what resources, if any, Aquinas offers for recognizing a Trinitarian vocation for various human *communities*.

References

Aquinas, St Thomas (1941), *Summa Theologiae*, Ottawa: Collège Dominicain (Translations of Augustine and Aquinas are mine.).

Aquinas, St Thomas, other works: consulted via http://www.corpusthomisticum.org/iopera.html.

Augustine, St Aurelius (1968), *De Trinitate libri XV* (Corpus Christianorum Series Latina L and LA), Turnhout: Brepols.

Ayres, L. (2014), *Augustine and the Trinity*, Cambridge: Cambridge University Press.

Cary, P. (2000), *Augustine's Invention of the Inner Self: The Legacy of a Christian Platonist*, Oxford: Oxford University Press.

Conrad, R., OP (2009), *7 Gifts of the Holy Spirit*, London: Catholic Truth Society.

Conrad, R., OP (2015), 'Wisdom and Sonship', in H. Goris, L. Hendriks and H. Schoot (eds), *Faith, Hope and Love: Thomas Aquinas on Living by the Theological Virtues*, 283–305, Leuven: Peeters.

Conrad, R., OP (2018), 'Humanity Created for Communion with the Trinity in Aquinas', in G. Westhaver (ed.), *A Transforming Vision: Knowing and Loving the Triune God*, 121–134, London: SCM.

Gilson, E. (1940), *The Mystical Theology of St. Bernard*, London: Sheed and Ward.

Hill, E., OP (1985), *The Mystery of the Trinity*, London: Geoffrey Chapman.

Jordan, M. D. (2017), *Teaching Bodies: Moral Formation in the* Summa *of Thomas Aquinas*, New York: Fordham University Press.

Merriell, D. J. (1990), *To the Image of the Trinity: A Study in the Development of Aquinas' Teaching*, Toronto: Pontifical Institute of Mediaeval Studies.

Pinsent, A. (2012), *The Second Person Perspective in Aquinas's Ethics: Virtues and Gifts*, London: Routledge.

Pius XII, Pope (1952), 'The Moral Limits of Medical Research and Treatment', address given 13 Sept. 1952 to the First International Congress on the Histopathology of the Nervous System, AAS 19, 779–789.

Sullivan, J. E., OP (1963), *The Image of God: The Doctrine of St. Augustine and Its Influence*, Dubuque: The Priory Press.

5

Human Dignity and Human Wretchedness from Irenaeus to Pico della Mirandola

John Loughlin

What we call today the 'Renaissance' stretched from around the end of the fourteenth century to the middle of the sixteenth century and is usually thought to have begun with the humanist Petrarch (1304–1374). It refers primarily to developments in Italy although other European countries such as France and England were involved. Renaissance studies have been divided between historians who emphasize a *rupture* between the Renaissance and the preceding Middle Ages – the so-called Dark Ages – and those who, by contrast, are aware of the *continuities* with that period. To some extent, this division coincides with broader ideological positions: those who regard Christendom as backward and rebarbative will emphasize the rupture, while those sympathetic to it will see continuity. The 'Renaissance' was, in fact, one of several European 'renaissances' such as that of Charlemagne in the ninth century or that of the twelfth century (Chenu 1964: 19–98; Mann 2001). This chapter will argue that the later Renaissance is marked more by continuity with previous periods of European history and could be seen as the high point of Christendom. This is particularly with regard to how it accepted the Christian framework of man's place in the world and its synthesis of the biblical understanding of man's creation in God's image and likeness with neo-Platonic and Ciceronian concepts. It is this synthesis that lies at the core of the concept of human dignity understood as the human being's distinctive character compared with the rest of creation. Nevertheless, this was not a mere Panglossian optimism as it was also aware of the wretched and misery of the human condition, although this was also tempered by hope. But the chapter will also show how, in some respects, the Renaissance was laying the foundation for the rupture with this Christian past caused by both the Protestant Reformation and the secular Enlightenment in the sixteenth and eighteenth centuries, respectively.

The notion that the Renaissance was a radical break with medieval Christendom was developed during the nineteenth century by anticlerical and anti-Catholic historians such as the Frenchman Jules Michelet (1798–1874), the Swiss Jacob Burckhardt (1818–1897) and the Oxford don Walter Pater (1839–1894). It was Michelet who, in his 1855 *Histoire de France*, first coined the term 'Renaissance' meaning 'rebirth'. Michelet was from a Protestant Huguenot background and shared the anti-Catholic and republican sympathies of this group. He loathed the medieval period. For him, 'Renaissance' was a term meant to celebrate the end of the Middle Ages and the arrival of a newer and better humanity. Michelet's massive 19-volume *Histoire de France* was written to support the ideals of the French Revolution and to attack the monarchy and the Catholic Church in France. Volume 7 of the history, published in 1855, was entitled *La Renaissance*. For him, the Renaissance meant 'the discovery of the world and the discovery of man. The sixteenth century … went from Columbus to Copernicus, from Copernicus to Galileo, from the discovery of the earth to the discovery of the heavens. Man refound himself' (quoted in Brotton 2002: 20). Brotton sums up Michelet's approach: 'This new spirit was contrasted with what Michelet viewed as the "bizarre and monstrous" quality of the Middle Ages. To him the Renaissance represented a progressive, democratic condition that celebrated the great virtues he valued – Reason, Truth, Art, and Beauty' (2002).

Burckhardt was born in Basel, the son of a Protestant clergyman. He published *The Civilisation of the Renaissance in Italy* in 1860. In this work, he developed the notion of a contrast between the Middle Ages and the Renaissance in which the latter was characterized by human individuality, while during the former, men were characterized by a lack of individual awareness: 'Man was conscious of himself only as a member of a race, people, party, family or corporation (quoted in Brotton 2002: 21).' There is, of course, a great deal of truth in the idea that Renaissance art and sculpture, under the influence of classical Greek and Roman statuary, developed a new awareness of the individual compared to the Byzantine and medieval European traditions. And Burckhardt's writings on Renaissance art were admired by historians such as Kenneth Clark, who could not be accused of denigrating medieval Catholicism (Clark 1974: 114). But Burckhardt exaggerated the differences and emphasized the rupture rather than the continuities. His interpretation of the Renaissance, however, became part of a popular narrative that is widespread even today. His major error was to extrapolate from developments in art and sculpture to making statements about the whole character of a period of civilization. Burckhardt was an admirer of the German pessimist philosopher Schopenhauer and was in turn admired by Nietzsche. All three were part of a movement that rejected Christianity and advanced the notion that 'Christendom' was characterized by 'darkness' and 'obscurantism', and this fitted their anti-Christian prejudices. Furthermore, this fed into a narrative that glorified the individual and personal autonomy that had developed since the Protestant Reformation in Germany and Switzerland, was intensified by Immanuel Kant and assumed a secularized form in the nineteenth century.

Walter Pater carried the positions of Michelet and Burckhardt to their logical conclusion in his book *The Renaissance*, published in 1873. Pater viewed the Renaissance primarily from an aesthetic point of view and eschewed its political, social and economic dimensions by stressing the notion of 'art for art's sake'. He saw figures such as Leonardo, Botticelli and Michelangelo as rebels against the conventions of the Church and concerned to develop their own individuality. At the same time, Pater was sometimes nostalgic for the Christian world he had left behind and, despite his aestheticism, was critical of what he regarded as amoral and solipsistic excesses such as Oscar Wilde's *The Picture of Dorian Gray*. Nevertheless, his individualistic and aesthetic method influenced a whole generation of subsequent writers on the period including Kenneth Clark and A. C. Benson (Brotton 2002: 21).

It is clear that the three writers discussed here interpreted the Renaissance from the perspective of nineteenth-century bourgeois individualism and its loss of faith in Christianity. Each could find examples that justified their own adopted positions with regard to philosophy, politics, ethics and art. But by emphasizing the rupture between the medieval period and the Renaissance, they seriously underestimated the continuities that exist between the two periods.

A key to understanding these continuities is to examine how the notion of the human being as created in the 'image and likeness of God' (Gen 1:27) was central to the Christian anthropology that developed throughout the entire period from the first encounter between Christian missionaries and the Greco-Roman world of the second and third centuries AD. The early Christian theologians were concerned both with preserving the biblical notion of the human being's special dignity as the summit of God's creation and with warding off the distortion of the Gospel message by the Gnostic movement (Daniélou 1973: 445–469). At the same time, they felt free to draw on the prevailing philosophical traditions of the time, especially on neo-Platonism with regard to the notions of image and likeness and on Stoicism, as mediated by Cicero, to explain the rational basis of man's dignity. But this was all couched in the framework of the Christian history of salvation: the human race, represented by Adam and Eve, had fallen from the state of grace through sin was restored to its original innocence in Christ, the image of the invisible God, and through Christ, who is the image of the invisible God, each man and woman was offered not only such restoration but the new and greater dignity of adopted sonship and eternal life (Col. 1:15-18).

Irenaeus of Lyon (*c.* AD 140–*c.* AD 202) was the first to make use of the biblical phrase 'in the image (*eikon*) and likeness (*homoiosis*) of God', distinguishing 'image' from 'likeness' (Phan 1988: 43–63). Most contemporary biblical scholars agree that in Hebrew the two terms are synonymous (see Day 2019 in this volume). But Irenaeus drew on the Greek translation of the Hebrew Bible known as the Septuagint and distinguished between the terms in a way that would develop a whole theology and spirituality (Lossky 1975). He taught that, after the Fall, human beings lost the 'likeness' but retained the 'image' of God. Irenaeus thought that 'image' also referred to man's body while 'likeness' is a supernatural gift (the *donum additum*) from God (Phan 1988: 49). Irenaeus's notion that the body is also in the image of God was probably to counteract the Gnostic teaching, prevalent at that time, that the body is evil. Irenaeus summed up his understanding of human dignity in the phrase 'the glory of God is the living man[1] (*Gloria Dei vivens homo*)', which is sometimes translated as 'the Glory of God is man fully alive' (*Adv. Haer.* IV, 20.6–7). Clement of Alexandria (AD 150–215) uses the distinction in a rather different way. Plato had distinguished between the *daimon*, the highest or governing part of the soul, and the *eudaimonia*, the state of perfection of the soul. Clement, in turn, distinguishes between *eikon* (equivalent of the *eudaimonia*) which is understood as the final state of likeness to God, while *homoiosis* denotes the dynamic, continuing process by which this goal is pursued (the *daimonia*) (Daniélou 1973: 409). Clement also argued that the *eikon* denoted man's participation in the Word through his faculty of reason: 'The divine and royal Logos is the image of God, the human mind (*nous*) is the image of the image' (*Strom.* V. 14: 94–95). Clement linked this to freedom. Human beings can make free choices because we have the capacity to reason while animals act through instinct. Thus, being endowed with reason by virtue of being made in God's image, man achieves the likeness only through the correct exercise of his freedom.

Not all the Greek and Latin Fathers used the distinction between image and likeness, but they were all conscious of the human being's great dignity. Among the Cappadocian Fathers, Gregory of Nyssa (AD 335–394) waxed lyrical about humanity:

Everything God created was very good. The story of creation witnesses to it. Man was also listed among those very good things, adorned with a beauty far superior to all of the good things. What else, in fact, could be good, on a par with one who was similar to pure and incorruptible beauty? ... The reflection and image of eternal life, he was truly good; no, he was very good, with the radiant sign of life on his face. (*Homilia in Canticum* 12: PG 44, 1020c)

Again:

The sky was not made in God's image, not the sun, not the beauty of the stars, no other things which appear in creation. Only you [human soul] were made to be the image of nature that surpasses every intellect, likeness of incorruptible beauty, mark of true divinity, vessel of blessed life, image of true light, that when you look upon it you become what He is, because through the reflected ray coming from your purity you imitate He who shines with you. Nothing that exists can measure up to your greatness. (*Homilia in Canticum* 2: PG 44, 805d)

But this beauty and greatness have been distorted by sin. Gregory sees the Beatitudes (Matt 5: 3–12; Lk 6: 20–22) as the way to restore this beauty: 'If, with a diligent and attentive standard of living, you wash away the bad things that have deposited in your heart, the divine beauty will shine in you' (*De Beatitudinibus* 6: PG 44 1272ab). Among the Western Fathers, Ambrose of Milan (*c.* AD 340–397) also did not distinguish between the two terms, and he drew more on Cicero's definition of human dignity, borrowed from the Stoics:

But it is essential to every enquiry about duty that we keep before our eyes how far superior man is by nature to cattle and other beasts; they [that is, other animals] have no thought except for sensual pleasure and this they are impelled by every instinct to seek; but man's mind is nurtured by study and meditation; he is always either investigating or doing, and he is captivated by the pleasure of seeing and hearing. (Cicero *De officiis* 105)

For Ambrose, echoing Cicero (but contradicting Irenaeus):

The flesh, therefore, cannot be made in the image of God. That is true, however, of our souls, which are free to wander far and wide in acts of reflection and counsel. Our souls are made to envisage and reflect on all things ... That, therefore, is made in the image of God which is perceived, not by the power of the body but by that of the mind. (*Hexaemeron* VI, 7, 42–6 quoted in Phan 1988: 215)

The notion of *imago Dei* remained influential in the West and was used by St Augustine, St Bernard of Clairvaux and St Thomas Aquinas. It provided an overarching anthropological framework for the understanding of the humanity's place in the world. Augustine of Hippo developed the notion that being made in God's image and likeness meant that we are made in the image of the Trinity (Sullivan 1963). As Augustine expresses it: 'Of all the animals on earth the main one is man. He was made to be the image of God' (*City of God*, 12:28). Instead of looking outside ourselves and trying to escape from the world of matter as the neo-Platonists of his day had done, Augustine argued that we should seek the transcendent realities they were searching for, and ultimately God, by looking within and discovering our memory, understanding and will; these give us the ability to know, understand and respond to God. Charles Taylor has called this the turn to 'inwardness' which would later evolve through the nominalism of Occam, the reformed theology of Luther and the subjectivism of Descartes to the modern cult of individualism (Taylor 1989: 128–129). Augustine was also aware of man's sinfulness and saw that the image of God within man has been damaged by the sin of disobedience so that the Christian life consists in seeking, with the help of God's grace, to return to it: 'When, therefore, we contemplate His image in our very selves, let us, like the younger son in the Gospel [Lk 15: 11–32] return to ourselves, rise and seek Him from whom we have departed by sin' (*City of God*, 11:28). Augustine's *City of God*, initially written as a response to the sack of Rome by the Barbarians in the early fifth century, was an attempt to refute the accusation made at the time that the fall of the city was a result of the adoption of Christianity in the Empire and the neglect of the traditional pagan gods. Augustine had no difficulty in refuting these charges and his great work was about much more than this, and, dealing with theology, philosophy and politics, it became the key work that largely shaped Western Christendom from that time until the modern period (Gilson 1960).

Other Latin writers continued to promote the notion of the special dignity of human beings. Boethius (*c.* AD 480–524) continued the synthesis in *De consolatione philosophiae* where he developed the concept of 'person'. In this work, he describes human beings as 'O felix hominum genus (Oh happy race of men!) (8: 25). Pope St Leo the Great (*c.* AD 400–61) related man's greatness to the Incarnation. In a sermon given on Christmas Day, he proclaimed: 'Rouse yourself, oh man, and recognize the dignity of your nature. Remember that you were made in God's image: though corrupted in Adam, that image has been restored in Christ' (*Sermo 7, In Nativitate Domini* 2: 6, PL 54).

Two theologians, although very different from each other, can be regarded as 'bridges' between the medieval period and the early centuries of the Renaissance: Bernard of Clairvaux (1090–1153) and Thomas Aquinas (1225–1274).

Bernard was a Cistercian monk whose influence was enormous during the first half of the twelfth century (Evans 2000; Gilson 2010 [1940]). He has been called 'the last of the Fathers', and his writings can be seen as the culmination of the great tradition of Western patristic thought that had begun with St Augustine (Merton 1954). The Mellifluous Doctor, as he was called by Pius XII in 1953, was active at a crucial turning point in the history of Western Europe, a period that has been called 'the long twelfth century' (Noble and Van Engen 2012). Several transformations were taking place during this period: new economic forces were reviving the cities (Nicholas 2012); universities were being founded in Bologna, Paris and Oxford; and the great Gothic cathedrals were being built. In the Church, too, important reforms were occurring driven by Pope Gregory VII in what Harold Berman has called the 'Papal Revolution': the Pope was centralizing power in Rome, standardizing canon law and reforming the secular clergy with the reimposition of compulsory celibacy especially on their senior members (Berman 1983). The Papal Revolution was primarily an attempt by the Church to wrest control over its institutions from the hands of secular rulers as well as the Holy Roman Emperor (1983). During this period, there was also a renewal of the monastic life: the Camaldolese hermits were founded in 1012 by a Benedictine monk St Romuald; the even stricter Carthusian hermits by St Bruno in 1084; and the Cistercians in 1098 as a more strict interpretation of the Rule of St Benedict. Bernard entered the Cistercians with thirty relatives and friends in 1115.

Bernard was a key actor in these developments but what interests us here is his 'mystical theology' based on the notions of 'image and likeness'.[2] Bernard asks how human beings differ from other animals and, like Augustine, says we can answer this question by looking at ourselves. There we can find positive attributes of the body but above these and much superior are the attributes of the spirit. St Bernard uses the term *dignitas* to describe the highest of these attributes: 'free will' (*liberum arbitrium*) which is human dignity par excellence. There are two reasons why this gives men and women dignity. First, it raises us above all other animals. Second, it gives us the authority to dominate them and to use them for our own purposes. But recognizing our possession of *liberum arbitrium* means that we also possess reason or understanding (*scientia*). One cannot exist without the other. It is easy to see here the synthesis of Augustine's concept of image and Cicero's definition of human dignity as reason or understanding. But Bernard does not leave it there. He also recognizes that this *scientia* of our own dignity is incomplete if we do not also have a knowledge of the One from whom we receive it. This gives us the desire to discover the author of our own dignity and to attach ourselves to Him. This desire leads to 'virtue'. Free will, knowledge or reason and virtue are the three components of human dignity which must always go together. Having free will and knowledge without virtue may give us a certain 'glory' but this would be vainglory. One can note here, in Augustinian style, the Trinitarian character of this conception of human dignity. Bernard argued that all human beings and not just Christians in principle possess this dignity. Christians, however, have the advantage of knowing Christ who has revealed it in all its fullness.

Bernard, like Augustine, believed that the human being is made for love (*amor*), and he devotes a great deal of attention to this notion. We should love ourselves and our neighbours but, above all, we should love God. He quotes the famous phrase of Augustine: 'the measure by which God should be loved is measureless' (*De diligendo Deo* 1:1). But because of original sin we usually remain at the first level, love of self, with rising to the second or third levels, the love of neighbour and the love of God respectively. Bernard uses the account of the expulsion of Adam and Eve from the Garden of Eden to explain why this is so. The human being henceforth lives in exile. God had created him a noble creature (*creatura nobilis*) because he created him in his own image. Expelled from the *regio similitudinis* (the country of 'likeness') he now inhabits the *regio disimilitudinis*, a phrase borrowed from St Augustine's *Confessions*. Adam thus introduced corruption into the world and all his descendants have inherited this corruption. But all is not lost because God has not abandoned his children and it is possible, through Christ, to recover the likeness.

Bernard follows Augustine in situating the 'image' in the mind (*mens*) of man but emphasizes the will (*voluntas*), and especially man's radical freedom, rather than the intellect. Man is a noble creature who cannot lose this radical freedom without ceasing to be a man. This does not mean that reason is absent. As we saw above, freedom is *liberum arbitrium*. The *arbitrium* refers to the faculty of reason allowing us to weigh up and judge before making our free choice. We can never lose this but there are two other liberties that we can lose: freedom from sin (*libertas a peccato*) and the freedom from suffering (*libertas a miseria*). It is these two liberties that constitute man's 'likeness' to God that was lost at the Fall. Bernard also points to an aspect of human dignity that will become important during the Renaissance: the notion of 'uprightness' (*rectitudo*). Following a notion that goes back to the classical authors such as Ovid, human dignity was shown by the upright posture of the human body. Bernard interpreted this also as a spiritual disposition (moral uprightness) but because of original sin, we are now 'bent over' (*curva*). Paradoxically, we straighten up again through the exercise of humility, following Christ who humbled himself to become man. As a Cistercian monk, Bernard saw the monastic life and the Rule of St Benedict as the means by which this straightening up takes place.

St Bernard lived in a period when the dominance of the monasteries as intellectual centres was being challenged by the schools associated with cathedrals such as Chartres and the new universities who were developing another method of learning that became known as scholasticism. At much the same time, the works of Aristotle, some of which had been preserved by Arab scholars, were rediscovered and translated into Latin. For a time, this challenged the predominance of Plato and neo-Platonism. Bernard and the Cistercians had opposed some of these developments as can be seen in his famous conflict with Peter Abelard (AD 1079–1142). But the new learning was embraced by the new movements of friars and especially by the Dominicans Albert the Great (AD 1200–1280) and his student Thomas Aquinas (Tugwell 1988). Albert had introduced the writings of Aristotle into the curriculum of Dominican students and this was fully developed by Thomas, particularly in the latter's great theological synthesis, the *Summa Theologiae* (Davies 2014). While Thomas broke new ground in applying Aristotelian concepts such as 'accident' and 'substance' as ways in which to conceptualize the doctrine of the real presence of Christ in the Eucharist, he remained faithful to Augustine and Bernard both of whom he quotes copiously. Aquinas follows the tradition by distinguishing 'image' and 'likeness' (*Summa Theologiae*, 1a, 93). He says that something can be *like* another thing because it resembles it 'in some way'. But it is the *image* of another thing if it resembles it 'quite precisely' (Davies 2014: 147–150). This image, according to Aquinas, resides in man's understanding and will: 'While all creatures bear some resemblance to God, only in a rational creature do you find resemblance to God in the manner of an image ... what puts the rational creature in a higher class than others is precisely intellect or mind' (quoted in 2014: 149). Aquinas also follows Augustine's insight that man is made in the image and likeness of God understood as Trinitarian (Conrad 2019 in this volume). At the same time, he stresses the role of intellect rather than the will as Bernard had done. We shall see below how Dante Alighieri (AD 1265–1321) remained faithful to this tradition.

From Augustine writing at the end of the fourth century to Dante at the turn of the fourteenth century, there are thus deep continuities of spiritual outlook and intellectual formation which extended beyond the Middle Ages. C. S. Lewis spoke of a common framework: 'the mediaeval synthesis ... the whole organisation of ... theology, science and history into a single, complex and harmonious Model of the Universe' (Lewis 1964: 11). Lewis believed that this 'Model' depended on two factors. First, the culture of the Middles Ages was *bookish* in character. They had inherited a vast and very heterogenous collection of books from Judaic, Pagan, Platonic, Aristotelian, Stoic and, of course, Christian and Patristic sources. Second, they had a love of systematization and much time was spent organizing these diverse materials (Lewis makes the amusing comment that among modern inventions they would have most loved the card index!). The two examples where this work of harmonious systematization can be most fully found are Aquinas's *Summa Theologiae* and Dante's *Divine Comedy* (1964: 12). Lewis goes on to remark that in this Model,

> everything links up with everything else; at one, not in flat equality, but in a hierarchical ladder.. (N)ot only is this Model of the Universe … a supreme mediaeval work of art but … it is in a sense the central work, that in which most particular works were embedded, to which they constantly referred, from which they drew a great deal of their strength. (Lewis 1964)

The Renaissance humanists

Dante's epic *Divine Comedy* was suffused with the spirituality of Bernard of Clairvaux who leads him into the highest reaches of heaven (*Paradiso*, Canto 31, 58ff) and the theology of Thomas Aquinas (*Paradiso*, Canto 10; Bouck 2014). We can thus regard him as a transitional figure between the Middle Ages and the Renaissance that begins with Petrarch (AD 1304–1374). It was Petrarch who coined the term 'Dark Ages' to describe the preceding period. But this referred to the methods, philosophy and language of scholasticism rather than to the theology and spirituality of Christendom. On the contrary, Petrarch is generally regarded as a devout and faithful son of the Church although, like Dante, he was critical of some aspects of the state of the Church in his day especially the location of the papacy in Avignon (Trinkhaus 1970: 3). Far from developing a new framework in which to view the human being's place in the universe, Petrarch and the humanists who followed him remained to a large extent within the 'Model' identified by C. S. Lewis. At the same time, from within this framework, they 'elaborated significant new conceptions of human nature, utilising both the unspoken precedents of the medieval attitudes that were built into their culture and the more self-consciously borrowed classical views' (1970). Petrarch, like Augustine, Bernard or Thomas Aquinas, was acutely aware of human greatness and nobility. But he was also aware of our fallen nature and misery, and his being caught between despair and grace. Petrarch saw life as a search for truth and fulfilment driven by desire. But he follows Augustine and the neo-Platonists rather than the 'dialecticians', as he called the Scholastics, in seeking a remedy to his plight. This is achieved through meditation and contemplation and not through mere verbal formulae such as those used by the Scholastics. Petrarch returns to the classical definition of the nature of the human being:

> If you see a man so potent in reason that he runs his life according to reason, subordinates his appetites to this alone, and checks his emotions by the brake of reason, and knows that he distinguishes himself from the wildness of animals by this alone and deserves this very name of man in so far as he lives according to reason. (quoted in Trinkhaus 1970: 13)

What also distinguishes us as human beings is our awareness of our own mortality.

Life in the Middle Ages and the early modern period, despite the great social and economic transformations that had marked the eleventh and twelfth centuries, was still marked by danger and disaster, and human mortality was vividly present in men's minds. At the end of the twelfth century, Cardinal Segni (AD 1198–1216), later Pope Innocent III, had written a treatise entitled *Liber de contemptu mundi, sive De miseria humanae conditionis* (*Contempt for the World: Or, The Wretchedness of the Human Condition*). Innocent spoke disparagingly of man's body, the disgusting circumstances of his birth (through lustful sex), of the fact that not only does he not dominate the earth as he did before the Fall but he is now the weakest of all the animals (Stark 2014: 182). Innocent saw work as a punishment and disparaged knowledge and technological progress. This perspective seemed to be confirmed when Europe and the Near East were struck by the Black Death (1346–1353) just at the time when the humanist movement was emerging. Nevertheless, the nobility of the human condition was never forgotten even in these darkest of times. Innocent III had promised to write a second treatise on human dignity but had not gotten around to doing so. It was the humanists, therefore, who sought to complete the first volume of Innocent's work by writing the missing second volume. According to Trinkhaus, 'They not only took the traditional exegesis concerning the meaning of man's creation "according to the image and likeness" of God, but they added to it several other themes that resulted in a much broadened version of the genre "The Dignity of Man"' (1970: 192). These themes included man's rule over the rest of creation, the beauties of the world at man's disposal, the capacities of the human mind, soul and body for the work of ruling over the subhuman universe, the erectness of man's posture pointing to the heavenly goal, the immortality of the soul, the gift of the Incarnation which honoured man, the consequent beatification of man and the resurrection of the body, man's ascent in dignity beyond the angels (1970).

The humanists thus set out to complement Innocent's pessimistic vision of the human condition with a more positive vision of man's greatness and nobility. Petrarch published *The Dignity of Man* in 1354 or 1357. Salutati, without explicitly devoting a text to human dignity as such, alludes to it in his *De nobilitate legum et medicinae* (1399), which states that 'human nature excels all corporeal creatures and any man transcends the dignity of his own body'. Facio published *De excellentia ac praestantia hominis* in 1447 or 1448. Manetti completed his four-volume treatise *De dignitate et excellentia hominis* in 1452 or 1453, the fourth volume of which is an explicit response to Innocent's pessimistic view of man (Stark 2014: 178). This is not to say that the humanists rejected completely Innocent's work on man's wretchedness. On the contrary, most of them shared the attitudes contained in it to some extent. Rather they were concerned to complement it by what they regarded as the fuller vision of humanity (Stark 2014).

Stark points out two areas where rebuttal of Innocent was essential to the development of Renaissance humanism. First, they developed a positive interpretation of the role of work in human life. For Innocent, work was simply a punishment for man's sin. Stark comments that 'Bonincontri and Pontano, drawing from the anthropologies in [the classical authors] Lucretius and Manilius, not only stress man's ability to overcome initial hardships but also emphasize the importance of labor and experimentation in his development' (2014: 187). Valla and Facio had also emphasized the importance of work and experience (2014: fn. 54). This was important during the Renaissance as artisans as well as artists were developing new techniques in art, architecture, building and town planning. Second, the humanists took a positive view of the role of knowledge. Stark notes that 'proponents of the "misery of man" school [such as Innocent] emphasize the futility of knowledge and the attendant ills of technological progress' (2014: 188). Indeed, this had been one of the points of conflict between some monastic traditions and the newly emerging schools and the new orders such as the Dominicans and Franciscans.[3] For Innocent, knowledge could be both futile and morally treacherous (Stark 2014: 189). For humanists such as Petrarch, Facio and Manetti, however, man's reason was what made him truly human and reflected the divine image in him. He should, therefore, use it to improve his lot on earth and prepare himself for the next world. Manetti illustrates this by drawing on both mythological and historical examples to show the many ways in which man's intellect has contributed to human history and well-being. He mentions three examples drawn from mythology as well as historical experience:

the creation of the first ship, the *Argo*; Brunelleschi's dome for the cathedral in Florence; and Archimedes's celestial sphere or planetarium (2014: 190). We find the same sentiment in the words of Shakespeare's *Hamlet*: '[man is a] beast no more. Sure, he that made us with such large discourse, looking before and after, gave us not that capability and godlike reason to fust in us unused' (*Hamlet*, Act 4, Scene 4). It is obvious how such attitudes to work and knowledge were important drivers for the intensive productivity and experimentation that marked Italian and other European cities from the fourteenth century onwards. This left its mark on literature and poetry, music (see Arnold 2014 in this volume), art and sculpture (see Verdon 2014 in this volume), and architecture. Some artists such as Michelangelo and Leonardo da Vinci excelled in all these fields and the term 'Renaissance Man' was coined to describe them.

Thus far we have emphasized the continuities that existed between the Renaissance and the previous Middle Ages. People throughout the long centuries of Christendom had viewed the world through the prism of Christian faith. From the early Fathers of the Church to the Renaissance humanists, classical philosophers such as Plato, Aristotle and Cicero and neo-Platonists such as Plotinus were used to complement and further develop the biblical story of creation which included both man's greatness because of his being made in the image and likeness of God (*gloria*) and his wretchedness caused by original sin and the Fall (*miseria*). Innocent III's work was the extreme expression of the 'misery' tradition. Bernard of Clairvaux and the Benedictine monastic tradition that he represented were also aware of man's '*miseria*', but they also believed that human beings could not lose the 'image' of God without ceasing to be human and also that the 'likeness' could be restored through the imitation of Christ in the monastic life. On the other hand, Dante, Petrarch and the humanists who came after emphasized human 'glory' but they too were conscious of human sinfulness. Dante, after all, takes us through hell and purgatory before reaching heaven. But there is no doubt that the more positive 'dignity' tradition became the dominant one from the fourteenth century onwards until the sixteenth-century Protestant Reformation when it was challenged by Luther and Calvin (see Witte 2019 in this volume).

Philosophy in the Renaissance

The Renaissance humanists were primarily concerned with issues of language, rhetoric and literary forms and less about philosophical questions (Kristeller

1948: 1). Some of them were, nevertheless, interested in philosophical issues and inherited most of the philosophical framework from their predecessors, especially Augustine's neo-Platonism (Gilson 1960) but also Aristotle, as mediated through the Dominicans Albert the Great and Thomas Aquinas (Davies 2014). Texts of these authors became available in the original Greek and more scholars were capable of reading them in that language.

The key questions were: What is the nature of this cosmos and what is the place of human beings in it? Two ideas, both drawn from Plato, were important here. The first was Plato's notion of the 'world-soul' which was found in the *Timaeus*.[4] Through the mouth of Timaeus, Plato observed that the world is characterized by beauty and order, and he sought to explain why this is so. He argued that it is because it was created by a benevolent creator, a 'demiurge', who is himself good. The world has a purpose which is to return to its creator. The cosmos has a body (the earth) and a soul (the world intellect). Plato believed that individual souls could be restored to unity and harmony by contemplating the harmony of the cosmos. The French Dominican and scholar of neo-Platonism, Festugière expressed it thus:

> The concrete world is joined to the world of ideas by the intermediary of the world-soul. The world, as a vast living thing, is possessed of self-movement, and this presupposes a soul. And the motion of the world, at least in the celestial regions, is a celestial motion that reveals a design, a rationale; and this fact invites the inference that the soul that moves the universe is an intelligent soul. In fact, the world-intelligence contemplates the beauty of the ideal-realm, and it is in virtue of this contemplation that it imposes upon the universe the ordered movement we see. In consequence, the world is truly an 'order', a *kosmos*. (Festugière 1966–1968 [quoted in Chenu 1964: 21])

It is easy to see how some aspects of this notion would appeal to Christian authors, especially the ideas of the beauty and harmony of the universe and its teleological character. Some schools of thought, such as that of St Victor, were, however, suspicious of it and others, such as Citeaux, denounced it as pagan. But it found a sympathetic home in the school of Chartres and in the University of Paris (Chenu 1964: 23). Thomas Aquinas, rather later, adopted Aristotle's conception of nature including his rejection of Plato's theory of creation. Nevertheless, the Platonic vision experienced an important revival during the Renaissance. This was stimulated by the founding of the Florentine Platonic Academy, a loose network of philosophers and humanists, at the end of the fifteenth century by Marsilio Ficino and sponsored by Lorenzo de Medici. Among its most important members was the young Pico della Mirandola (see below).

The second key notion refers to the human being's place in this created cosmos. In contrast to modern mechanistic notions of nature which derive from Descartes and to those existentialist conceptions that see man as a kind of alien spiritual being lost in the world, the neo-Platonists, as we saw above, experienced the world as itself spiritual and thought of human beings, themselves both spiritual and material, as being in profound relationship to it. One way of expressing this was that the human is a microcosm at the centre of the macrocosm which is the universe. Pseudo-Dionysius and Duns Scotus Eriugena both incorporated this into a hierarchical system in which the human being occupied a central place:

> From the middle of the [twelfth] century on, the 'hierarchical' conception of the universe would cast over men's minds a spell comparable to that cast by the scientific *mythos* of evolution in the nineteenth century. The key to the understanding of the universe, and of man in the universe, was taken to be the ordered, dynamic, and progressive chain of all beings – a chain in which causality and meaning fall together, and in which each being is a 'theophany', a revelation of God'. (Chenu 1964: 23)

This corresponds to the above-mentioned 'Model' identified by C. S. Lewis. The place of man in the world was seen as not merely physical but also metaphysical and mystical and underlay the various mystical theologies of authors such as Bernard of Clairvaux (Gilson 2010) – and even of St Thomas Aquinas. Man's place in the world was a dynamic one – he could rise *or* fall. By God's grace he could ascend to mystical union with God, but he could also, as a result of sin, fall back to the lowest rungs of the hierarchy.

Pico della Mirandola: Continuity and innovation

The 'dignity' tradition reached its climax in the famous work of Pico della Mirandola which was posthumously entitled *Oratio de hominis dignitate*, published in 1486. The *Oratio* was a preface to Pico's 900 'theses' in which he sought to synthesize the teachings of the Bible with almost all the philosophical and religious traditions known at the time. The theses had originally been written in order to hold a public 'disputation' with theologians and philosophers in Rome. The disputation was not held after the Pope forbade it when some of the 'theses' were denounced as heretical. Pico then fled from Rome and wrote the *Oratio* to justify his position. It is this, however, which has become his most famous writing even if the 900 theses are interesting in their own right.

Pico summarizes his position under two points: (i) the dignity of man and (ii) the unity of all truth. With regard to the second point, the theses attempt to show the elements of truth in all religious and philosophical traditions and how these can be harmonized with biblical revelation. In particular, he attempts to harmonize the metaphysical systems of Plato and Aristotle and thus also justifies the use of Aristotle by the Scholastics such as St Thomas. In fact, Pico defended the latter against attacks by other humanists. But it is his notion of human dignity where Pico both demonstrates continuity with the traditional notions drawn from both Genesis and the classical authors and develops a distinctively new set of ideas about humanity. In the first pages of the *Oratio* he summarizes the usual justifications of man's dignity such as his position as the mediator between the different heavenly and earthly spheres, his intelligence and power of reason, his being made 'a little lower than the angels' according to David in the psalms [Ps 8]. While not rejecting these arguments, he advances another which would have important consequences for future philosophical developments. He presents God speaking to humans in this way: 'In conformity with your free judgement, in whose hands I have placed you at the centre of the world, you are confined by no bounds; and you will fix limits of nature for yourself ... you, like a judge appointed for being honourable, are the moulder and maker of yourself; you may sculpt yourself into whatever shape you prefer' (della Mirandola 1965: 4–5). This notion of man's dignity consisting in his capacity to 'make himself' and of fixing his own limits would appeal to later generations and lead to a new and different kind of humanism. But despite the apparent 'openness' of his conception, Pico in fact thought that there were just two paths he could follow both of which were in harmony with the traditional Christian and biblical conception of the Fall as well as with the neo-Platonic notion of 'falling' from the spiritual to the material world or vice versa: 'You can grow downwards into the lower natures which are brutes. [Or] you can again grow upward from your soul's reason into the higher natures which are divine' (1965).

The Reformation and the Enlightenment

The new learning, in particular the emphasis on linguistic studies and returning to the original sources of the Bible (both the Hebrew and Septuagint versions) and the classical authors (especially newly discovered works of Plato and Aristotle as well as the early Greek Fathers), had a profound impact on European culture and religion. Most of the humanists, such as Petrarch and, later, Erasmus, remained within the Catholic Church. This was also true of the Italian painters and sculptors such as Brunelleschi and Michelangelo (see Verdon 2019 in this volume). Nevertheless, it also impacted on those who, in the sixteenth century, would launch the Reformation which destroyed the unity of Christendom. Luther (1483–1546) rejected Renaissance humanism but used some of its linguistic techniques such as returning to the original languages of the Bible to produce his own translation based on these rather than on the Vulgate. He also rejected the interpretation of 'image and likeness' that had dominated Western theology from the time of Irenaeus by stating that both image and likeness were destroyed at the Fall and, consequently, man was 'utterly depraved'. The Catholic position had been that at least the 'image' remained and this was a vestigial goodness. Aquinas had argued that grace built on nature, including human nature. Calvin shared Luther's theological position but, in his own writings, he was more open to using some of the classical authors such as Seneca's writings on law and mercy. Nevertheless, both authors and subsequent Protestant writers were more aware of man's *miseria* than of his natural dignity and glory. The latter would be true only after man was completely remade through Christ although modern Protestant writers also emphasize that it was from within Protestantism, and especially Calvinism, that modern forms of democracy and human rights became possible (see Witte 1979 in this volume).

As we saw in the opening paragraphs of this chapter, some modern authors interpreted, wrongly in my opinion, Renaissance humanism as a break with Europe's Christian past. They tried to omit the Christian element of the story and emphasize simply the return to the classical authors rather than the Bible and the Fathers. But they were not entirely wrong. At least one humanist began to follow this path, even if his was very much a minority position. Machiavelli (1469–1527) looked to Ancient Rome rather than the Gospel for inspiration in advising political rulers and advocated a cynical realism rather than the Beatitudes. In *The Prince* (1513) he advocated lying, dishonesty and murder of opponents as methods of governing. Although he was rejected by the Florentine Medici government of the time, he was subsequently admired by Enlightenment authors such as Spinoza, Rousseau and Diderot. The Wars of Religion in the fifteenth and sixteenth centuries hastened the decline of Christianity's influence on the modern state which overthrew the central position of the Church as the regulator of society. But it was Pico's notion that man makes himself that was an important precursor of modern secular or atheist humanism, although he himself was far removed from this. This combined with the growing role of the sciences to promote a notion of humanism that sought to replace God as man's creator. After Descartes (1596–1650), the physical universe itself was regarded as a vast mechanistic system which bore little resemblance to the neo-Platonic 'spiritually infused' world of the Renaissance. In the eighteenth century among key intellectual elites, religion took the form of Deism which thought that God had created the world but then had, as it were, set it adrift and left it up to human beings to run it. Gradually, this turned into true atheism with philosophers such as David Hume (1711–1776) explicitly declaring themselves atheist. By the end of the nineteenth century, Nietzsche had proclaimed the 'death of God' but, far from man replacing him, what remained was nihilistic despair.

Conclusions

Christianity, in both its Byzantine and Latin versions, has been a fusion and synthesis of the biblical message that human beings, male and female, are created in God's image and likeness with elements of Greek and Roman philosophy. While we share aspects of the material world with animals and other creatures, we also possess a divine spark because of this image and likeness. The notion that humans have something divine about them existed in ancient mythology but Genesis made the startling claim that we are made in God's very image. The Stoics and, following them, Cicero also recognized this divine spark in the form of 'reason'. Aristotle too defined man as a 'rational animal'. In the long history of Christianity, these pagan ideas combined with the biblical messages of creation, Fall, Incarnation and redemption in Christ to develop a sublime notion of human dignity and greatness. It is this synthesis which underlies the concept of human dignity that has been at the heart of Western civilization. It has led to the most wonderful flourishing of forms of communal living in monasteries, parishes and cities; architecture in the form of Gothic cathedrals and Baroque Churches; and statuary and paintings from Giotto to Michelangelo and Leonardo. Its sacred music has evolved for more than a thousand years from the early Gregorian chant committed to manuscript form in Notre Dame in Paris in the twelfth century, to the choral masterpieces of Bach and Handel, the oratorios of Mendelssohn and the music of Elgar in the nineteenth century and, today, the music of James Macmillan and John Rutter, among many others. All of this vast creativity has been a celebration of human beings understood as quasi-divine and as God's creatures, created by God and redeemed by Christ.

The central notions of the Christian understanding of human dignity include reason, freedom and a will that allows us to choose our own destiny. For Christians of all ages, this means choosing to be like God or choosing to reject him. The first leads to dignity and *'gloria'*. But the Western understanding of human dignity is also realistic. It recognizes that because of our freedom, we can reject *gloria* and opt instead for wretchedness and *miseria*. This basic existential capacity to choose is also the basis of human equality. This 'equality', however, does not mean that we are simply interchangeable and exist on a flattened plane. Rather it means that we relate to each other according to our unique characteristics. The notion of human rights contained in this view does not see human beings as isolated individuals each carrying his or her little bundle of 'rights' which he or she can exercise provided they do not interfere with the rights of others as a certain type of liberalism would have us believe. Rather, it sees us as members of a community of persons, each individual unique but existing only in relation to the others and bringing to the community a set of gifts as well as duties and responsibilities. The Renaissance view, in continuity with all previous generations of Christian thought, also recognized that we are sinners and therefore capable of injuring the human community as well as the rest of creation. But although it was aware of our wretchedness, it preferred to emphasize our greatness and the possibility of forgiveness and redemption. This is what we call today a holistic view of the dignity of the human person.

Notes

1   Most translations of classical texts use the generic term 'man' to mean the human race, including men and women. We shall use this term in such quotations to avoid tedious circumlocutions.

2   The following section follows closely Gilson (2010 [1940]: 48–77).

3   Although the Benedictines and Cistercians also developed their own scholarly and intellectual traditions and one can speak, for example, of a Benedictine and Cistercian humanism (Fracheboud 2000: 94–111).

4   'Then God, having decided to form the world in the closest possible likeness to the most beautiful of intelligible beings, and to a Being perfect in all things, made it into a living being, one, visible, and having within itself all living beings of like nature with itself' (Plato, *Timaeus* 30d. 2–5).

References

Berman, H. J. (1983), *Law and Revolution: The Formation of the Western Legal Tradition*, vol. 1, Cambridge, MA: Harvard University Press.

Bouck, J., OP (2014), 'The Summa in Verse, or Why You Should Read All of Dante's Divine Comedy'. Dominicana Blog, Dominican Studium of the St. Joseph Province of the Order of Preachers. http://www.dominicanablog.com/2014/05/12/the-summa-in-verse-or-why-you-should-read-all-of-dantes-divine-comedy.

Brotton, J. (2002), *The Renaissance Bazaar: From the Silk Road to Michelangelo*, Oxford: Oxford University Press.

Burckhardt, J. (1990 [1860]), The Civilization of the Renaissance in Italy, London: Penguin Classics.

Chenu, M-D. (1964), *Nature, Man and Society in the Twelfth Century*, Toronto: University of Toronto Press.

Clark, K. (1974), *Another Part of the Wood: A Self-Portrait*, London: Murray.

Daniélou, J. (1973), *Gospel Message and Christian Culture: A History of Early Christian Doctrine before the Council of Nicaea*, vol. 2, London/Philadelphia, PA: Darton, Longman & Todd/The Westminster Press.

Dante Aligheri, (2012), *The Divine Comedy*, translated by Robin Kirkpatrick, London: Penguin Classics.

Davies, B. (2014), *Thomas Aquinas's Summa Theologiae: A Guide and Commentary*, Oxford: Oxford University Press.

Evans, G. R. (2000), *Bernard of Clairvaux*, Oxford: Oxford University Press.

Festugière, A. J. (1966–1968), *Proclus: commentaire sur le Timée*, vol. 2, Paris: J. Vrin.

Fracheboud, M-A. (2000), *The First Cistercian Spiritual Writers*, Philadelphia, PA, Xlibris Corporation.

Gilson, E. (1960), *The Christian Philosophy of Saint Augustine*, New York, Random House.

Gilson, E. (2010 [1940]), *The Mystical Theology of Saint Bernard*. Whitefish, Montana: Kessinger Publishing.

Kristeller, P. O. (1948), 'Introduction', in E. Cassirer, P. O. Kristeller and J. H. Randall Jr. (eds), *The Renaissance Philosophy of Man*, 1–20, Chicago, IL: The University of Chicago Press.

Lewis, C. S. (1964), *The Discarded Image: An Introduction to Mediaeval and Renaissance Literature*, Cambridge: Cambridge University Press.

Lossky, V. (1975), *In the Image and Likeness of God*, London: Mowbrays.

Mann, N. (2001), 'The Origins of Humanism', in Jill Kraye (ed.), *The Cambridge Companion to Renaissance Humanism*, 1–19, Cambridge: Cambridge University Press.

Merton, T. (1954), *The Last of the Fathers: Saint Bernard of Clairvaux and the Encyclical Letter, Doctor Mellifluus*, New York: Harcourt Brace Jovanovic.

Michelet, J. (1855), *Histoire de France*, vol. 7, Paris: Chamerot.

Nicholas, D. (2012), 'Lords, Markets, and Communities: The Urban Revolution of the Twelfth Century', in T. F. X Noble and J. Van Engen (eds), *European Transformations: The Long Twelfth Century*, 259–278, Notre Dame, IN: University of Notre Dame Press.

Noble, T. F. X. and J. Van Engen (eds) (2012), *European Transformations: The Long Twelfth Century*, Notre Dame, IN: University of Notre Dame Press.

Pater, W. (1873), *The Renaissance: Studies in Art and Poetry*, Auckland, New Zealand: Floating Press.

Phan, P.C. (1988), *Grace and the Human Condition*, Wilmington, Delaware: Michael Glazier.

Pico della Mirandola (1965 [1486]), *On the Dignity of Man*, Introduction by P. J. W. Miller, translations by C. G. Wallis, P. J. W. Miller and D. Carmichael, Reprinted 1998 with new bibliography, Indianapolis, IN/Cambridge: Hackett Publishing Company, Inc.

Stark, C. (2014), 'Renaisance Anthropologies and the Conception of Man', in A. Moudarres and C. P. Moudarres, (eds), *New Worlds and the Italian Renaissance: Contributions to the History of European Intellectual Culture*, 172–194, Leiden: Brill; Biggleswade: Extenza.

Sullivan, E. (1963), *The Image of God: The Doctrine of St Augustine and Its Influence*, Dubuque, IA: The Priory Press.

Taylor, C. (1989), *Sources of the Self: The Making of Modern Identity*, Cambridge: Cambridge University Press.

Trinkhaus, C. (1970), *In Our Image and Likeness: Humanity and Divinity in Italian Humanist Thought*, 2 vols, London: Constable & Co.

Tugwell, S., ed. (1988), *Albert & Thomas: Selected Writings*, Mahwah, NJ: Paulist Press (Writings translated, edited and introduced by Simon Tugwell OP).

6

The Beauty of the Person in Christian Thought and Art

Timothy Verdon

The Western concept of human dignity became visible in Italian art of the late Middle Ages and Renaissance, when – particularly in the neo-Platonist environment of fourteenth- and fifteenth-century Florence – a new sensitivity to the person expanded the Scholastic focus on nature (Trinkaus 1970). This is clear above all in depictions of Jesus Christ (Verdon 2006), whom artists, following the poets of ancient Israel, imagined as beautiful, in physical and above all moral terms. 'Of all men you are the most handsome', said the author of Psalm 43 to the Messianic King whom he addressed in a wedding song: 'Gracefulness is a dew upon your lips, for God has blessed you forever. Warrior, strap your sword at your side, in your majesty and splendour advance, ride on, in the cause of truth, gentleness and uprightness' (Ps. 43.2-4). And in another psalm, similarly addressed to the future King of Israel, the poet says: 'Royal dignity has been yours from the day of your birth, sacred honour from the womb, from the dawn of your youth', and adds: 'Yahweh has sworn an oath he will never retract: you are a priest forever of the order of Melchisedek' (Ps. 110.3-4).

Christ as mirror

An early image of the Saviour as royal bridegroom, warrior in the cause of right and eternal priest is the *Blessing Christ* of an altarpiece attributed to Giotto and dateable to the second decade of the fourteenth century, today in the Museum of Art in Raleigh, North Carolina (Tartuferi 2008: 88–90; Verdon 2009: 11–16). This work (see Illustration 1) both preserves the solemnity of the Eastern icon-tradition, which had dominated Italian art in the thirteenth century, and speaks the new language of which Giotto was author, with a softness in the modelling of the body and warmth in the flesh tones far from the flattened forms and enamel tints of Byzantine paintings.

Giotto's more realistic style alludes to the Incarnation of God's Word in the man Jesus, a truth of faith that in Giotto's day was again central to Christian thought, thanks to the influence of Franciscan theologians; the *Blessing Christ* in fact was painted for the Franciscan church in Florence, Santa Croce. At the same time, in Giotto's *Christ* human bodiliness coexists with divine attributes codified in earlier sacred art: the fixed gaze and hieratic air and robes of colours symbolizing the Lord's two natures (red for man's earth, blue for God's heaven). The overall effect is that of a bodiliness that is '*capax Dei*', capable of divinity.

Analogous equilibrium is evident in the symmetry of facial lineaments, which, together with the flush of health and the tender, well-shaped lips, make this Christ the divine 'lover' described in the Song of Songs, 'fresh and ruddy, to be known among ten thousand' (Sg. 5.10), and the Bridegroom to whom, in the Apocalypse, with intense yearning 'the Spirit and the Bride say: "Come!"' (Rev. 22.17). Giotto, that is, imagined a physically desirable person, in whom human allure expresses the dignity of God.

A final detail qualifies Giotto's icon of incarnate divinity: the wound at the centre of Jesus's right hand. The blood on the open palm recalls Christ's death on the cross, investing his dignity with vulnerability and his beauty with the drama of sacrifice. Indeed, in this exchange of sensory and mystical solicitations, Christ's bodily attractiveness is not only a simple physical fact but the expression of a complex moral dynamic. For the body, which God created good and found worthy to bear his own divinity, was assumed by Christ for a purpose, the Word taking flesh in order to suffer and die for sinful human beings. To this dignity of self-offering, we then add the idea of 'beauty' because in Catholic theology, Christ's cross was also a wedding chamber and the gift of his body an act of passionate love. The New Testament affirms that 'Christ loved the Church' as a husband does his wife 'and sacrificed himself for her to make her holy' (Eph. 5, 25). In Him, that is, bodily attractiveness was not meant for sin but for sanctification, and the beauty with which artists endow his person is an earnest of something greater, the sacrament of a *pulchritudo* known only to the soul.

The entire image, of which the *Christ* is the central panel, shows similar half-figures of four other personages, all involved with the Saviour's life and death: at Christ's right (our left), Mary, the mother from whom he received his body; at his left (our right) St John the Baptist, who identified him as God's sacrificial 'lamb'; at our far left, then, St John the Evangelist, who wrote: 'The Word became flesh'; and at our far right St Francis of Assisi, who reproduced Christ's bodily wounds in his own stigmata. In the work's original position upon an altar in the Franciscan church in Florence, these five half-figures looked towards the celebrant and towards those taking part in Mass in a 'face-to-face' encounter above the bread and wine.

In its original situation, Giotto's Christ was thus a mirror for those who would receive his body and blood. Showing his wounded hand, he seems to utter the words which a Father of the Church, St Peter Chrysologus, ascribed to him, inviting believers to contemplate him and recognize themselves. 'Look at me and see your own body, your limbs, your heart, your blood', Chrysologus's Christ says (*Discourse 108*). 'And', he continues, 'if you fear what belongs to God, why not love at least what is your own? If you flee before the master, why not run to meet your brother?'. Moved by this idea, Peter Chrysologus then exclaims: 'O immense dignity of the Christian priesthood! Man has become his own victim and his own priest. He does not seek what he must immolate to God outside of himself, but carries with himself and in himself all that he must sacrifice.' Finally, urging us to imitate Christ, Peter Chrysologus exhorts: 'O man, be both sacrifice and priest ... make an altar of your heart, and thus confidently present your body as a victim to God.' For, he concludes, 'God seeks your faith, not your extinction; he thirsts for your prayer, not your blood. He is placated by your will, not by your death.'

Spiritual transformation

A second work will help develop these ideas. According to Peter Chrysologus, God thirsts for our prayer, and in fact another of the ways in which art has communicated the dignity and beauty of the human being is through images of people praying. Even Jesus prayed: the New Testament says that 'during his life on earth, he offered up prayer and entreaty, aloud and in silent tears, to the One who had power to save him out of death, and he submitted so humbly that his prayer was heard' (Heb. 5.7).

That is why, in a painting done around 1450 depicting the Saviour's baptism (see Illustration 2), the artist Piero della Francesca shows Christ with hands joined and gaze turned inward, totally focused on 'the One who had power to save him out of death' (Verdon 2010: 15–19). Jesus's baptism in the Jordan in fact prefigured the Cross, and the seriousness with which Piero characterizes his face alludes to Christ's awareness that he must die, just as the Lord's utter calm suggests his 'humble submission' to God's will. Jesus's serenity here is also obviously due to the fact that, when he accepted baptism (and with it the Cross), a voice came from heaven recognizing him as God's beloved Son, in whom the Father was well pleased (Mt. 3.17, Mk. 1.11, Lk. 3.22). There is no higher dignity.

Piero della Francesca thus presents prayer as an occasion of existential commitment and a place of enduring identity. The identity (in Christ's case divine as well as human) is visible in the beauty of the Saviour's youthful body, similar to that of an ancient statue of the kind the Renaissance so admired. The commitment – the willingness to accept death – transpires in Christ's overall gravity and, if we look at the entire image, in the tree growing beside him, which alludes to the Cross. These iconographic features translate the second part of the New Testament passage relative to the prayer and entreaty offered by Christ: the assertion that 'although he was Son, he learnt to obey through suffering; but having been made perfect, he became for all who obey him the source of eternal salvation and was acclaimed by God with the title of high priest of the order of Melchisedek' (Heb. 5.8-10).

High priest. Piero della Francesca's painted panel, today in the National Gallery in London, originally stood on the altar of a monastic church, the no longer extant Camaldolese Priory of St John the Evangelist at the gates of the artist's home town, Borgo San Sepolcro, between Tuscany and Umbria. This priestly Christ was thus created for a semi-eremitical prayer-community and normally seen during Mass and the celebration of the Divine Office, which suggests that the moral and spiritual criteria applied to Christ in the just quoted passage from the *Letter to the Hebrews* – humble submission to God, obedience learned through suffering and achieved perfection – were also applicable to those for whom the image was intended, the monks, who – in this young man in prayer seen above an altar – would have contemplated the sense of their own life.

What did they feel as they looked at the painting? No historical source provides such information, but we can imagine – indeed, we *have to* imagine – the monks' probable reactions. In evaluating images and especially sacred images, we should always ask what their *moral* as well as aesthetic impact was – what power they possessed, in their original context, to lead viewers to measure their lives with what they saw in the artwork. For the monks for whom this *Baptism of Christ* was destined, the body of the young hero, seen above the raised host at the consecration of the Mass, must have constituted a challenge, in the spirit of the New Testament, to be 'in your minds ... the same as Christ Jesus: his state was divine, yet he did not cling to his equality with God but emptied himself to assume the condition of a slave, and became as men are; he was humbler yet, even to accepting death, death on a cross' (Ph. 2.5-8).

In Piero della Francesca's painting, above Christ the monks also saw a white dove, and it would have seemed to them that the Holy Spirit was descending both on the man represented and on the bread and wine of the Mass. They would have known moreover that just as Christ rose from the dead in the Spirit, and the same Spirit changes the bread and wine into Christ's body and blood, so too all who eat and drink of Christ are destined to undergo a change; according to St Paul, 'We who have been modelled on the earthly man, will be modelled on the heavenly man [... and] we shall all be changed. This will be instantaneous, in the twinkling of an eye, when the last trumpet sounds' (1 Co. 15.49-52). In the case of paintings like this one, rather than speak generically of 'moral impact' we should imagine specific spiritual tension – the monks' expectation that their lives be changed on the model of Christ.

Such interior transformation is the hope of every Christian. Explaining the effects of baptism, St Gregory of Nyssa claimed that 'our nature itself has undergone a change', so that we now have 'a different life and a different way of living' (*Discourse on the Resurrection of Christ*: 1). In the same vein, St Cyril of Alexandria affirmed that 'the Spirit transforms those in whom he dwells in another image, so to speak' (*Commentary on the Gospel of St John*: 10) and quoted St Paul, according to whom 'we, with our unveiled faces reflecting like mirrors the brightness of the Lord, all grow brighter and brighter as we are turned into the image that we reflect' (2 Co. 3.18). This painting too was meant to be a mirror, I mean, showing the monks the beauty to which all Christians are called.

A significant component of Piero della Francesca's painting is the natural world evoked by the foreground tree and the beautiful distant landscape (Verdon 2001: 158–166). Nature always invites a prayerful response, in fact, and St John Damascene would say that 'the spectacle of the countryside spurs my heart to glorify God' (*De sacris imaginibus orationes*: 1.27). Vice versa, prayer heightens human sensibility to nature, allowing people to perceive themselves as part of a divine plan whose order transpires in the varied beauty of the cosmos.

Scripture teaches man to read his life in relation to the cosmos. The first psalm, for instance, describes the man of God as being 'like a tree that is planted by water streams, yielding its fruit in season, its leaves never fading; success attends all he does' (Ps. 1.3), and this similitude suggests a second, complementary reading of the tree that Piero put next to Christ: not only an allusion to the future Cross but also a sign in nature of the human being's potential. As the tree is fruitful, so can the man of God bear fruit.

In the Christian view, however, the relationship of human beings with the natural world goes beyond mere analogy: 'The whole creation is waiting with eagerness for the children of God to be revealed', St Paul states, and develops his argument by noting that 'it was not for its own purposes that creation was subjected to frustration, but for the purposes of him who imposed it – with the intention that the whole creation itself might be freed from its slavery to corruption and brought into the same glorious freedom as the children of God' (Rm. 8.18-21). Nature too is destined for salvation, that is, and right up to 'this time has been groaning in labour pains', as Paul continues (Rm. 8.22); it will be freed of corruption only when 'the children of God' are revealed. Piero della Francesca's Christ – posed next to the tree and in front of a broad, sunlit landscape – is the first 'child of God' revealed to the world, acknowledged as such by his Father in this very moment, when, in the thinking of the Church Fathers, his immersion in the natural element of water, at baptism, in fact purified all of nature (Verdon 2001: 158–166).[1]

The dignity of the human person thus implies a responsible relationship with the cosmos, an acceptance of responsibility vis-à-vis the natural order. Creation, which speaks to us of our own potential, waits for us to step forth, as Christ did at the Jordan. We legitimately share nature's beauty when with Christ we accept the dignity of being *salvatores mundi*, saviours of the world.

Unwavering resolve

The third image I will discuss is better known than the preceding two, a veritable icon of Western art, Leonardo da Vinci's *Last Supper*, executed in the mid-1490s and still in its original setting in the Dominican friary of Santa Maria delle Grazie in Milan: a wall painting in the friar's dining hall, showing Jesus's final meal before his arrest and subsequent torture and death (Verdon 2001: 200–209). Unlike Giotto's *Christ* and Piero's *Baptism*, the *Last Supper* was not made for an altar, but it has obvious Eucharistic content, depicting the institution of the sacrament, when Jesus gave bread and wine to his disciples as his body and blood. It transfers reflection on the Eucharist from the ritual context seen in the preceding works to a narrative one, the Passover repast described in the Gospels, inviting the Dominicans who ate in the refectory to imagine themselves at table with Christ. Through a masterful use of linear perspective, Leonardo in fact suggests that the event depicted unfolds in an extension of the friars' dining room and at the centre of his perspective system positions Christ (see

Illustration 3): all the lines drawing our eye into the depth of the pictorial space lead to him. He is not the final vanishing point, though, for the lines converge *beyond* him, in the sweet evening air, at a point that remains hidden. Seeking infinity, our gaze finds only Christ, who in fact said: 'He who has seen me has seen the Father' (Jn. 14.9).

Like many artists before him, Leonardo represents the moment during the Supper in which the apostles react to Jesus's shocking announcement: 'One of you will betray me' (Jn. 13.21). To strengthen the dramatic impact, instead of showing each of the twelve as a separate unit, as earlier artists had usually done, Leonardo unites the apostles in four groups of three, two to the right, two to the left of the Saviour. He suggests what would have happened to twelve men who had been living together for three years: their natural subdivision into groups, each different from the other yet interconnected. Within each group, the members discuss the meaning of Christ's shocking words, many of them looking towards the Lord and gesturing in his direction.

This centripetal movement on the painting's surface, like the perspective lines leading into depth, inexorably focuses our attention on the main actor, Christ, in the very moment of his great discourse and of his mysterious gesture, the giving of bread and wine as his body and blood. In the groups immediately to Christ's right and left the overall movement towards him is inverted: the apostles nearest him pull back, that is, and the flow of their feelings does not reach the Saviour, who remains in majestic solitude.

Yet Leonardo makes us feel that the emotional intensity of these men – their capacity to act 'with one heart and soul', their shared desire for transparency before a Master who has made himself their servant and spoken to them of his coming death – all derive from Jesus, are born in relation to Him, and that it is He who makes possible the sincerity with which, for example, St Philip, on our right, invites the Lord to read his heart. Jesus has opened himself to them, letting them see his anguish, of which he has spoken, giving himself to them in a new way, and now the apostles discover that they too are able to be open – are willing, they too, to offer themselves. In contact with this Servant-Lord, with this man who speaks like God, his followers discover a capacity to respond beyond the normal limits of nature: a supernatural capacity, similar to Jesus's own. A thousand years before Leonardo, St Gregory Nazianzen described what the Renaissance artist would paint, saying: 'The new and great mystery which embraces our existence is this participation in Christ's life. He communicated himself entirely to us: everything that he is has become entirely ours. Under every aspect we are him: through him we bear in ourselves the image of God, by whom and for whom we were created. The physiognomy impressed upon our features is now that of God' (*Discourse 7*).

As in a mirror, again, we see ourselves in Leonardo's Christ, in whom converge the lines of infinity, the sentiments of many hearts and – woven together, interpenetrating, united in a single life – the nature of God and that of man. In this extraordinary figure the artist gathers together all the various threads of the Last Supper narrative: Jesus's 'ardent desire' to share a meal with his friends; his full awareness of what would happen to him afterwards; the sense that he had come to a supreme moment and that, as he accomplished an everyday action, giving bread and wine to those around him, he was situating this act against a totally new horizon.

The pyramidal composition chosen by Leonardo to convey all this – the eloquent open-armed pose of Christ, whose right hand reaches for the glass of wine, while his left indicates the bread – derives from a common type of fifteenth-century devotional image: the *Imago pietatis* ('Image of Pity') or *Vir dolorum* ('Man of Sorrows'). The clear allusion to the Passion makes sense in the Dominican dining hall because on the opposite wall, at the end of the room opposite the *Last Supper*, in the same years Leonardo worked another artist, the Milanese master Donato Montorfano, painted a *Crucifixion*, also still in place.

Montorfano's forgotten *Crucifixion* in fact completes the meaning of Leonardo's famous *Last Supper*, the event of Friday afternoon fulfilling that of Thursday evening, and if Leonardo's Christ, whose gaze is turned downwards and inwards, were to raise his eyes, he would see his own immediate future at the other end of the room. The Gospels assure us that he knew what awaited him and was 'sad unto death', yet – and this is my point – he went on with the meal, offering sacramentally the body and blood he would give the next day physically, authorizing Judas to proceed with his betrayal.

This means that the dignity and beauty of Leonardo's Christ are those of an unwavering resolve, even in the face of death. This message was also meant for the Dominican friars who took meals between these two wall paintings, in the space of the dining hall between Jesus' commitment (at the Supper) and its fulfilment (on the cross). The friars too had made a solemn commitment and were called to remain faithful, fulfilling what they had promised by vow.

Failure as *kenosis*

After three paintings a masterpiece of sculpture can help develop our argument: a late work by Michelangelo in which paradoxically the dignity and beauty of the person are conveyed through failure – through the experience that theologians call 'kenosis', self-emptying.

The work is an unfinished *Pietà* (see Illustration 4), begun around 1547 and abandoned, unfinished, in 1555 when Michelangelo was eighty years of age (Wasserman 2003). Carved in Rome, where the artist spent the last decades of his life, this group of four figures, now in the Opera del Duomo Museum in Florence, was meant for Michelangelo's funerary chapel, which he imagined in a Roman church, perhaps Santa Maria Maggiore. Had it gone where its sculptor wanted, this *Pietà* would probably have been set on a plinth or in a niche just beyond the altar of the intended chapel (in any other position so large a work would interfere with movement and sight lines) and thus once again must be discussed in relation to the Eucharist, since in the placement intended by Michelangelo Christ's muscular body, lowered by an old man into the arms of Mary, at your right, and of Mary Magdalene, at your left, would have appeared to be laid on the altar table (Verdon 2003). The first years of Michelangelo's work on this group are in fact those in which the council fathers at Trent were writing the Catholic *Decree on the Eucharist*, with its reiteration of traditional belief in the real presence of the Saviour's body and blood in the consecrated bread and wine of Mass, in rebuttal of new interpretations of the sacrament from the Protestant north. In positioning the *Pietà* in the Opera del Duomo Museum in Florence, which I direct and whose new installation is my project, I asked our architects to create a base for it with the height and shape of an altar and to give the hall in which it stands the character of a sacred space.

This *Pietà* is an intensely personal work not only because it was meant for Michelangelo's tomb but above all because it contains his self-portrait in the figure of Nicodemus, the Pharisee who went to Christ by night, because hearing the Lord speak of the need to be born again, he wondered: 'How can anyone who is already old be born? Is it possible to go back into the womb again and be born?' (Jn. 3.4). These are important questions for an old man, such as Michelangelo was when he carved his own features into Nicodemus's face, and, as he worked on the *Pietà*, Michelangelo in fact was thinking of his own death: in one of the sonnets he wrote in those years, which I have had displayed on the entry wall of the same room, he says that his life journey is now at its end, on a stormy sea in a frail barque. Fear of damnation and hope for Christ's mercy loomed large in the old artist's mind (Verdon 2017).

There is much more, however, for Michelangelo not only left this work unfinished – his Christ has no left leg – but actually tried to destroy it: the clear signs of breakage on the Saviour's left arm were made by the artist himself, with the same hammer, we suppose, which he had hitherto used to drive his chisel through the stone. The Florence *Pietà* thus bears witness to a fury so great that it led the greatest sculptor of his time to try to obliterate his own monument in frustration, I believe, at not being unable to complete it.

The problem was not one of waning physical strength – Vasari, one of Michelangelo's sixteenth-century biographers, says that even in old age the sculptor could carve marble more energetically than a man much younger; the problem rather was of concept and of will. The famous artist had not planned the work well, and when he reached the point we see must have understood that to add the left leg, which would have protruded over Mary's thigh and then bent down, would destroy the harmony of the composition he had created. You may ask: 'How could Michelangelo commit such an error?', but the answer is evident: this is a sculpture he did for himself alone, never having to show a patron drawings or models; he worked at it sporadically, across eight years, his main task in Rome in that period being the Basilica of St Peter's and its dome; and he worked in less than ideal circumstances. Vasari says he visited Michelangelo in his studio in Rome at night and found the old man carving the *Pietà* in the dark, with only a candle attached to a paper hat he had made for himself, able to see only the few inches he was actually cutting.

And so, this famed master, who all his life had believed he had from God the gift of intuiting in any marble block the perfect statue that it could become, at eighty years of age had to acknowledge he could no longer do it. That was the first failure: his inability to plan the work through, which would be apparent again in his last sculpture, the *Pietà* now in Milan which he began when he abandoned this one but could not decide how to finish before he died in 1564.

The second failure was still worse, though: a failure of will or perhaps we should say of self-image. For, as he says clearly in the sonnet quoted above, the one I have put on the wall of the museum, he no longer believed in art as an adequate expression of his life, accusing himself of having made it his 'idol' and his 'monarch' and voicing the fear of losing his soul. In the sonnet's last *terzina* he says: 'Let neither painting nor sculpting any longer calm my soul, turned to that Divine Love who opened his arms for us upon the cross' – '*Nè pinger nè scolpir fia più che quieti/l'anima, volta a quell'Amor divino/c'aperse, a prender noi n' croce, le braccia*' (Verdon 2015: 65–66). Facing death, he could no longer conceive works of sculpture, not even intimate works like these late Pietàs, because he had ceased to believe they were sufficient to express his life.

It was a genuine *kenosis*, an 'emptying' like that of Christ in the works Michelangelo sought to carve, who had 'emptied himself, taking the form of a slave, becoming as human beings are', as the New Testament tells us, 'and being in every way like a human being, he was humbler yet, even to accepting death, death on a cross'. But as the same text continues, precisely 'for this God raised [Christ] on high and gave him the name which is above all other names' (Phil. 2.7-8). In the Christian view, the highest dignity and ultimate spiritual beauty in fact belong to those who accept the humiliation and disfigurement of defeat, trusting in Him who alone gives victory, the God and Father of the Crucified.

Surrender and reciprocity

Defeat itself becomes victory, of course, and humiliation triumph when – fear cast out by perfect love – one spontaneously surrenders, as a woman does to the man who wins her. 'Let him kiss me with the kisses of his mouth', says the Bride of the Song of Songs, speaking of a loved one whom the Fathers and Doctors of the Church have identified with Christ (Sg. 1.2a). Experiencing his ardour, the Bride tells her Bridegroom: 'delicate is the fragrance of your perfume, your name is an oil poured out, and that is why the maidens love you' (Sg. 1.3). Among these 'maidens' have been many saintly women, and in the seventeenth and eighteenth centuries the visionary intimacy with Christ of the great female mystics became a standard subject of Catholic art, in part in reaction to Protestant scepticism about the possibility of such total union of the human person with God.

The best-known representation of this kind is the grand Baroque 'machine' created by Gianlorenzo Bernini for the noble Venetian family of the Cornaro beginning in 1647 (Verdon 2012: 222–223): a chapel dedicated to the Spanish mystic Theresa of Avila in the Roman church of Santa Maria della Vittoria (see Illustration 5). There, above the altar in a sort of 'chapel within the chapel', we see *Saint Theresa of Avila in Ecstasy*: a sculptural group comprised of an angel bearing the arrow which Theresa said was plunged several times into her entrails, and the woman so wounded. The overwhelming force of this experience is conveyed by the architecture of the niche, which bends forward, and by the heavy fabric of Theresa's Carmelite habit, which flows around her like molten lava. Love's force is communicated above all by the swoon into which she falls, going limp before the divine onslaught.

The decidedly theatrical impression of this masterpiece is confirmed by two loge-type boxes, at right and left of the altar, from which members of the Cornaro family assist, privileged witnesses of the intimate union of Theresa's soul with God. And the light in the chapel, filtered from a hidden source above St Theresa, descends along 'rays' of gilded wood to the saint's body, while frescoes in the chapel ceiling simulate the open sky, with clouds of painted stucco overlaying the architecture: an illusory heaven invading the material universe.

I have spoken of 'surrender', but it is worth recalling that surrender is not a passive act. Here in fact Bernini illustrates the reciprocity found in the Song of Songs: a dialogue that to the chosen soul reveals not only the partner's beauty but its own as well. To the woman of his heart the Bridegroom of the Song says: 'How beautiful you are, my love, how beautiful you are! Your eyes are doves', and she responds: 'How beautiful are you, my Beloved, and how delightful! All green is our bed. The beams of our house are of cedar, the panelling of cypress' (Sg. 1.15-17).

In this shared confession of beauty there is dignity as well, the insuperable value of the absolute. For, as the closing lines of the Song of Songs assert, 'Love is as strong as death, passion as relentless as the underworld. Its flash is a flash of fire, a flame of God himself. No flood can quench love, nor torrents drown it. Were a man to offer all his family wealth to buy love, contempt is all he would gain' (Sg. 8.6-7). Human worth, indeed, springs from love's free exchange and beauty from looking into eyes which return our gaze with love – ultimately into God's eyes, even if in another's face.

Jubilation

The final work I will discuss is a painting by the contemporary Florentine artist Filippo Rossi, well known in Italy for his abstract icons – one of the masters called by Benedict XVI to a famous meeting in the Sistine Chapel in 2009. The painting, a triptych entitled *Magnificat* (see Illustration 6), is the property of the Community of Jesus, an ecumenical monastic family in the Benedictine tradition at Orleans, Massachusetts, on Cape Cod (Verdon 2010: 65–67).

Rossi himself interprets the work:

> My triptych *Magnificat* imagines Mary's prayer … [it] expresses the three-fold unity of a movement which is also stillness, like the New Testament event the work evokes, which involved the angel Gabriel, Mary and the Holy Spirit. The disk in the upper part of the triptych is a material visualization of the God who is love, radiant and intense but also unchanging, still.
>
>   But what can art perceive of so deep a mystery? How can art become its voice and its sign? My triptych responds in terms of a felt inner vibration which can be translated in musical terms: everything becomes sacramental cosmic harmony.

That is why I designed three pentagrams on which notes ascend and descend like golden petals. These are God's seeds, rich in fruit. Here where the subject is the Father and the Son, we also have Mary, fecundated by grace, and so the theme includes a woman who is at once mother and daughter, as Dante said, addressing the Virgin as '*figlia del tuo Figlio*' [daughter of your son]. She is the humble servant on whom the Lord turned his gaze, touched with his Spirit, lifted up, casting down the mighty from their thrones.

If we break the New Testament Incarnation account into its various moments, this painting evokes that in which Mary raises her song of praise to God. It is also the moment when God's power to save those who fear him reveals his mercy. God in fact speaks and calls each of us in different ways, planting the treasure of his response in us – the response which, when we utter it, perfectly realises us. (quoted in Verdon 2010: 65–67)

The painting is like a two-part choir. Mary, in the work's lower zone, is represented as 'full of grace' and foreshadowed in various kinds of gold. And, rising from Mary, harmonic notes shimmering on the pentagrams move towards God in the upper zone. 'I tried', Rossi says, 'to translate into visual terms a perceived interior vibrato, configuring a "musical" experience in which everything becomes "sacrament" of a harmony. I wanted this "symphony" to irradiate the whole work, and indeed that the joyous music flow beyond the image to enfold the viewer'.

In this abstract yet clear image, Filippo Rossi celebrates the creature's potential, expressed perfectly in Mary, to respond to the Creator. He eschews the figurative style in which most Christian art has been done because he is convinced that the harmonic vibrancy of the Virgin's response – of her soul 'magnifying' the Lord – cannot be expressed in descriptive language. Rossi's belief that more than description is called for recalls what St Augustine said in a memorable page on the 'new song' that Psalm 33 [32] invites every believer to intone (Verdon 2012: 262–264). 'Give thanks to Yahweh on the lyre, play for him on the ten-stringed lyre. Sing to him a new song, make sweet music for your cry of victory', verses 2 and 3 command, and Augustine exhorts his readers:

Divest yourselves of what has become old, for you have learned the new song: a new man, a new testament, a new song. The new song is not for old men: it can be learned only by new men, men who have been renewed, through grace, and freed of what was old, men who now belong to the new testament, which is the kingdom of heaven. All our love yearns for this and sings a new song. Raise a new song not with your tongue, however, but with your life! (*Commentary on Psalm 32*: 1.7-8).

According to Augustine, this song – performed not with the believer's tongue but with his life – is 'non-figurative', 'abstract', using only sounds, not words. The Bishop of Hippo, asserting that it is God himself who gives the tone, enjoins on all who would sing in this way to

> not go in search of words, as if you were able to translate with articulated sounds a song in which God will delight. Sing, rather, with jubilation. What does it mean to sing with jubilation? It means to comprehend without being able to explain in words that which we sing with our heart. In fact, those who sing during the grain or grape harvest, or as they do some other hard work, at first take pleasure in their song's words, but then, as emotion grows, feel it no longer possible to vent their feelings in words and so express themselves with the simple modulation of notes. And this song they call 'jubilation'.

Rossi's non-figurative icon seeks to transmit an emotion impossible to convey adequately in words, visually evoking the modulation of notes produced by a jubilant heart, a new song of praise to God in Christ. This too is beauty, this too dignity: silent joy and pulsing knowledge of Him whom words cannot describe and whom our theology diminishes – the God whom only life itself, and love, and perhaps art, can express.

For, as revealed in Jesus Christ, God is the beauty which embraced, ennobles, enriching all who accept this dignity with prayerful inwardness, forging a bond with cosmic reality. As revealed in Christ, God opens the heart to relationships in a self-giving that is fully conscious, even when to give implies defeat, and that in surrender discovers joy, a song without words.

The context – of the beauty, of the dignity, of the prayer, of the dying for love and rising for life, of the joy and the song – is most often the Eucharist, the ultimate creative act, in which material things become spiritual ones, bread a body, wine blood. Not only has most Christian art been made to accompany this transformation – made for altars in churches – but artists in a special way obey Christ's command to 'Do this in memory of me', taking pigments or stone and saying: 'This is my body, this is my blood, this is my life, given for you.' Artists in fact can teach us the beauty and the dignity of being human.

Note

1   Cf. also Gregory Nazianzen, Discourse 39 for the Baptism of Christ (PG 36,350–359) and Maximus of Turin, discourse 100 on the Epiphany, 1,3 (CCL 23, 398–400).

References

Augustine of Hippo, *Comment on Psalm 33 [32]*, in *Corpus Christianorum series latina*, Tournhout 1953-, 38, 253ff., and V. Tarulli (ed.), *Opere di Sant'Agostino, xxviii : Esposizioni sui Salmi*, Rome 1993.

Chrysologus, Peter, *Discourse 108*, in Migne, J.-P. (1854–1865), *Patrologia Cursus completus, series latina*, 52, 499–500.

Cyril of Alexandria, *Commentary on the Gospel of St. John*, in Migne, J.-P. (1857–1867), *Patrologia Cursus completus, series graeca*, 74, 434.

Gregory Nazianzen, *Discourse 7*, in Migne, J.-P. (1857–1867), *Patrologia Cursus completus, series graeca*, 35, 786–787.

Gregory of Nissa, *Discourse on the Resurrection of Christ*, in Migne, J.-P. (1857–1867), *Patrologia Cursus completus, series graeca*, 46, 603–606.

John Damascene, *De sacris imaginibus orationes*, in Migne, J.-P. (1857–1867), *Patrologia Cursus completus, series graeca*, 94, 1268.

Tartuferi, A. (2008), *L'eredità di Giotto. Arte a Firenze 1340-1375* (catalogue of the exhibit at the Uffizi, 10 June–2 November 2008).

Trinkaus, C. (1970), *In Our Image and Likeness. Humanity and Divinity in Italian Humanist Thought*, 2 vols, Chicago: University of Chicago Press.

Verdon, T. (2001), *L'arte sacra in Italia. L'immaginazione religiosa dal paleocristiano al postmoderno*, Milan: A. Mondadori.

Verdon, T. (2003), 'Michelangelo and the Body of Christ. Religious Meaning in the Florence Pietà', in J. Wasserman (ed.), *Michelangelo's Florence Pietà*, 127–148, Princeton, NJ: Princeton University Press.

Verdon, T. (2006), *Cristo nell'arte europea*, Milan: Mondadori Electa (translated as *Le Christ dans l'art européen*, Paris: Citadelles & Mazenod, 2008).

Verdon, T. (2009), *Il catechism della carne. Corporeità e arte cristiana*, Siena: Cantagalli.

Verdon, T. (2010), *Arte della preghiera*, Vatican City: Libreria Editrice Vaticana (cf. also Idem. (2014), *Art and Prayer*, Brewster, MA: Paraclete Press).

Verdon, T. (2012), *Breve storia dell'arte sacra cristiana*, Brescia: Editrice Queriniana.

Verdon, T. (2015), *The New Opera del Duomo Museum*, Florence: Mandragora (the sonnet is cited in C. Guasti, *Le rime di Michelangelo*, Florence 1863, p. 230).

Verdon, T. (2017), 'The Infancy, Passion and Resurrection of Christ in Michelangelo', in M. Wivel (ed.), *Michelangelo and Sebastiano* (catalogue of the exhibition at the National Gallery, London, 15 March–25 June 2017), London: National Gallery Company.

Wasserman, J., ed. (2003), *Michelangelo's Florence Pietà*, Princeton, NJ: Princeton University Press.

Illustrations

1. Giotto, *Altarpiece*. Raleigh, North Carolina, Museum of Art. Detail: The figure of Christ (https://www.flickr.com/photos/universalpops/11175468243).
2. Piero della Francesca, *Baptism of Christ*. London, National Gallery (https://artuk.org/discover/artworks/the-baptism-of-christ-115457).
3. Leonardo da Vinci, *Last Supper*. Milan, Santa Maria delle Grazie (https://en.wikipedia.org/wiki/The_Last_Supper_(Leonardo_da_Vinci)#/media/File:%C3%9Altima_Cena_-_Da_Vinci_5.jpg).
4. Michelangelo, *Pietà*. Florence, Museo dell'Opera del Duomo (https://www.wikiart.org/en/michelangelo/pieta).
5. Gianlorenzo Bernini, *St. Theresa in Ecstasy*. Rome, Santa Maria della Vittoria. Detail: The Angel and St Theresa (https://uploads0.wikiart.org/images/gianlorenzo-bernini/the-ecstasy-of-st-teresa(1).jpg).
6. Filippo Rossi, *Magnificat*. Orleans, Massachusetts, Church of the Transfiguration (https://www.artfree.it/opera_edit.php?id=132).

7

Western Christian Sacred Music and Human Dignity

Jonathan Arnold

I am convinced that music really is the universal language of beauty which can bring together all people of good will on earth.[1]

Introduction

'No culture so far discovered lacks music. Making music appears to be one of the fundamental activities of mankind.' So writes Anthony Storr in his book *Music and the Mind*, which acknowledges music's ubiquitous presence in all parts of the world (1992: 1). In every country music plays a role in social bonding and community by promoting good mental health and well-being within a cohesive society. The work of Robin Dunbar and others shows us that music, and especially singing, is not 'auditory cheesecake' as Steven Pinker would have it, a kind of sweet extra to life that has no evolutionary function, but is rather a fundamental part of our make-up as human beings (Pearce et al. 2015; Weinstein et al. 2016). The great medieval philosopher and music theorist Boethius was aware of music's essential nature to the human experience when he wrote in his *Fundamentals of Music* in about AD 520: 'Music is so naturally united with us that we cannot be free from it even if we so desired.' Music is one of the most potent ways we can both be fully human and encounter something numinous or transcendent, however loosely we define these terms. The physical, embodied, experiential and communal qualities of music can have profound social consequences: 'Music brings about similar physical responses in different people at the same time. This is why it is able to draw groups together and create a sense of unity' (Storr 1992: 24).

The integral place of music in the human experience is consistent with Jacques Maritain's notion that 'true' or 'integral Christian humanism' is the essence of human dignity – that which brings life in its totality, both materially and spiritually (Maritain 1973). For Maritain, human beings are 'individuals' who contribute to the wider community; moreover, they are also 'persons' with a spiritual identity and destiny. In both the spiritual and physical realms humans contribute to the 'common good'. Maritain brings the notion of the individual and person together as a unified and integral whole. The individual 'is subordinate to the (temporal) common good of the community'. However, as a person 'with a supernatural end, one's "spiritual good" is superior to society – and this is something that all political communities should recognize'.[2] Thus, in this chapter, I wish to address how these characteristics of human dignity, both the physical/material and spiritual/transcendent, relate to sacred music in its composition, performance and reception, contributing to life in its totality. I shall examine the role of sacred music within the history of music theory, philosophy and theology, including its influences on the mind, morality, education, culture and ideas of the human soul. I will also consider the importance of sacred music to human communities, especially in a post-secular West, and explore why singing has been central to human evolution and identity. I will also briefly investigate the healing properties of music for both the individual and society. But first, we must decide what sacred music is and what it means to civilization.

Sacred music and Western civilization

Music is central to civilization. Evidence, including fossil records, suggests that music predated language and was even the basis for language. McGilchrist's research reveals that 'the control of voice and respiration needed for singing came into being long before they [early humans] would ever have been required by language' (McGilchrist 2012: 102). Even today, children develop simple musicality before speech: 'intonation, phrasing and rhythm develop first; syntax and vocabulary come only later' (2012: 103). The fact that music expresses our emotions implies that 'our love of music reflects the ancestral ability of our mammalian brain to transmit and receive basic emotional sounds' (2012).

McGilchrist opines that music, being the ancestor of language, developed mostly in the right hemisphere of the brain that is concerned with communication and social cohesion. Even though language and words have dominated Western society for many centuries, when we hear or perform music, we naturally regain the harmonious and cohesive experience of community – and community fosters dignity (McGilchrist 2012: 105). According to McGilchrist, therefore, long before historical records began music was at the heart of community, consciousness and culture.

Music is also at the heart of the material world, built into the fabric of the physical universe. The Greek mathematician Pythagoras (sixth century BC) discovered that the most harmonious of consonant simultaneous sounds were those that complied with a simple mathematical ratio (1:2, 2:3, etc.). Pythagoras is also known for his idea of the music of the spheres. He considered earthly music to be a reflection of cosmic harmony. A second-century treatise by Plutarch (1967) argued that Pythagoras was not so much enamoured with music as a sensual experience but rather as a phenomenon to be understood by the mind: 'The grave Pythagoras rejected the judging of music by the sense of hearing, asserting that its excellence must be apprehended by the mind. This is why he did not judge it by the ear, but by the scale based on the proportions, and considered it sufficient to pursue the study no further than the octave' (quoted in Begbie 2004: 319, n. 15). For Pythagoras then, music engaged with one of the essential features of human identity and dignity: the conscious mind. Regarding the improvement of the mind, Aristotle (384–322 BC) questioned whether music ought to be taught for the advancement, or 'decorum', of the individual and society in Book 8 of his *Politics*. Of course, he concluded that it was of great benefit. Of the possible states of being that music might appeal to (pleasure seeking, the active life in civic service and the contemplation) music related to all three (Hankins: 233 and 238). But it was a philosopher, Plato, who was to begin exploring music's connection with another fundamental element of human dignity, namely, morality.

Plato (427–347 BC) was strongly influenced by Pythagorean thought regarding music and developed it in his *Republic* and *Timaeus*, where he took the mathematical cosmology of music theory and applied it to his notion of a world soul: for Plato, 'Music gives us not only a model of harmonious balance, unity, and integrity, it actually implants cosmic harmony into the soul of humans' (Begbie 2004: 80). Music could help achieve virtue by balancing the soul's rational, spiritual and bodily elements; it could be a 'means to correct any discord that may have arisen in the courses of the soul ... our ally in bringing it into harmony and agreement with herself' (Begbie 2004, quoting Plato, *Timaeus*, 47d.). Indeed, musical modes (*harmoniai*) were considered able to influence moral behaviour. For instance, the Phrygian and Dorian modes could give people courage and temperance, whereas the Ionian and Lydian modes could be detrimental to the human character (2004: 81). Thus, it was crucial for Plato that the listener engaged with the correct form of music, for the sake of our souls, in order that we may participate in the balance of the cosmic harmoniousness: 'heard music for Plato has a positive ethical, political, and social potential'. Plato, however, was deeply suspicious of music's emotional power; it could calm, but it can also excite and damage the soul. Thus, listening alone was not enough when engaging with music. The mind must be employed in order to interpret the sounds in a rational way.

The most important of Plato's followers in the third century, Plotinus (*c.* AD 205–270) provided a link between Plato's Greek world and the Christian world. Plotinus took Plato's sharp distinction between the world of ideals and forms and the lesser world of material things, and created what we now call a 'neo-Platonic' scheme whereby the highest of ideal forms, the 'One', is the Supreme Being from which, or from whom, emanates the created order in a series of hierarchies, down to the lowest material. At the top of this hierarchy is intellect, or mind (*Nous*). As the full extent of Platonic writings came to be translated, commented upon and circulated, the intellectual importance of music grew. These pedagogical treatises all aimed to improve their readers' attainment of a virtuous life; in order to do so one needed to live by reason. But questions were still to be answered concerning Christian notions, in the West, of the human soul.

Aristides Quintilianus (*c.* third century AD?) wrote one of the most important treatises on music of his age, *De Musica*. He considered music to be both a science and an art (Begbie 2004 citing Thomas Mathiesen 2002: 112–120). It was essential to education but also a means to elevate the soul beyond this world: 'the object of music is the love of the beautiful (cited in MacDiarmaid 2018: 296)'. He drew upon Platonic and Pythagorean ideas that, in turn, informed early Christian thinking on music, such as Augustine of Hippo's (AD 350–430) own *De Musica* (387–391).

Augustine, from North Africa and Bishop of Hippo, was the most influential theologian in Western Christianity to assimilate Platonic and Hellenistic thought, not least in his theology of music. Augustine echoed the notions of the Platonic One and the hierarchical ladder of beings below, down which emanates the goodness of the absolute being. *De Musica* contained a 'vocabulary that would be mined for the next one and half millennia' (Van Deusen 1999: 577). Augustine concurred with the Platonic idea that the cosmos was ordered by numerical ratios and proportions. Thus, music was more of a mathematical discipline than an aural, sensual pleasure. It was a science of '*bene modulandi*', of a 'good measuring' of the world, involved in its numerical ratios. However, fallen humanity cannot tune in to the music of the heavens, *musica caelestis*. In Augustine's sixth volume of *De Musica* he perceived God, the supreme musician, to have created the cosmos from nothing and, in so doing, gave it form or music. Fallen humanity, imprisoned by its love of inferior beauty, must strive to hear beyond the corporeal and temporal sound of earthly music and hear instead the incorporeal and eternal music of the transcendent divine (*Confessions*, 10.33, 49–50). Every aspect of the created order reflects the One who created it. Thus, as Carol Harrison observes, for Augustine, creation praises the *Deus Creator Omnium* and becomes purified by loving the source of all harmony and music (2011: 31–39 and 45; cf. St Augustine, *De Musica*, 6.14-46 and 6.4-7). Because music is part of God's universal order, its performance literally binds both performer and listener to a divine cosmic order that wards off sin and chaos (Horne 1985; Harrison 2011: 31–32). But Augustine's suspicion of the sensuality of music was never far from his mind, as he fought his own inclinations towards idolatry and secular pleasure (*Confessions*, 9.2.14).

But there was also considerable inner tension in Augustine regarding music's power: 'I fluctuate between the danger of pleasure and the experience of the beneficent effect [of music]' (*Confessions* 10.33.50). Thus, it was therefore necessary for any devotional listener to music not to reject music altogether but to move towards God through the music and beyond it, beyond the 'temporal' (Harrison 2011: 41–42), rather like looking at an Icon and moving towards God through and beyond it, rather than worshipping the object of beauty for itself. In Augustine's own words:

> All the diverse emotions of our spirit have their various modes in voice and chant appropriate in each case, and are stirred by a mysterious inner kinship. But my physical delight, which has to be checked from enervating the mind, often deceives me ... It tries to be first and in the leading role, though it deserves to be allowed only as secondary to reason. (*Confessions* 10.33.49; cf. Harrison 2011: 42 and Begbie 2004: 320–321).

Beyond Augustine, Europe gained the foundation of medieval music theory from the Roman poet, philosopher and politician Boethius (*c.* AD 480–525), who placed sacred music at the heart of human dignity and development by emphasizing its importance to human education (Boethius 1989). His *De Institutione Musica* held music in the highest regard. For Boethius, as for Augustine and his predecessors, music was primarily a mathematical, rational and intellectual activity and was divided into three levels: the cosmic music (of the spheres, elements and seasons) is *musica mundana*; the harmonizing of our human bodies and souls is *musica humana*; and the music we hear is *musica instrumentalis*. This latter category was only an entry level to the higher forms, as Bower has noted: 'The goal of learning *musica* is to ascend to the level of reason. The fundamental principle motivating Platonic music theory is *knowing*, the acquisition of pure knowledge, and Boethius' threefold division of music and three classes of musicians resonate consistently with this principle' (2002: 147).

For many centuries, the supremacy of the philosopher who wrote *about* music above the singer or player who *performed* it was accentuated in music theory, but with the weakening of the Carolingian Empire, the Platonic tradition was brought into the musical life of the monasteries, which were the backbone of the Church's musical life. Plainchant's eight modes, performance practice and music theory gradually moved closer together by necessity and practicality. From the twelfth century and the rise of polyphony onwards, the Pythagorean-Platonic tradition of musical thought as adopted by the Christian world pervaded until its waning in the sixteenth and seventeenth centuries.

Platonic thought on the nature of the human soul drew in many eras and places on Pythagorean ideas that centred on musical harmony. For instance, the Renaissance Italian humanist Leonardo Bruni (*c.* 1370–1444) was aware of this, stating that harmony and number were best suited to softening and delighting the soul. For Bruni, 'Good music projected powerful "representations" of the virtues into the soul' (Hankins 2015: 238). Moreover, towards the end of the fifteenth century, with Marsilio Ficino's (1433–1499) influential translations and commentaries circulating across Italy, music's role in Platonic cosmology and theology became well established and intellectual circles once again affirmed music's place among the liberal arts (Ficino 1989). Ficino was the most influential Italian philosopher of his time, who brought Platonic and neo-Platonic thought back into the consciousness of Italian culture and, by extension, to Northern European humanism. Ficino's philosophy emphasized the dignity of man, a favourite theme for humanists from Francesco Petrarch (1304–1374) to Pico della Mirandola (1463–1494) seeking to extol humanity's scientific and political capacities and achievements, but Ficino added a cosmological and metaphysical aspect, particularly by his insistence, following Plato, on the immortality of souls, which became an extension of the dignity doctrine: 'It was not for small things but for great that God created men' (Letter to Giovanni Calvalcanti, quoted in Salaman 1996: 25).

In the arts, Ficino had a passion for music and extolled its positive effect on the mind. He played the 'orphic lyre' (lute). He was also a music theorist and one of the first to treat the interval of a third and a sixth as consonant (Voss 2006: 10). Ficino believed beauty to be divine in itself, which, through art, philosophy and religion, could transform humanity (Ficino, *Opera Omnia*, quoted in Voss 2006: 12). Concerning music in particular, a letter to Domenico Benivieni (1460– *c.* 1507), 'a master musician', illustrates Ficino's esteem of the art, which derives from his knowledge of Plato and Hermes Trismegistus (dates unknown):

> Plato thinks that true music is nothing other than harmony of mind: natural, insofar as its powers are consonant with the powers of mind, and acquired, insofar as its motions are consonant with the motions of the mind … Hermes Trismegistus says that both have been assigned to us by God, so that through the former we may continually imitate God Himself in our reflections and dispositions and through the latter we may regularly honour the name of God in hymns and sounds. (Voss 2006: 179)

For Ficino, music could perform an intermediary role between the body and the soul, and exercise a beneficial effect on both the emotions and the senses. Thus, musical sound becomes a bridge between heaven and earth.

Fifteenth-century humanist theorists could also see the benefits of music for the dignity and decorum of the political system and the state. Good music was a 'civilizing influence, spreading harmony [and] checking barbarism' (Hankins 2015: 240). The underlying assumption of musical scholarship was that the Greco-Roman world of antiquity was essentially good; that the present had become corrupted; and that what had been lost needed to be recaptured (Hankins 2015: 241). This assumption applied to all the liberal arts, or the *bonae artes*, that is, 'arts that gave the individual moral worth and dignity, arts that served the commonwealth by making its leaders virtuous' (Hankins 2015: 231). In the fifteenth century, regarding the role of music, particularly in its function of setting and communicating text, there emerged an emphasis upon elegance, dignity and clarity of style which resulted in harmony, echoed in Pico's *Oratio* or *Oration on the Dignity of Man*, which extolled the liberal arts as a means of uplifting humanity through the exercise of the soul and mind. As with Ficino, his tutor Pico's ambition for humanity was an ascent to God and a return to 'the One'. Music played an important role in facilitating this ascent. Fine examples of early humanist musical text-setting are by Johannes Ciconia (*c.* 1370–1412) and Guillaume Dufay (1397–1474). Such composers had the task of embellishing their chosen texts with musically expressive devices in order most eloquently to communicate the meaning and morality of the words. Bose has called this an 'aesthetic vocabulary':

> By providing a reliable and authentic aesthetic vocabulary, this elaborately codified system should conduct musicologist and performer alike to the source of the genre's well-attested affectivity, thereby permitting the reconstruction of a possible performance aesthetic. (Bose 1996: 2)

One of the outcomes of such an aesthetic vocabulary in singing was to effect the emotions by calming mind and body. Here we must distinguish between domestic and church music:

> Unlike clerical vocalists in churches and palatine chapels, who sang to God on behalf of the immortal souls of mankind, the humanist singer sang to men and women in courts and academies to entertain them, but also for their moral benefit in this life. (Hankins: 258)

As for ecclesiastical music in the fifteenth century, the humanists tolerated the multi-voiced polyphony, so long as it retained the 'dignity and gravity of the plainchant and avoided the excesses of rhythmic intricacy' (Wegman: 19). For instance, Giovanni Caroli (1428–1503), the Florentine Dominican friar opined, in the late fifteenth century, that hymns and psalms should be sung 'with dignity and devotion, and fervour of heart, with reverence and honour of the deity' (quoted in Wegman: 27).

But this was clearly not always adhered to. In the sixteenth century, humanists such as Desiderius Erasmus (1467–1536) criticized the way in which church choirs ruined music, for the listener, by their unsophisticated delivery. This sort of criticism, grounded in the classical rules of rhetoric and prosody, was commonplace throughout the humanists' writings on music and the liturgy. Its essence lies in the matter of 'delivery' (*pronuntiatio*) that ancient writers viewed as the most important in oratory. According to Marcus Fabius Quintilian (*c.* AD 35–*c.* 100), whose teachings served as the best guide to classical rhetoric for Renaissance humanists, the four features of delivery are accuracy, clarity, elegance and compatibility (Russell 2001: 99–119, cited in Kim 2008: 11–12; Harrán 1997: 25, 28–37).

Erasmus shared Ficino's neo-Platonic idea that music operated as a mystical agent between the human spirit and the divine (Cobussen 2008: 44). From the teachings of the early Church, Erasmus surmised that the most important kind of music was communal singing of an entire congregation: 'The most beautiful harmony is when all the members of Christ sing the same song as their head' (*Collected Works of Erasmus*, 64: 321). Moreover, the biblical text and its clarity and intelligibility, as well as the unity and simplicity of the music, were the most important characteristics in sacred music. However, what he heard in contemporaneous church and monastic choirs was 'thundering and raucous yelling, so that the sounds obscure everything and nothing can be understood' (Kim 2006: 294, quoting Erasmus, *Declarationes*). The issue of comprehensibility was also evident in England. John Case's 1587 *The Praise of Musicke* stated that 'the singing of so many parts together, causeth the ditty not to be understood' (quoted in Wegman: 60).

Therefore, what developed, through the late medieval and Renaissance periods, in the humanist programme of philological, rhetorical and dialectical experimentation, was an emphasis upon the word of poetry and eloquent expression of it, which became fundamental in the performance and interpretation of music. It was surely not the intention of any musical humanist philosopher or composer that this verbal emphasis would be so useful to those reformers, such as Ulrich Zwingli, who would radically change the nature and role of music within religion. Nevertheless, that was the case, leading to music's eventual liberation from religion and sacred function in the eighteenth century (Blanning 2010). But in the Catholic Church, the Council of Trent decreed that sophisticated polyphonic music could be the medium by which to communicate divine words, so long as the 'entire manner of singing ... should be calculated not to afford vain delight to the ear, but so that the words may be comprehensible to all; and thus may the hearts of the listeners be caught up into the desire for celestial harmonies and contemplation of the joys of the blessed' (Council of Trent, 1562, 22nd session, Canon 8).

The most notable composer to implement the reforms was Giovanni Pierluigi da Palestrina (*c.* 1525–1594), composing in a purer and more restrained style than his predecessors. In his Mass, composed in honour of Pope Marcellus (*Missa Papae Marcelli*), one can hear beautiful, pure lines of the text clearly among the voices of the choir. Legend has it that this single composition saved sacred choral polyphony for the Catholic Church. The Spanish composer Tomás Luis de Victoria (1548–1611) also wrote music which conformed to this specification. His intense mystical approach to composition, like a musical echo of the spiritual writings of the Spanish Carmelite Teresa of Ávila (1515–1582), draws the listener into the meaning of the text and into a deeper contemplation of the divine. In England, the sixteenth-century Elizabethan injunctions that demanded more syllabic and homophonic musical settings of text, in order to appreciate the words, was embraced by the genius of Thomas Tallis (1505–1585) and William Byrd (1539/40 or 1543–1623). Despite Tallis's Catholic leanings and Byrd's outright recusancy, they were equally adept at composing in the 'old' Latin polyphonic style, during the reign of Mary Tudor, or in the 'new' vernacular style of the first Elizabethan age.

What is sacred music today?

The Council of Trent's decrees demanded that no 'profane' melodies be mixed with sacred music. But perhaps in the West today, we might be more willing to acknowledge that a great deal of music, if not all music, that prompts an affective response might also appeal to our consciousness and culture, mind and morality, soul and sacrality. Of course, Western culture owes its inheritance to the Judaeo-Christian tradition, and this cannot be ignored. But, if music touches our hearts and minds, desires and doubts, and evokes a creative participation from those who listen attentively or 'seriously', as Rowan Williams emphasizes (1994: 249), then music defies definition as an object of reverence in itself. Music ennobles human dignity because it can point towards something far greater than itself, but which it alone can express. Arguably, therefore, 'sacred music' is now *all* music that addresses, in whatever manner, themes essential to human existence, not only that music is religious by its intention, text or context. The atheist, Christian or agnostic can all feel the benefits of great music for their mind, heart and soul.

In this 'post-secular' context (a term that will be explained in the following section), greater accessibility to sacred music through digital media greatly benefits human dignity because it leads those who find resonance in sacred music to a better intuitive knowledge of themselves as human beings and of society as a whole. Music can satisfy a longing for something greater than ourselves. Beautiful and profound harmonies may evoke an echo of the Christian faith or appeal to our deepest human desires, a humanity united by shared frailty, doubt, which seeks desire to admire the transcendent. The boundaries between sacred and secular music are now blurred, for so many now find that music of all kinds leads to a sense of admiration and reflection that might, potentially, lead back to the object of that admiration, the 'divine' source of love, which is the greatest of all human qualities. I will now continue the theme of how music relates our human dignity as 'life in totality' by exploring the importance of sacred music to community.

Music, community and post-secularism

We live in a world where community is more important than ever. Although individualism predates Margaret Thatcher's declaration that 'there is no such thing as society, only families and individuals', nevertheless in the past few decades in the United Kingdom, there has been an increasingly individualist and consumerist approach to our wider communities. However, we are now moving into a post-secular age, where individualism is giving way to a greater search for relationship and belonging. As Ian Mobsby writes:

> Our post-Reformation, post-Enlightenment inheritance is the cult of the individual, and in short we desire community but often have no idea how to seek it. As a result, our culture has become less humane … [This] individualism gravely impoverished the quality of our spiritual communities. (2008: xii)

Post-secular culture has emerged in the complexity of religious decline and an increase in those seeking spiritual nourishment. If secularization is 'the process of reducing religious, spiritual and philosophical belief in general society', then post-secularism is 'a time when the forces of secularization have not only stopped, but where social forces have driven a renewed appreciation for the place of spirituality in general society' (Mobsby 2008). A post-secular society has become one in which holistic spirituality is flourishing, while Sunday church attendance declines. This holistic experience contains a number of factors, Mobsby argues, including 'the return to the importance of the subjective and experiential over the rational'; 'a return to the appreciation of the sacred and enchantment of life'; 'and a world view informed by postmodern sensibilities' (Mobsby 2018). This phenomenon has seen a huge increase in the number of people calling themselves 'spiritual but not religious', and whom Nancy Ammerman has labelled 'extra-theistic', that is, people who have either never been to church or have stopped attending church but still seek transcendence in nature and beauty; seek to make sense of unity and connection; seek meaning to life's journey and the mystical truth that lies within (2013a, b, quoted in Mobsby 2018).

For such seekers music often becomes an important conduit for meaningful human experience and being. Thus, the strand of scholarship advocating that music can be listened to in a self-contained, pure, aesthetic way without the need for any reference to any other aspect of existence for its meaning has given way to the notion that music is always interconnected with other temporal phenomena in our society (Norris 1989; Kivy 1990; Dahlhouse 1991; Higgins 1991; Hargreaves and North 1997; Cook 1998; Bonds 2006).

For instance, music can become meaningful through its performance 'through the interplay between its temporal processes and a vast range of temporal processes which shape our lives in the world – from the rhythm of breathing to the coming and going of day and night' (Begbie 2000: 13). Music is embedded in social and cultural practices (Cook 1998: 117; Begbie 2000: 13 n. 16); our physical surroundings influence how music is performed and sounds (Begbie 2000: 15);

music is both corporeal (physiological and neurological) and emotional. Thus, music is heard through the filter of our social, cultural, physical, psychological, emotional and communal humanity, not to mention theological factors: 'Music is something that should happen whenever people feel a need to speak through sounds, to thank God they are on the earth or to curse him for what they are suffering' (Mellors 1946: 18). The most fundamental and enduring music that connects to our sense of community, consciousness, feelings and souls is singing.

The singing voice and human dignity

Why do we sing? One answer is the dignity and fulfilment that arises from social bonding because 'humans are a cultural species' (Mesoudi 2011: 1). We inherit and acquire a plethora of cultural practices, which fundamentally affect our behaviour. We may agree with Mesoudi that culture changes and evolves but, with regard to music, we may also agree with Davidson that throughout human history, the creation and performance of music through singing has had a constant and unchanging characteristic and aim – it has almost always involved a level of social communication (Davidson 2004: 57). The 'real or implied presence of others', even when music is practised alone, points to the human need for social interaction. Music's social purpose has been a constant feature of faith communities throughout history, but even outside of any religious context, music, and especially singing, implies interaction: 'singing a lullaby, a work song, a hunting song, or a school song; chanting as a member of a football crowd' and so on (2004). A wide spectrum of research techniques in the psychology of music has developed in order to examine music as social behaviour. In the story of evolution, the problem of how human beings create and maintain social bonds in large groups has been ongoing. Weinstein et al. have argued that 'evidence from historical and anthropological records suggests that group music-making might act as a mechanism by which this large-scale social bonding could occur' (2016: 152). In an experiment, individuals from a community choir who met in both small and large groups

> gave self-report measures of social bonding and had pain threshold measurements taken (as a proxy for endorphin release) before and after 90 min of singing. Results showed that feelings of inclusion, connectivity, positive affect, and measures of endorphin release all increased across singing rehearsals and that the influence of group singing was comparable for pain thresholds in the large versus small group context … The finding that singing together fosters social closeness – even in large group contexts where individuals are not known

to each other – is consistent with evolutionary accounts that emphasize the role of music in social bonding, particularly in the context of creating larger cohesive groups than other primates are able to manage. (2016)

Overall, therefore, they discovered that the 'social bonding effects of singing are actually more substantial in larger group settings compared to smaller, more familiar groups' (Weinstein et al. 2016). The remarkable aspect of this phenomenon is that it doesn't matter whether the people you are singing with are friends or not. Even with complete strangers, the resulting rise in endorphin levels is still the same. Communal singing, especially in large groups, gives you a feeling of well-being even to the extent that your pain threshold is increased.

The phenomenon of the community choir developed in the mid- to late twentieth century, with choirs such as Joan Taylor's 'Can't Sing Choir' at Morley College in London, Polly Barton's 'Singing for the Terrified' and Frankie Armstrong's 1988 Natural Voice Network,[3] which seeks to build 'accepting, non-judgmental communities that sing together' (Morgan and Boyce-Tillman: 24). These organizations and many others like them have all played an important part in introducing people to communal singing who don't necessarily have musical training or be able to read music but who, through a process of aural and oral learning, gain a sense of the joy of inclusive, embodied, nourishing music making through communal singing (Weinstein et al. 2016: 24, 26). The Birmingham 'Wellbeing Choir',[4] for instance, promotes itself thus: 'Attending a choir rehearsal is an uplifting and friendly experience' (2016: 28).

In their work exploring the community choir, Boyce-Tillman and Morgan have found that there has been an 'opening up' of the idea of 'choir' over the past fifty years and that the 'fragmented nature of contemporary society' has brought a need for 'creating communities based on the valuing of difference' (2016: 31). Moreover, 'by concentrating on the experiencing of music and the processes involved in creating events rather than musical products, music has been seen as a way of enabling people to encounter and respect difference in order to create a unity based on encompassing diversity' (2016). Boyce-Tillman and Morgan go further still and suggests that 'it is in the community choir that some people are finding some answers to their spiritual search' (2016: 53). Don Saliers further explores this search, positing some reasons why singing might be so spiritually fulfilling:

The act of singing is a deeply human act, found in every culture. This is so because singing activates things that seem so central to human life itself: bodily, emotional, intellectual, and moral animation ... Singing *enacts* the praise, thanksgiving, and blessing. Singing also *enacts* sorrow, anger, lament, and the questioning of God. (2007: 63)

Music is an 'embodied' art form and singing connects the physical body with a spiritual one, thus changing the status of the singer or listener to an elevated level of human dignity. Pope Benedict explains his Trinitarian understanding of the role of singing within the liturgy and its source of love:

> The singing of the Church comes ultimately out of love. It is the utter depth of love that produces the singing. "*Cantare amantis est*", says St. Augustine, singing is a lover's thing. In so saying, we come again to the Trinitarian interpretation of Church music. The Holy Spirit is love, and it is he who produces the singing. He is the Spirit of Christ, the Spirit who draws us into love for Christ and so leads to the Father. (2014: 142)

My own experience of singing with professional choirs and directors who specialize in performing sacred repertoire reflects this. It is just one testament to the fact that sacred music today, at its best, is in the hands of specialists who over the past few decades have been responsible for its growth in popularity, which is itself quite possibly a contributing factor to the rise in cathedral attendance.[5] But singing together, at whatever level, brings great benefits to human dignity, both individually and communally. It is not merely an ornament to society but is essential for social cohesion. I now turn to explore how sacred music can bring us healing, a fundamental aspect of any dignified and caring society.

Music as healing the individual

Music is good for our health. Music therapy in hospitals, hospices and in many areas of public health is well known and documented. For instance, music can have a noticeable effect on brain activity in remarkable ways: it can ease the symptoms of neurological diseases as well as prompt less therapeutic consequences, such as epileptic fits ('musicogenic epilepsy') (Storr 1992: 34–37). The work of Oliver Sacks has been important in charting music's effects on the brain (1973, 1985, 2007). Sacks has worked for decades analysing how music affects patients with various neurological problems, such as Parkinson's disease, aphasia, dementia, epilepsy and melancholia. He writes that 'our auditory systems, our nervous systems, are indeed exquisitely tuned for music'. However, discerning how this might be so, physiologically and neurologically, is not clear: 'How much this is due to the intrinsic characteristics of music itself … and how much to special resonances, synchronizations, oscillations, mutual excitations, or feedbacks in the immensely complex, multilevel neural circuitry that underlies musical perception and replay, we do not yet know' (Sacks 2007: xii).

Robert Jourdain has attempted to demonstrate how music leads us from sound, to tone, to melody, to harmony, to rhythm, to composition, to performance, to listening, to understand and, finally, to ecstasy: 'Music seems to be the most immediate of all the arts, and so the most ecstatic' (2007: 328). Jourdain draws upon Sacks's work with Parkinson's patients to demonstrate how music 'possesses' us. In trying to articulate the nature of this 'possession', Jourdain uses the language of encounter, relationship and experience:

> By providing the brain with an artificial environment, and forcing it through that environment in controlled ways, music imparts the means of experiencing relations far deeper than we encounter in our everyday lives ... Thus, however briefly, we attain a greater grasp of the world ... It's for this reason that music can be transcendent. For a few moments it makes us larger than we really are, and the world more orderly than it really is. (Jourdain 1997: 331)

Jourdain also gives a definition of this specific, musical experience of transcendence:

> We respond not just to the beauty of the sustained deep relations that are revealed, but also to the fact of our perceiving them. As our brains are thrown into overdrive, we feel our very existence expand and realize that we can be more than we normally are, and that the world is more than it seems. That is cause enough for ecstasy. (Jourdain 1997: 331)

Music expands our horizons by helping us to experience life beyond mere materiality and thus opens new potentialities for human growth and dignity. But music can also heal communities on a larger scale.

Healing a broken society

The Scottish composer Sir James MacMillan has said that music gives us 'a glimpse of something beyond the horizons of our materialism or our contemporary values'.[6] Whether we imagine such music reaching the divine ear or not, we can take MacMillan's point that all music is good for society and for our human dignity. He suggests that serious music holds the key to healing our broken culture:

> Music, as the deep mathematics of creation and cosmos, connects our over-stimulated lives in the modern world with an archetypal sense of order in nature.

> Music, when it speaks directly and profoundly to the human psyche, can provide
> a transformative sense to human life in all its corporeal, intellectual and spiritual
> parameters.

Music is an essential expression of what it means to be human, including the numinous and spiritual in all of us. As MacMillan puts it: 'I believe it is God's divine spark which kindles the musical imagination now, as it has always done, and reminds us, in an increasingly dehumanized world, of what it means to be human.' Other composers have recognized, such as Sir John Tavener:

> The fact that I've been given this Universalist vision of the world makes it a
> possibility that I might be able to contribute, just fractionally, toward the healing
> of a planet that's torn to pieces at the moment, by strife, by war, by different
> religions warring with each other. Now through the Universalist language of
> music perhaps there is a possibility to bring about a healing process and, after
> all, music was originally this function.[7]

For both MacMillan and the late, lamented Tavener, all music can lead to a deeper intuitive understanding of our sacrality, as Tom Service has written: 'All music, according to MacMillan, is a means of "searching out the sacred."'[8] Moreover, it is a continuing phenomenon that if music of any kind leads people towards the numinous and transcendent, people still look for religious language to describe the experience of it.

Conclusions

Sacred music lies at the heart of human evolution, language and civilization, as well as our consciousness, community, culture, morality and spirituality. The presence of sacred music in our society exemplifies Maritain's notion that human beings are 'individuals' who contribute to the wider community but who are also 'persons' with a spiritual identity and destiny. Through singing, a fundamental feature of human life throughout evolution, humans have been able to contribute, both physically and spiritually, to the 'common good'. In music, the individual submits to the common good and community as music requires listening, yielding to the needs of the ensemble and communal harmony. But music allows each person to express their 'spiritual goodness' and ultimate destiny to the gathered community. I end where I began, with the words of Anthony Storr:

Music exalts life, enhances life, and gives it meaning. Great music outlives the individual who created it. It is both personal and beyond the personal ... Music is a source of reconciliation, exhilaration, and hope which never fails ... It is irreplaceable, undeserved, transcendental blessing. (1992: 188)

As we intuit, as far as our brains will allow, the 'vastness and complexity of a world that we cannot represent to ourselves', Storr's words give us hope that in music we have the means by which we may approach, with some kind of meaning, the awesome mystery of our existence.

Notes

1   Pope Benedict XVI, address given at Paul VI Audience Hall, Vatican City, 16 April 2007.
2   https://plato.stanford.edu/entries/maritain. Accessed 12 July 2018.
3   Natural Voice Practitioners Network: http://www.naturalvoice.net.
4   Wellbeing Community Choir: http://www.ukrw2013.co.uk/wellbingcommunitychoir.
5   http://www.churchofengland.org/media-centre/news/2012/03/cathedral-attendance-statistics-enjoy-over-a-decade-of-growth.aspx.
6   http://www.aosm.org.uk/index.php/archive/item/sacred-music-can-heal-our-broken-culture. Accessed 7 September 2018.
7   Interview with John Tavener by David McCleery, transcribed from 'John Tavener Reflects ... A Recorded Interview' on the CD recording *John Tavener: A Portrait* (Naxos, 2004).
8   Tom Service, 'On the Trail of the Sacred', *Guardian* blog, 11 March 2010: https://www.theguardian.com/music/2010/mar/11/sacred-music-simon-russell-beale. Accessed 12 July 2018.

References

Ammerman, N. (2013a), *Sacred Stories Spiritual Tribes: Finding Religion in Everyday Life*, New York: Oxford University Press.

Ammerman, N. (2013b), 'Spiritual but Not Religious? Beyond Binary Choices in the Study of Religion', *Journal for the Scientific Study of Religion*, 52: 258–278.

Begbie, J. (2000), *Theology, Music and Time*, Cambridge: Cambridge University Press.

Begbie, J. (2004), *Resounding Truth, Christian Wisdom in the World of Music*, Grand Rapids, MI: Baker Academic.

Benedict XVI (J. Ratzinger) (2014), *The Spirit of the Liturgy*, San Francisco, CA: Ignatius Press.

Blanning, T. (2010), *The Triumph of Music*, Cambridge, MA: Harvard University Press.

Boethius, Anicius Manlius Severinus (1989 [*c.* AD 520]), *Fundamentals of Music*, edited by C. V. Palisca and translated by C. M. Bower, New Haven, CT and London: Yale University Press.

Bonds, M. (2006), *Music as Thought: Listening to the Symphony in the Age of Beethoven*, Princeton, NJ: Princeton University Press.

Bose, M. (1996), 'Humanism, English Music and the Rhetoric of Criticism', *Music & Letters*, 77: 1–21.

Bower, C. (2002), 'Transmission of Ancient Music Theory into the Middle Ages', in T. Christensen (ed.), *The Cambridge History of Western Music Theory*, 136–167, Cambridge: Cambridge University Press.

Cobussen, M. (2008), *Thresholds: Rethinking Spirituality through Music*, Aldershot: Ashgate.

Cook, N. (1998), *Music: A Very Short Introduction*, Oxford: Oxford University Press.

Dahlhaus, C. (1991), *The Idea of Absolute Music*, trans. Roger Lustig, Chicago: Chicago University Press.

Davidson, J. W. (2004), 'Music as Social Behaviour', in E. Clarke and N. Cook (eds), *Empirical Musicology: Aims, Methods, Prospects*, Oxford: Oxford University Press.

Erasmus, D. (1532), *Declarationes ad censuras Lutetiae vulgatus sub nomine facultatis theologie Parisiensis*, Basil.

Ficino, M. (1989), *De Vita Coelitus Comparanda: Marsilio Ficino, Three Books on Life*, A Critical Edition and Translation with Introduction and Notes by Carol V. Kaske and John R. Clark, Binghamton, NY: Medieval and Renaissance Texts and Studies, Book 3, Chapter XXI.

Hankins, J. (2015), 'Humanism and Music in Italy', in A. M. B. Berger and J. Rodin (eds), *The Cambridge History of Fifteenth-Century Music*, 231–262, Cambridge: Cambridge University Press.

Hargreaves, D. and A. North (1997), *The Social Psychology of Music*, Oxford: Oxford University Press.

Harrán, D. (1997), 'Toward a Rhetorical Code of Early Music Performance', *The Journal of Musicology*, 15: 19–42.

Harrison, C. (2011), 'Augustine and the Art of Music', in J. Begbie and S. Guthrie (eds), *Resonant Witness: Conversations between Music and Theology*, 27–45, Grand Rapids, MI: Eerdmans.

Higgins, K. (1991), *The Music of Our Lives*, Philadelphia, PA: Temple University Press.

Horne, B. L. (1985), 'A Civitas of Sound: On Luther and Music', *Theology*, 88: 21–28.

Jourdain, R. (1997), *Music, the Brain and Ecstasy: How Music Captures Our Imagination*, New York: Avin Books.

Kim, H-A. (2006), 'Erasmus on Sacred Music', *Reformation and Renaissance Review*, 8: 277–300.

Kim, H-A. (2008), *Humanism and the Reform of Sacred Music in Early Modern England: John Merbecke the Orator and the Booke of Common Praier Noted (1550)*, Aldershot: Ashgate.

Kivy, P. (1990), *Music Alone: Philosophical Reflections on the Purely Musical Experience*, Ithaca, NY: Cornell University Press.

MacDiarmid, F. (2018), 'De Utilitate Cantorum: Unitive Aspects of Singing in Early Christian Thought', *The Anglican Theological Review*, 100: 291–309.

Maritain, J. (1973), *Integral Humanism: Temporal and Spiritual Problems of a New Christendom*, Notre Dame, IN: University of Notre Dame Press.

Mathiesen, T. (2002), 'Greek Music Theory', in T. S. Christensen (ed.), *The Cambridge History of Western Music Theory*, Cambridge: Cambridge University Press.

McGilchrist, I. (2012), *The Master and His Emissary*, New Haven, CT and London: Yale University Press.

Mellers, W. (1946), *Music and Society: England and the European Tradition*, London: Dobson.

Mesoudi, A. (2011), *Cultural Evolution: How Darwinian Theory Can Explain Human Culture and Synthesize the Social Sciences*, Chicago: Chicago University Press.

Mobsby, I. (2008), *God Unknown: The Trinity in Contemporary Spirituality and Mission*, Norwich: Canterbury Press.

Mobsby, I. (2018), 'The Place of New Monasticism in a Post-Secular Culture': lecture delivered at the *Diocesan Spirituality Advisors' Conference*, Launde Abbey, Leicestershire, 10 April.

Morgan, S. and J. Boyce-Tillman (2016), *A River Rather Than a Road: The Community Choir as Spiritual Experience*, Oxford, Bern: Peter Lang.

Norris, C. ed. (1989), *Music and the Politics of Culture*, London: Lawrence and Wishart.

Pearce, E., J. Launay, and R. I. M. Dunbar (2015), 'The Ice-breaker Effect: Singing Mediates Fast Social Bonding', *Royal Society Open Science*, 2: 1–9. Available at: http://rsos.royalsocietypublishing.org/content/2/10/150221.

Plutarch (1967 [*c.* AD 100]), *Plutrach's Moralia*, trans. P. H. de Lacy and B. Einarson, Cambridge, MA: Harvard University Press.

Russell, D. (2001), *Quintilian: The Orator's Education*, 5 volumes. The Loeb Classical Library. Cambridge, MA: Harvard University Press.

Sacks, O. (1973), *Awakenings*, London: Duckworth.

Sacks, O. (1985), *The Man Who Mistook His Wife for a Hat*, London: Duckworth.

Sacks, O. (2007), *Musicophilia: Tales of Music and the Brain*, London: Picador.

Salaman, C. (1996), 'Introduction', in *Meditations of the Soul: Selected Letters of Marsilio Ficino*, translated from the Latin by Members of the Language Department of the School of Economic Science, London: Shepheard-Walwyn.

Saliers, D. (2007), *Music and Theology*, Nashville: Abingdon Press.

Storr, A. (1992), *Music and the Mind*, London: Harper Collins.

Van Deusen, N. (1999), 'Musica, De', in A. D. Fitzgerald et al. (eds), *Augustine through the Ages: An Encyclopedia*, Grand Rapids, MI: Baker Academic.

Voss, A., ed. (2006), *Marsilio Ficino*, Berkeley, CA: North Atlantic Books.

Wegman, R. C. (2005), *The Crisis of Music in Early Modern Europe, 1470–1530* (2005), New York: Routledge.

Weinstein, D., J. Launay, E. Pearce, R. I. M. Dunbar and L. Stewart (2016), 'Singing and Social Bonding: Changes in Connectivity and Pain Threshold as a Function of Group Size', *Evolution and Human Behavior*, 37: 152–158.

Williams, R. (1994), *Open to Judgement: Sermons and Addresses*, London: Darton, Longman & Todd.

8

Human Dignity, Equality and Liberty in Protestant Thought

John Witte Jr.

This chapter tests the meaning and takes the measure of human dignity in the Protestant tradition. My main argument is that sixteenth-century Protestants had a deep and distinctive understanding of human dignity, equality and liberty, which still shapes Protestant understandings today. The essence of human dignity, Protestants have long taught, lies in the juxtaposition of human depravity and human sanctity. Human dignity is something of a divine fulcrum that keeps our depravity and sanctity in balance. The essence of human equality lies in our radical calling to be God's prophets, priests and kings with divinely appointed vocations to discharge. Human equality is a standing rebuke to all false hierarchies within church, state and society alike. And the essence of human liberty lies in our right and duty to serve God, neighbour and self, and to do so with the ominous assurance of divine judgement. Human liberty is the divine calling that keeps our individuality and community in balance.

These Protestant teachings, I argue, were already adumbrated in Martin Luther's famous little tract *Freedom of a Christian* (1520) and then elaborated by Protestants over the next century. Luther's tract was something of a Protestant *Dignitatis Humanae*[1] in its day, an enduring theological statement on the essence of human dignity in and on distinctly Protestant terms. Several theological teachings in this little tract were filled with radical political, social and legal implications. While Luther did not draw out these implications, later sixteenth- and seventeenth-century Protestants did, particularly followers of John Calvin who faced persecution and genocide that were killing their coreligionists by the tens of thousands, even with the primitive weaponry of the day. Their political transformation of Luther's original teachings helped render Protestantism a formidable agent of democratic revolutions fought in the name of human rights.

The last part of this chapter reflects on how these early teachings still shape Protestant instincts about human dignity, human equality and human rights today.

It must be stressed that I am presenting only one Protestant stream of reflection on human dignity, albeit a deep and enduring one. Other Protestants over the centuries have taken their departure more directly from those famous biblical texts proclaiming that persons are created in the 'image of God' with reason, will and memory; that they are the apex and lords of creation made 'a little lower than the angels'; that they are stewards called to 'subdue the earth' and 'to dress and keep the garden'; that they are called to partake of the universal spiritual dignity of Christ and the cruciform sacrificial ethic of 'the Word made flesh'. All these and other Protestant views of human dignity tend to resonate more closely with prevailing Patristic, Catholic and Humanist constructions that are featured elsewhere in this volume. And some of them are considerably better known and more frequently proffered today, especially in ecumenical discussions (Baker 1961; Trinkhaus 1970; Tinder 1981; Moltmann 1984; McCrudden 2014). My rendering of the Protestant teaching on human dignity herein is not meant to deprecate these other Protestant contributions but to complement them.

Sinner and saint, servant and lord

Martin Luther's *Freedom of a Christian* (1520) was one of the defining documents of the Protestant Reformation, and it remains one of the classic tracts of the Protestant tradition still today.[2] Written on the eve of his excommunication from the Church, this was Luther's last ecumenical gesture towards Rome before making his incendiary exit. Much of the tract was written with a quiet gentility and piety that belied the heated polemics of the day and Luther's own ample perils of body and soul. Luther dedicated the tract to Pope Leo X, adorning it with a robust preface addressed to the 'blessed father'. He vowed that he had to date 'spoken only good and honourable words' concerning Leo and offered to retract anything that might have betrayed 'indiscretion and impiety'. 'I am the kind of person', he wrote in seeming earnest, 'who would wish you all good things eternally' (LW 31:334–336).

Luther was concerned, however, that the papal office had saddled Leo with a false sense of dignity. 'You are a servant of servants (*servus servorum*) within the Church', Luther wrote to Leo, citing the classic title of the Bishop of Rome (LW 31:341). And as a 'servant of God for others, and over others, and for the sake of others', you properly enjoy a 'sublime dignity' of office (LW 31:341–342).³ But those 'obsequious flatterers' and 'pestilential fellows' of your papal court do not regard you as a humble servant. Instead, they treat you as 'a vicar of Christ', as 'a demigod [who] may command and require whatever you wish'. They 'pretend that you are lord of the world, allow no one to be considered a Christian unless he accepts your authority, and prate that you have power over heaven, hell and purgatory'. Surely, you do not believe any of this, Luther wrote to Leo, tongue near cheek. Surely, you can see that 'they err who ascribe to you alone the right of interpreting Scripture' and 'who exalt you above a council and the church universal'. 'Perhaps I am being presumptuous' to address you so, Luther allowed at the end of his preface. But when a fellow Christian, even a pope, is exposed to such 'dangerous' teachings and trappings, God commands that a fellow brother offer him biblical counsel, without regard for his 'dignity or lack of dignity' (LW 31:341–342).⁴

In later pages of the *Freedom of a Christian* and in several other writings in that same crucial year of 1520, Luther took aim at other persons who were, as he put it, 'puffed up because of their dignity'.⁵ He inveighed at greatest length against the lower clergy, who, in his view, used the 'false power of fabricated sacraments' to 'tyrannize the Christian conscience' and to 'fleece the sheep' of Christendom.⁶ He criticized jurists for spinning the thick tangle of special benefits, privileges, exemptions and immunities that elevated the clergy above the laity, and inoculated them from legal accountability to local magistrates (LW 44:157ff., 202ff.). He was not much kinder to princes, nobles and merchants – those 'harpies', as he later called them, 'blinded by their arrogance' and trading on their office, pedigree and wealth to lord it over the languishing commoner (LW 7:182ff.; LW 44:203ff.).⁷ What all these pretentious folks fail to see, Luther wrote, is that 'there is no basic difference in status ... between laymen and priests, princes and bishops, religious and secular' (LW 44:129.). Before God all are equal.

Luther's *Freedom of a Christian* thus became, in effect, his *Dignitatis Humanae* – his bold new declaration on human nature and human freedom that described all Christians in his world regardless of their 'dignity or lack of dignity' as conventionally defined. Pope and prince, noble and pauper, man and woman, slave and free – all persons in Christendom, Luther declared, share equally in a doubly paradoxical nature. First, each person is at once a saint and a sinner, righteous and reprobate, saved and lost – *simul iustus et peccator* in Luther's signature phrase (LW 31:344–347, 358–361).⁸ Second, each person is at once a free lord who is subject to no one and a dutiful servant who is subject to everyone.

Only through these twin paradoxes, Luther wrote, can we 'comprehend the lofty dignity of the Christian' (LW 31:355).

Every Christian 'has a two fold nature', Luther argued in expounding his doctrine of *simul iustus et peccator.* We are at once body and soul, flesh and spirit, sinner and saint, 'outer man and inner man'. These 'two men in the same man contradict each other' and remain perennially at war (LW 31:344). On the one hand, as bodily creatures, we are born in sin and bound by sin. By our carnal natures, we are prone to lust and lasciviousness, evil and egoism, perversion and pathos of untold dimensions (LW 31:344, 358–361).[9] Even the best of persons, even the titans of virtue in the Bible – Abraham, David, Peter and Paul – sin all the time (LW 19:47–48, LW 23:146). In and of ourselves, we are all totally depraved and deserving of eternal death. On the other hand, as spiritual creatures, we are reborn in faith and freed from sin. By our spiritual natures, we are prone to love and charity, goodness and sacrifice, virtue and peacefulness. Even the worst of persons, even the reprobate thief nailed on the next cross to Christ's, can be saved from sin. In spite of ourselves, we are all totally redeemed and assured of eternal life (LW 31:344–354, 368–377).

It is through faith and hope in the Word of God, Luther argued, that a person moves from sinner to saint, from bondage to freedom. This was the essence of Luther's doctrine of justification by faith alone. No human work of any sort – even worship, contemplation, meditation, charity and other supposed meritorious conduct – can make a person just and righteous before God. For sin holds the person fast and perverts his or her every work. 'One thing, and only one thing, is necessary for Christian life, righteousness, and freedom', Luther declared. 'That one thing is the most holy Word of God, the gospel of Christ' (LW 31:345). To put one's faith in this Word, to accept its gracious promise of eternal salvation, is to claim one's freedom from sin and from its attendant threat of eternal damnation. And it is to join the communion of saints that begins imperfectly in this life and continues perfectly in the life to come.

A saint by faith remains a sinner by nature, Luther insisted, and the paradox of good and evil within the same person remains until death. But there is 'a difference between sinners and sinners', Luther wrote: 'There are some sinners who confess that they have sinned but do not long to be justified; instead, they give up hope and go on sinning so that when they die they despair, and while they live, they are enslaved to the world. There are other sinners who confess that they sin and have sinned, but they are sorry for this, hate themselves for it, long to be justified, and under groaning constantly pray to God for righteousness. This is the people of God', the saints who are saved, despite their sin.[10]

This brought Luther to a related paradox of human nature – that each Christian is at once a lord who is subject to no one and a priest who is servant to everyone. On the one hand, Luther argued, 'every Christian is by faith so exalted above all things that, by virtue of a spiritual power, he is [a] lord' (LW 31:354). As a redeemed saint, as an 'inner man', a Christian is utterly free in his conscience, utterly free in his innermost being. He is like the greatest king on earth, who is above and beyond the power of everyone. No earthly authority – whether pope, prince or parent – can impose 'a single syllable of the law' upon him (LW 36:70, echoing LW 31:344–346). No earthly authority can intrude upon the sanctuary of his conscience, can endanger his assurance and comfort of eternal life. This is 'the splendid privilege', the 'inestimable power and liberty' that every Christian enjoys (LW 31:355–358).

On the other hand, Luther wrote, every Christian is a priest, who freely performs good works in service of his or her neighbour and in glorification of God (LW 31:355–356).[11] 'Christ has made it possible for us, provided we believe in him, to be not only his brethren, co-heirs, and fellow-kings, but also his fellow-priests', Luther wrote. And thus, in imitation of Christ, we freely serve our neighbours, offering instruction, charity, prayer, admonition and sacrifice even to the point of death (LW 31:355; see also LW 36:241). We abide by the law of God so far as we are able so that others may see our good work and be similarly impelled to seek God's grace. We freely discipline and drive ourselves to do as much good as we are able, not so that we may be saved but so that others may be served. 'A man does not live for himself alone', Luther wrote, 'he lives only for others' (LW 31:364–365; see also LW 51:86–87). The precise nature of our priestly service to others depends upon our gifts and upon the vocation in which God calls us to use them (LW 38:188; LW 28:171–172). But we are all to serve freely and fully as God's priests.

'Who can then comprehend the lofty dignity of the Christian?' Luther wrote. 'By virtue of his royal power he rules over all things, death, life, and sin.' The person is entirely free from the necessity of doing good works and fully immune from the authority of any one. But by virtue of 'his priestly glory, he is omnipotent with God because he does the things which God asks and requires' (LW 31:355; see also LW 17:209ff.). He devotes himself entirely to doing good works for his neighbour, he submits himself completely to the needs of others.

Such are the paradoxes of the Christian life in Luther's view. We are at once sinners and saints; we are at once lords and servants. We can do nothing good; we can do nothing but good. We are utterly free; we are everywhere bound. The more a person thinks himself a saint, the more sinful in fact he becomes. The more a person thinks herself a sinner, the more saintly she in fact becomes. The more a person acts like a lord, the more he is called to be a servant. The more a person acts as a servant, the more in fact she has become a lord. This is the paradoxical nature of human life. And this is the essence of human dignity.

Luther intended his *Freedom of a Christian* to be a universal statement for his world of Christendom – a summary of 'the whole of the Christian life in a brief form', as he put it in his preface to Leo (LW 31:343). He grounded his views in the Bible, liberally peppering his tract with all manner of biblical citations and quotations. He wove into his narrative several strong threads of argument pulled selectively from a number of Church Fathers and late medieval Christian mystics. He published his tract both in Latin and in simple German, seeking to reach both the scholar and the commoner alike. He wrote with a pastoral directness and emotional empathy, convinced that if he could point out the Jekyll and Hyde in everyone, his readers would find both ample humility and ample comfort. So convinced was Luther of the veracity and cogency of his views that he believed even the Jews, the one perennial sojourner in his world of Christendom, would convert en masse to the Gospel once they heard it in this simple form.[12] Though this latter aspiration proved fanciful, Luther's views on human dignity did command an impressive readership among Christians. *Freedom of a Christian* was a best seller in its day – going through twelve printings in its first two years and five editions by 1524. It remained a perennial favourite of commentaries and sermons long after Luther's passing and well beyond the world of Lutheranism (Edwards Jr. 1981: 39, 64, 100–101).[13] It is no small commentary on the enduring ecumenical efficacy of Luther's views of human nature, dignity and freedom that they lie at the heart of the *Joint Declaration on the Doctrine of Justification*, signed by Catholic and Evangelical leaders on 31 October 1999.[14]

Human dignity and human freedom in later Protestant thought

What all this elegant dialectic theology meant for the nature of freedom of the Christian in this world, Luther's little tract did not so clearly say. Luther did make clear that all Christians have the freedom and duty to follow the Bible conscientiously and to speak out against human ideas and institutions that conflict with the Bible. The Bible was for Luther the great equalizer of Christians – to the remarkable point of allowing Luther, a lowly Augustinian friar from an obscure German town, to address His Holiness Leo X as if he were the pope's equal. Luther also made clear that clergy and laity are fundamentally equal in dignity and responsibility before God. The traditional assumption that the clergy were superior to the laity and entitled to all manner of special privileges, immunities and exemptions was anathema to Luther. Luther at once laicized the clergy and clericalized the laity, treating the office of preaching and teaching as just one other vocation alongside many others that a conscientious Christian could properly and freely pursue.[15]

Luther's *Freedom of a Christian*, however, was no political manifesto on freedom. Spiritual freedom may well coexist with political bondage, Luther insisted. The spiritual equality of persons and vocations before God does not necessarily entail a social equality with all others (LW 31:354–356, 364–365). Luther became doubly convinced of this discordance after witnessing the bloody Peasants' Revolt in Germany in 1525 and the growing numbers of radical egalitarian and antinomian experiments engineered out of his favourite theological doctrines of the priesthood of all believers and justification by faith alone. In the course of the next two decades, Luther defended with increasing stridency traditional social, economic, political and ecclesiastical hierarchies as a necessary feature of this earthly life.

Luther came to defend this disparity between the spiritual and temporal dimensions of human freedom, dignity and status with his doctrine of the two kingdoms. God has ordained two kingdoms or realms in which humanity is destined to live, Luther argued, the earthly or political kingdom and the heavenly or spiritual kingdom. The earthly kingdom is the realm of creation, of natural and civic life, where a person operates primarily by reason, law and passion. The heavenly kingdom is the realm of redemption, of spiritual and eternal life, where a person operates primarily by faith, hope and charity. These two kingdoms embrace parallel forms of righteousness and justice, truth and knowledge, but they remain separate and distinct. The earthly kingdom is distorted by sin and governed by the law. The heavenly kingdom is renewed by grace and guided by the Gospel. A Christian is a citizen of both kingdoms at once and invariably comes under the distinctive jurisdiction of each kingdom. As a heavenly citizen, the Christian remains free in his conscience, called to live fully by the light of the Word of God. But as an earthly citizen, the Christian is bound by law and called to obey the structures and strictures of ecclesiastical, political and parental authority, even if they are sometimes hard and abusive (Witte 2002: 87–118).

Later Protestants, however, retreated from this quietism, especially as they faced pogroms, inquisitions and genocides that were killing their co-religionists by the tens of thousands from the later sixteenth century on. Particularly

Lutherans in Magdeburg and Calvinists in France, the Netherlands, Scotland, England and America went from turning cheeks to swinging swords against their tyrannical oppressors. And they used their writing desks and pulpits to work out a logic of democratic revolution in protection of their basic rights.[16]

Many Calvinist writers converted Luther's famous doctrine that a person is at once sinner and saint into a firm anthropological foundation for later Western theories of democracy and human rights. On the one hand, these Reformed Protestants argued, every person is created in the image of God and justified by faith in God. Every person is called to a distinct vocation, which stands equal in dignity and sanctity to all others. Every person is a prophet, priest and king, and responsible to exhort, to minister and to rule in the community. Every person thus stands equal before God and neighbour. Every person is vested with a natural liberty to live, to believe, to love and serve God and neighbour. Every person is entitled to the vernacular Scripture, to education, to work in a vocation. On the other hand, these Reformed Protestants argued, every person is sinful and prone to evil and egoism. Every person needs the restraint of the law to deter him from evil and to drive him to repentance. Every person needs the association of others to exhort, minister and rule her with law and with love. Every person, therefore, is inherently a communal creature. Every person belongs to a family, a church, a political community.

From the later sixteenth to the later eighteenth centuries, various Reformed groups recast these Protestant doctrines of the person and society into democratic social forms. Since all persons stand equal before God, they must stand equal before God's political agents in the state. Since God has vested all persons with natural liberties of life and belief, the state must ensure them of similar civil liberties. Since God has called all persons to be prophets, priests and kings, the state must protect their constitutional freedoms to speak, to preach and to rule in the community. Since God has created persons as social creatures, the state must promote and protect a plurality of social institutions, particularly the church and the family.

In this same period, they recast Protestant doctrines of sin and its limits into democratic political forms. The political office must be protected against the sinfulness of the political official. Political power, like ecclesiastical power, must be distributed among self-checking executive, legislative and judicial branches. Officials must be elected to limited terms of office. Laws must be clearly codified and discretion closely guarded. If officials abuse their office, they must be disobeyed. If they persist in their abuse, they must be removed, even if by revolutionary force and regicide. These Protestant teachings were among the driving ideological forces behind the revolts of the French Huguenots, Dutch Pietists and Scottish Presbyterians against their monarchical oppressors in the later sixteenth and seventeenth centuries. They were critical weapons in the arsenal of the Puritan revolutionaries in seventeenth-century England and eighteenth-century America. They remained important sources of inspiration and instruction during the great modern age of democratic construction on both sides of the Atlantic.

Protestants instincts about dignity, equality and liberty today

Half a millennium after its publication, Luther's *Freedom of a Christian* still shapes many Protestants' instincts about human dignity and human freedom.

First, Luther's doctrine of *simul iustus et peccator* renders many Protestants instinctively sceptical about too optimistic a view of human nature and too easy a conflation of human dignity and human sanctity. Such views take too little account of the radicality of human sin and the necessity of divine grace. They give too little credibility to the inherent human need for discipline and order, accountability and judgement. They give too little credence to the perennial interplay of the civil, theological and pedagogical uses of law, to the perpetual demand to balance deterrence, retribution and reformation in discharging authority within the home, church, state and other associations. They give too little insight into the necessity for safeguarding every office of authority from abuse and misuse. A theory of human dignity that fails to take into account the combined depravity and sanctity of the human person is theologically and politically deficient, if not dangerous.

This cardinal insight into the twofold nature of humanity was hardly unique to Martin Luther and is readily amenable to many other formulations. Luther's formula of *simul iustus et peccator* was a crisp Christian distillation of a universal insight about human nature that can be traced to the earliest Greek and Hebrew sources of the West. The gripping epics of Homer and Hesiod are nothing if not chronicles of the perennial dialectic of good and evil, virtue and vice, hero and villain, in the ancient Greek world. The very first chapters of the Hebrew Bible paint pictures of these same two human natures, now with Yahweh's imprint on them. The more familiar picture is that of Adam and Eve who were created equally in the image of God and vested with a natural right and duty to perpetuate life, to cultivate property, to dress and keep the creation (Gen. 1:26-30; 2:7, 15-23 [Revised Standard Version]). The less familiar picture is that of their first child

Cain, who murdered his brother Abel and was called into judgement by God and condemned for his sin. Yet 'God put a mark on Cain', Genesis reads, both to protect him in his life and to show that he remained a child of God despite the enormity of his sin (Gen. 4:1-16.).[17] One message of this ancient Hebrew text is that we are not only the beloved children of Adam and Eve, who bear the image of God, with all the divine perquisites and privileges of Paradise. We are also the sinful siblings of Cain, who bear the mark of God, with its ominous assurance both that we shall be called into divine judgement for what we have done and that there is forgiveness even for the gravest of sins we have committed.

Luther believed that it is only through faith and hope in Christ that we can ultimately be assured of divine forgiveness and eternal salvation. He further believed that it was only through a life of biblical meditation, prayer, worship, charity and sacramental living that a person could hold his or her depravity in check and aspire to greater sanctity. I believe that, too, as do many Christians today. But this is not to say that, in this life, Christians have the only insights into the twofold nature of humanity and the only effective means of balancing the realities of human depravity and the aspirations for human sanctity. Any religious tradition that takes seriously the Jekyll and Hyde in all of us has its own understanding of ultimate reconciliation of these two natures and its own methods of balancing them in this life. And who are we Christians to say how God will ultimately judge these?

Luther also believed that the ominous assurance of the judgement of God is ultimately a source of comfort, not of fear. The first sinners in the Bible – Adam, Eve and Cain – were given divine due process: they were confronted with the evidence, asked to defend themselves, given a chance to repent, spared the ultimate sanction of death and then assured of a second trial on the Day of Judgment, with appointed divine counsel – Christ himself, our self-appointed 'advocate before the Father' (1 John 2:1). The only time that God deliberately withheld divine due process was in the capital trial of His Son – and that was the only time it was and has been necessary. The political implications of this are very simple: if God gives due process in judging us, we should give due process in judging others. If God's tribunals feature at least basic rules of procedure, evidence, representation and advocacy, human tribunals should feature at least the same. The demand for due process is a deep human instinct, and it has driven Protestants over the centuries, along with many others before and with them, to be strident advocates for procedural rights.

Second, Luther's doctrine of the lordship and priesthood of all believers renders many Protestants instinctively jealous about liberty and equality – but on their own quite distinct theological terms. In the modern liberal tradition, liberty and equality are generally defended on grounds of popular sovereignty and inalienable rights. The American Declaration of Independence (1776) proclaimed it a 'self-evident truth' 'that all men are created equal [and] ... are endowed with certain unalienable rights'. The Universal Declaration of Human Rights (1948) proclaimed 'that all men are born free and equal in rights and dignity'. Protestants can resonate more with the norms of liberty and equality in these documents than with the theories of popular sovereignty and inalienable rights that generally undergird them.

The heart of the Protestant theory of liberty is that we are all lords on this earth. We are utterly free in the sanctuary of our conscience, entirely unencumbered in our relationship with God. We enjoy a sovereign immunity from any human structures and strictures, even those of the church when they seek to impose upon this divine freedom. Such talk of 'sovereign immunity' sounds something like modern liberal notions of 'popular sovereignty'. And such talk of 'lordship' sounds something like the democratic right to 'self-rule'. Protestants have thus long found ready allies in liberals and others who advocate liberty of conscience and democratic freedoms on these grounds. But when theologically pressed, many Protestants will defend liberty of conscience not because of their own popular sovereignty but because of the absolute sovereignty of God, whose relationship with his children cannot be trespassed. Many Protestants will defend certain unalienable rights not in the interest of preserving their personal privacy but in the interest of discharging their divine duties.

The heart of the Protestant theory of equality is that we are all priests before God. 'You are a chosen race, a royal priesthood, a holy nation, God's own people' (1 Pet. 2:9; Rev. 5:10, 20:6). Among you, 'there is neither Jew nor Greek, there is neither slave nor free, there is neither male nor female; for you are all one in Christ Jesus' (Gal. 3:28; Col. 3:10-11; Eph. 2:14-15.). These and many other biblical passages, among Luther's favourites, have long inspired a reflexive egalitarian impulse in Protestants. All are equal before God. All are priests who must serve their neighbours. All have vocations that count. All have gifts to be included. This common calling of all to be priests transcends differences of culture, economy, gender and more.

Such teachings have led a few Protestant groups over the centuries to experiment with intensely communitarian states where life is gracious, lovely and long. Most Protestant groups, however, view life in such states as 'brutish, nasty and short', for sin invariably perverts them. Structures and strictures of law and authority are necessary and useful, most Protestants believe. But such structures need to be as open, egalitarian and democratic as possible. Hierarchy is a danger to be indulged only so far as necessary. To be sure, Protestants over the centuries have often defied these founding ideals and have earnestly partaken of all manner of elitism, chauvinism, racism, antisemitism, tyranny, patriarchy, slavery, apartheid and more. And they have sometimes engaged in outrageous hypocrisy and casuistry to defend such shameful pathos. But an instinct for egalitarianism – for embracing all persons equally, for treating all vocations respectfully, for arranging all associations horizontally, for levelling the life of the earthly kingdom so none is obstructed in access to God – is a Lutheran gene in the theological genetic code of Protestantism.

Finally, Luther's notion that a person is at once free and bound by the law has powerful implications for our modern understanding of human rights. For Luther, the Christian is free in order to follow the commandments of the faith – or, in more familiar and general modern parlance, a person has rights in order to discharge duties. Freedoms and commandments, rights and duties, belong together in Luther's formulation. To speak of one without the other is ultimately destructive. Rights without duties to guide them quickly become claims of self-indulgence. Duties without rights to exercise them quickly become sources of deep guilt.

Protestants have thus long translated the moral duties set out in the Decalogue into reciprocal rights. The First Table of the Decalogue prescribes duties of love that each person owes to God – to honour God and God's name, to observe the Sabbath day and to worship, to avoid false gods and false swearing. The Second Table prescribes duties of love that each person owes to neighbours – to honour one's parents and other authorities, not to kill, not to commit adultery, not to steal, not to bear false witness, not to covet. Church, state and family alike are responsible for the communication and enforcement of these cardinal moral duties, Protestants have long argued. But it is also the responsibility of each person to ensure that he and his neighbours discharge these moral duties.

This is one important impetus for Protestants to translate duties into rights. A person's duties towards God can be cast as the rights to religious exercise: the right to honour God and God's name, the right to rest and worship on one's Sabbath, the right to be free from false gods and false oaths. Each person's duties towards a neighbour, in turn, can be cast as a neighbour's right to have that duty discharged. One person's duties not to kill, to commit adultery, to steal or to bear false witness thus gives rise to another person's rights to life, property, fidelity and reputation. For a person to insist upon vindication of these latter rights is not necessarily to act out of self-love. It is also to act out of neighbourly love. To claim one's own right is in part a charitable act to induce one's neighbour to discharge his or her divinely ordained duty.

Nearly half a century ago, the great American jurist Grant Gilmore put what he took as the most enduring legal lesson of Protestantism: 'The better the society the less law there will be', Gilmore said. 'In Heaven, there will be no law, and the lion will lie down with the lamb. In Hell, there will be nothing but law, and due process will be meticulously observed' (Gilmore 1977: 110–111). This is a rather common Protestant sentiment, which Luther did much to propound in some of his early writings. But a Protestant, faithful to Luther's more enduring insights, might properly reach the exact opposite projection. In Heaven, there will be pure law, and thus the lamb will lie down with the lion. In Hell, there will be no law, and thus all will devour each other eternally. Heaven will exalt due process, and each will always receive what's due. Hell will exalt pure caprice, and no one will ever know what's coming.

Notes

1   *Dignitatis Humanae:* 'Declaration on Religious Freedom'. On the right of the person and of communities to social and civil freedom in matters religious. Promulgated by Pope Paul VI, 7 December 1965.

2   *De Libertate Christiana* (1520), in *D. Martin Luthers Werke: Kritische Gesamtausgabe* (Weimar: H. Boehlaus Nachfolger, 1883–), 7:49–73 [hereafter WA], translated in Jaroslav Pelikan et al., eds., *Luther's Works* (Philadelphia: Muhlenberg Press, 1955–), 31:327–377 [hereafter LW]. A shorter German edition, *Die Freiheit eines Christenmenschen*, appears in WA 7:20–38.

3   The quote is from Luther, M. (1961 [1515–1516]: 8). Many of the teachings from these *Lectures* are repeated in Luther's *Freedom of a Christian*.

4   See similar sentiments in Luther's *Address to the Christian Nobility of the German Nation concerning the Reform of the Christian Estate* (1520), LW 44:123–217, at 136.

5   Quotation is from Luther's *Lectures on Genesis 38–44* (1544), LW 7:182.

6   See esp. LW 44:126–155; *The Babylonian Captivity of the Church* (1520), LW 36:11–126; *Treatise on Good Works* (1520), LW 44:21–114, at 87–94, with expansion in *The Keys* (1530), LW 40:321–370. In LW 44:158, Luther recommended that a new imperial law be passed against papal appointments of clergy so that 'no confirmation of any dignity whatsoever shall henceforth be secured from Rome'. In LW 44:129 and LW 36:117, Luther attacked the notion that the clergy were special because of the 'indelible mark' of their ordination, terming this 'a laughingstock'.

7   See also Luther's fuller statement in *Temporal Authority: To What Extent It Should Be Obeyed* (1523), in LW 45:75–129.

8   The theme recurs repeatedly in Luther's later writings. See, e.g., LW 12:328, 27:230ff., 32:173; WA 39/1:21, 492, 552.

9   See also LW 25:120–130, 204–213.

10   *Lectures on Romans*, 120. See also LW 23:146; LW 12:328–330; LW 8:9–12. In his later *Commentary on Genesis*, Luther argued that the teaching of *simul iustus et peccator* was a better way to understand human dignity than to focus on the familiar creation story that humans are created 'in the image and likeness of God'. Luther, a former Augustinian friar, was well aware of St Augustine's view that 'the image of God is the power of the soul – memory, the mind or intellect, and will'. He knew the traditional teaching that 'the similitude of God consists in this, that the memory is provided with hope, the intellect with faith, and the will with love'. 'Memory, will, and mind we have indeed', Luther allowed. And yes, 'the image of God was something most excellent, in which were included eternal life, everlasting freedom from fear, and everything that is good. However, through sin this image was so obscured and corrupted that we cannot grasp it even with our intellect'. *Commentary on Genesis*, LW 1:60–65. Hence the need to hold sinner and saint in dialectical tension.

11   See also LW 36:112–116, 138–140, LW 40:21–23; LW 13:152, and esp. the long diatribe in LW 39:137–224.

12   See *That Jesus Christ Was Born a Jew* (1523), in LW 45:129.

13   See also the remarkable propaganda work on Luther done by the Cranach family, discussed in Ozment (2013).

14   *Joint Declaration on the Doctrine of Justification by Faith* (Grand Rapids, MI: Wm. B. Eerdmans, 1999).

15   See further Martin Luther, *Concerning the Ministry* (1523), in LW 40:21ff.

16   This and the next three paragraphs are distilled from (Witte 2007).

17   See alternative exegeses in Mellinkoff (1981) and Westerman (1990).

References

Baker, H. (1961), *The Image of Man: A Study of the Idea of Human Dignity in Classical Antiquity, The Middle Ages, and the Renaissance*, New York: Harper & Bros.

Gilmore, G. (1977), *The Ages of American Law*, Chicago: University of Chicago Press.

Luther, M. (1520), *De Libertate Christiana*, in *D. Martin Luthers Werke: Kritische Gesamtausgabe* (Weimar: H. Boehlaus Nachfolger, 1883–), 7: 49–73[WA], translated in Jaroslav Pelikan et al., eds., *Luther's Works* (Philadelphia, PA: Muhlenberg Press, 1955–), 31: 327–377 [hereafter LW]. A shorter German edition, *Die Freiheit eines Christenmenschen*, appears in WA 7:20–38.

Luther, M. (1961 [1515–1516]), *Luther: Lectures on Romans* [1515–1516], trans. Wilhelm Pauck, Philadelphia, PA: Westminster Press.

McCrudden, C., ed. (2014), *Understanding Human Dignity*, Oxford/New York: Oxford University Press.

Mellinkoff, R. (1981), *The Mark of Cain*, Berkeley, CA: University of California Press.

Moltmann, J. (1984), *On Human Dignity, Political Theology and Ethics*, trans. M. Douglas Meeks, Philadelphia, PA: Fortress Press.

Ozment, S. (2013), *The Serpent and the Lamb: Cranach, Luther, and the Making of the Reformation*, New Haven, CT: Yale University Press.

Tinder, G. (1981), *Against Fate: An Essay on Personal Dignity*, Notre Dame, IN: University of Notre Dame Press.

Trinkhaus, C. (1970), *In Our Image and Likeness: Humanity and Divinity in Italian Humanist Thought*, 2 vols, London and Chicago: University of Chicago Press.

Westerman, C. (1990), *Genesis 1–11: A Commentary*, repr. ed., Minneapolis, MN: Augsburg Publishing House.

Witte, J. Jr. (2002), *Law and Protestantism: The Legal Teachings of the Lutheran Reformation*, Cambridge: Cambridge University Press.

Witte, J. Jr. (2007), *The Reformation of Rights: Law, Religion, and Human Rights in Early Modern Calvinism*, Cambridge: Cambridge University Press.

9

The Dignity of the Ancients and the Dignity of the Moderns

John Milbank

Dignity and rights today

The current academic debate about human dignity has a strange feature. Unlike most such debates, it scarcely commences with any obvious, given theoretical importance of the topic. Instead, it begins with the circumstance that 'dignity' and its verbal cognates have increasingly entered into our legal and media descriptions of human nature and its predicaments. For some, this usage is a superficial ornament to a more basic discourse of 'rights', and therefore 'dignity' should be a subject of at best rhetorical and not substantive consideration. At worst, it is a cipher for outmoded, hierarchical and essentialist dogmas that tend to dilute a recognition and extension of the rights of humanity. For others, 'dignity' is held in some way to supplement 'rights', while for a small intellectual minority (myself included) it is seen as a more valid alternative to 'rights'.

Yet all parties to this obscure debate concerning dignity (Should there be a debate at all? What is this debate about?) agree that it arises not initially from academic reflection or first principles – ironically enough, since *dignitas* in one sense of scholastic usage denoted 'first principle' – but from academic reflection on recent public usage.

This usage can be doubly dated. Primarily, 'human dignity' was newly (for the twentieth century) yoked to 'human rights' after 1948 in both the United Nations' Declaration of Human Rights and the old German Federal Republic's provisional (in view of the division of the country) *Grundgesetz* (Rosen 2012a: 38–47, 77–104). One can understand this yoking loosely in terms of a double rejection both of totalitarian suppression of human freedom and of unprecedentedly brutal treatment of certain classes of human beings which deliberately or effectively denied their human status.

But more precisely, one can understand this yoking in terms of the coming together of two quite different and indeed fundamentally opposed traditions of political and ethical reflection. The first is the liberal, eventually secular tradition of human rights that had been made the basis of the American Constitution and more fitfully of the various French constitutions since the Revolution (Rosen 2012b: 89–98; Moyn 2013; Rosen 2013: 143–154). For this tradition, the high status of human beings is self-given, whether because they 'own themselves' (the Lockean tradition of 'possessive individualism') or because they are divinely constituted as originally free and must therefore accord themselves a sacred respect as the trustees of an untradeable liberty (the Rousseauian tradition). It should be noticed here that the French tradition of rights is more emphatically civil-religious – and even residually Christian – than the American one. But in either case right is derived from the exercise of subjective freedom or from human autonomy and requires no other foundation. If dignity is also invoked, then it is essentially secondary to right understood in the higher sense of the value of spiritual freedom in itself. Key to understanding this unlikely marriage of rights and dignity is the crucial importance of Kantian thought after the Second World War, especially in Germany. For Kant had assumed and further spiritualized the Rousseauian and Republican approach to right and liberty: we do not own our own freedom which is a divine gift, trumping the mutability and tradeability of the material sphere (McCrudden 2008).[1] Hence it is morally illicit to commit suicide, tell a lie or surrender to sensuality for its own sake. Just for this reason Kant had spoken of human dignity or *würde* (2012 [1785]). So both in terms of the rhetoric of the dignity of the person and in terms of substantive moral commitments, the Kantian legacy was able to mediate between the liberal and the Catholic positions. However, I agree with both Samuel Moyn and Michael Rosen that this fusion is much more unstable than has often appeared to be the case. One can point to this instability in three ways.

First, one can refer to the second datable upsurge of discourse about 'human dignity'. This has occurred since 2001. The reasons for this 'second wave' are somewhat more obscure, but it can plausibly be taken that they parallel the reasons for the first wave. People have been horrified by the scant respect for human life, human suffering and the accepted modes of human existence and human interaction exhibited by both terrorists and states since 9/11. One senses a concern that respect for 'rights' does not sufficiently cover what counts as humane and respectful treatment of people, especially in circumstances of incarceration – also, an anxiety that 'rights' supposedly based upon autonomy and contract can logically be suspended in the case of 'terrorists' who refuse that contract and the basis of contract in respect for human liberty as such. Even refugees who have been accidentally placed outside state and legal contract often seem to fall in consequence beyond the sway of 'right'. And in either case loss of 'right' seems to result in a loss of humanity, a casting out into a limbo status unworthy of either the respect we accord to humans or the sympathy we sometimes accord to animals. For even though rights are deemed 'natural', if no pre-political divine establishment and enforcement of rights is admitted, then natural rights must, paradoxically, be positively instituted by human law. They are only 'natural' in the Hobbesian sense of being founded upon a supposedly natural condition of pre-contractual egotism, which was not, in itself, a state of 'right'. In a usually inchoate and inexplicit way, the resurgence of appeal to dignity besides right or even as the foundation of right seems to register an anxiety about the limits of secular recognition of human worth as 'right', as just indicated.

The second reason for the instability of the alliance between right and dignity concerns the nature of Catholic social teaching. Both Moyn and Rosen somewhat exaggerate the ruptures that have occurred here and play down a ground bass of continuity. While it is true that papal support for the dignity of rule, law, labour and women rested on hierarchical assumptions, it is nevertheless the case that the emphasis on the dignity of labour was a novel response to the collapse of the alliance of throne and altar. In the face of this collapse, a deliberate, bold and wholly novel overture was made towards the common people. If labour remained subordinate, its role was nevertheless vastly elevated in theory and in enabling practice. Much more of early Catholic social teaching shared assumptions and borrowed terms with the legacy of pre-1848 – often religiously inspired – socialism than is often allowed, precisely because the latter also understood itself as 'a third way' between reactionary invocation of the *ancien régime* on the one hand and predatory and iconoclastic liberalism on the other (Milbank 1997: 268–292; Michéa 2007).

Moreover, this overture was by no means merely opportunistic, because it was realized that the political theologies that had supported or defended the *ancien régime* were by no means authentically in continuity with a classical Catholic Aristotelian-Thomistic legacy. To the contrary, they tended to be based upon theological voluntarisms and positivisms which elevated the power of the one ruler to absoluteness and conceived of hierarchy as given, fixed and arbitrary. This was validly read as a betrayal of the Thomistic support for mixed constitution and a dynamic hierarchy based upon virtue and function benefiting the common good and so each and every member of the political community (Milbank 2006: 51–100).

Such an outlook was already inseparable from the Thomistic understanding of the dignity of the individual person who 'exists for himself' (though not with an absolute, modern self-ownership) in terms of his or her possession of rationality and freedom (*Summa Theologiae* II. II. q. 64 a.2 ad 2).[2] This dignity requires in some sense the political participation of all.

It is therefore wrong to say that Catholic corporatism contained no personalist dimension or that the dignity of the group was entirely disconnected from the dignity of the person, even in the nineteenth century. Within a Catholic outlook, it would have been impossible to speak of the dignity of labour without invoking the dignity of the human person, because this thesis announces that labour is an authentic way to be human – not to be a labourer, which would be tautologous. If, nevertheless, the dignity of the human being as such was less spoken of in that era, then this is because neo-Thomistic thought, in keeping with both Aristotle and Aquinas, did not think of human universality as something that could be atomically and empirically instanced as an abstract property that is literally the same and equal in all (as liberalism does), but rather as something always analogically differentiated in various conditions of life (including diversity of gender, of talent, ascribed and elected social role). In other words, Catholic social teaching realistically considered that it would be *vacuous* to focus in practice on the dignity and rights of human beings as such and not on the several dignities of human being in their various functions as they actually are *in the specifically modern world.*

For this understanding, personalism and corporatism are complementary rather than in tension with each other. For to value the dignity of the person is not to value an abstract bearer of free will, equivalent to all other such bearers, but to value the individual both as rationally free and as possessing an irreplaceably specific character. It is for this latter reason that each and every person is 'more' than the mere totality of people. But character – as Aristotle, Cicero and Aquinas make clear – is not just given by nature but is also habitually acquired, ascribed and chosen. It therefore does not exist outside relationality and social reciprocity. In consequence, one cannot respect a man and despise him as miner, son, father, cricket-player or lover.

It might seem as if stressing the dignity of his role would run the danger of subordinating him to his function for the social organism; but this only follows for traditionalism and positivism, not for an Aristotelian and Thomistic view which defines the purpose of the social and political whole as securing reciprocal justice and the always specific virtuous flourishing of each of its members. Indeed, one can turn the tables on liberalism here: if we mainly respect a man as a man per se, then this formalism can readily turn out to be compatible with all and every exploitation of him qua miner, son, father, fast bowler, etc. In consequence, these functions do indeed get reduced to merely instrumental functions of a machinic totality. Functions cease to be personally infused if, with false idealism and piety, we try to divorce personhood from function or, better, 'role'.

This false idealism informs every liberal constitutionalism (in the modern, Lockean sense) insofar as it only recognizes persons as bearers of abstract rights as individuals and otherwise regards social and economic life as 'politically indifferent'. This means that it only interferes with the latter in terms of laying down ground rules for fair play between independent human freedoms. It does not seek to ascribe any inherently desirable goals for social and economic activities. This 'asocial' and 'aneconomic' theory of the state (wildly discordant with even modern political realities) involves as its concomitant an 'apolitical' theory of the social and the economic. However, if, as for Aristotle, the aim of politics is to produce virtuously flourishing citizens, then, since people only develop characters through social and economic relations, the nature of these relations and their aims cannot be treated as a matter of political indifference. Inversely, the goal of social and economic relating will not be mainly the satisfaction of private predilections but relationship as such and the good of the other in the widest possible range (as both Aristotle and Cicero affirm). The widest possible range is the *polis* seen as the 'biggest society' and the widest scope of just reciprocity (for Aristotle) or the obscure international society of the *cosmopolis* (for Cicero).

This rejection of 'the separation of political from socio-economic powers' is a necessary conclusion of any authentically Christian political thinking, and yet it is the simple core of corporatism. To nurture the person one must nurture social groups and economic vocations. In order to widen personal political participation or *democracy*, one must ensure that every individual can exercise political influence through the workplace and with those with which he shares a common purpose. By contrast, merely representative democracy (which nevertheless has its place) assumes that there is in any case little impact to be made on most of human life through the political process, which indeed is for liberalism *undemocratically* defined as primarily the upholding of contractual rights, which as 'natural' do not need voting on, and the securing of social and economic 'fair play'. Democratic decision is here reduced to mass adjudication concerning the endless 'hard cases' to be decided within these terms of reference, while liberal constitutions (above all that of the United States) are devised to prevent any representation of a collective will from rejecting the ground rules of liberalism itself.

To the new circumstances of the twenty-first century and the continued non-liberalism of Catholic social teaching, one must add, as a third factor inciting tension in the enforced nuptial of right and dignity, the truth that Kantian mediation is unstable. Basically, where Kantian freedom degenerates into possessive individualism, or mere consumer freedom of choice, it ceases to be of strict ethical relevance or therefore to offer any ethical criterion in Kantian rather than Lockean terms, which quickly reduce to the securing of property rights and private material utility. Rawls's Kantian pupils, Christian Korsgaard and Onora O'Neill, simply reduce Kant to Locke, as Rosen rightly indicates (Rosen 2012a: 87–89, 145–147). But where to the contrary Kantian freedom remains 'dignified' and 'sublime', then it is of little practical and material relevance.

This is because Kant admitted that it is actually impossible to know whether one has acted out of a pure categorical imperative that treats people only as ends and can be universalized, and not out of a contingent imperative contaminated by sensual spontaneity and utility. One can only 'will to will' and be justified after all by Lutheran faith and not ethical action. This is why, as Rosen argues, Kant does not offer a humanist but a noumenal ethics (applying most of all to angels) and yet we only have a compromised human access to this ethics, mediated by a 'sublime feeling' for the moral law which should be willed (but cannot be so willed by us because of 'radical evil') purely dispassionately (Milbank 2003: 1–25).

Kantian ethics are then, in theory, religious. But even in terms of Kantian practice according to Kant they have always to be supplemented, compromised and at times betrayed by a mere aesthetics of sympathy and pursuit of utility, including a basic positivism in the realm of political legality. Inevitably then (and whether one is an atheist or not), the Kantian respect for free will as freedom, since one is the guardian of the divine gift of freedom, reduces after all in social practice to the willing *of something*, which may always be an impure will and so to a Lockean and 'consumerist' freedom of choice, which may be swayed by all sorts of sensual and selfish or utilitarian impulses now rendered legitimate. Certainly, in Kantian terms we must always keep our word and tell the truth *in the ethical world*, but not necessarily in the pragmatic-political one in which we always also live. And how can we be sure that we are telling the truth for the right reasons or telling it in the right way that really respects the other's freedom?

Therefore, the admitted sublimity of Kantian freedom is without real ethical effect, and his notions of human dignity fail to derive right from the dignity of freedom rather than from its sheer autonomy. What is more, any atheist construal of Kant will prove unable to explain why a free-willing against one's freedom does not still uphold a self-derived freedom. In consequence, it no longer knows, as we increasingly see, why we should not be allowed to kill ourselves or sell ourselves into erotic bondage.

So all the above considerations lead to a strong conclusion about the impact of the life, death, sex and gender issues which are driving a new wedge between right and dignity. They do not tend to show a merely 'residual' area of disagreement between these two perspectives, nor that the Catholic Church retains a different conception of dignity despite its full acceptance of the priority of the individual. Instead, they expose to view what has always secretly been the case: namely, that 'right' and 'dignity' stand for two radically opposed political philosophies and indeed for the two *most* opposed political philosophies: namely, the politics of the moderns and the politics of the ancients. For the Catholic conception of personal dignity continues to imply that universal dignity can only be expressed by the dignity of group, rank and status, while the Kantian notion of dignity is impotent to dislodge the liberal founding of dignity or worth upon right and so upon subjective autonomy.

One could say that the liberal view sees dignity as an 'internal' phenomenon of concealed willing, while the Catholic view sees dignity as an 'external' phenomenon of human position within the cosmic order and equally of individual human position within the social order.

Liberal dignity as duty or utility

In that sense, 'internal' versus 'external' would seem to express two *divergent* conceptions of dignity.[3] However, I shall now show why this is far too simplistic. For first, modern conceptions of dignity after all split internally between interior and exterior in their own specific way. And second, so do ancient and medieval ones, but in a different way, that trace back to an etymological and cultural ambiguity in the notion of *dignitas* as such. Eventually I will try to show that the key contrast turns out to be not after all between internal and external, but rather between a modern incapacity to *mediate* these two aspects, compared with the ancient perspective, especially in its Catholic Christian variant.

First, consider the modern division and disjunction of the dignified. Take the notion of 'dying with dignity'. This refers in part to the interior dimension of human life: our capacity for a rational exercise of freedom. A dignified death is, supposedly, a death whose place and hour has, in theory, been freely chosen by the individual who is mortally ill, at a point before he has lost all capacity for autonomous decision and so, for this perspective, all dignity.

Yet dignity with respect to death also refers in part to the most external circumstances of human life. A 'dignified death' is taken to be one that involves a minimum of pain, discomfort, physical mess or distressing circumstances.

This split clearly reflects a more general modern split between deontological and utilitarian approaches to ethics – especially if we take the 'utile' to refer in the widest possible sense to the convenient and pleasurable. Thus the same duality of dignity is extended from death to life in general. On the one hand, to live with dignity is to live not in any sense as a slave but as an autonomous being who has chosen or at least assented to her career, dwelling place, friendships and economic contracts. On the other hand, a 'dignified' life is taken to be one where we enjoy enough food, decent shelter and clothing, protection from the natural environment, mechanized transport and access to professional healthcare, educational expertise and informational and social media.

Again we see the contrast between, and yet typical combination of, the deontological and the utilitarian. Deontological aspects of dignity more readily apply to human adults, while utilitarian ones extend to children and to a lesser degree are extended to certain animals. 'To treat with dignity' as an according of respect to others tends to mean a respect for both their freedom and their comfort in a sense that extends to their being able to adopt a normative style of behaviour and dress that typifies human status. Michael Rosen struggles to explain how he personally requires a dignified treatment of dead bodies in secular terms outside these ethical frameworks – that is to say, even when no human freedom is at issue and no pleasure or displeasure to the living (2012a: 129–160). More to the point might be the observation that in fact respectful treatment of the dead (as of the dying) is increasingly violated in secular society.

It is therefore not simply the case that liberalism thinks of dignity as invisible right, while Catholicism thinks of dignity as visible status. For it also turns out that liberalism combines the invisible dignity of right with the visible dignity of style and convenience. A lack of integration between the two is revealed in the fluctuations of public policy where we possess no criterion by which to decide whether to concentrate on making people freer or more comfortable, ecstatically liberated or soberly healthy. In consequence we often end up contradictorily pursuing libertinism in one domain and Spartan discipline in others: for example liberalizing drug laws while extending draconian bans on smoking or permitting adult pornography while forbidding children from even touching each other (as in at least one Australian state today). The most synthesis we can ever achieve is a banal one that divides and rules the two incompatible modern ethical theories: thus people are rendered freer 'to choose' between ferociously marketed different versions of comfortable indulgence and programmes for self-discipline. The same pseudo-synthesis also works a dialectical reversion: austere deontology deconstructs into self-indulgent choice; sympathetic utilitarianism deconstructs into the rigours of hedonistic spectacle.

The Christian mediation between interior and exterior dignity, dignity and grace

Is it possible to affirm the dignity of human beings in universal and yet effectively concrete terms and thereby to hold together absolute invisible value with specific visible valuation?

In order to do so one must ensure that citizenry of the *cosmopolis* is not plausibly given simply by natural birth outside cultural and political relation. In doing so, Cicero already threatened to make subjective right the foundation of political order. Just like Aristotle, he allowed that there were pre-political communities involving justice and friendship. He agreed with the Greek philosopher that the basis of these communities lay in the needs of human beings not just to fulfil their material needs but also to enjoy friendship. However, unlike Aristotle he declared (no doubt in conditions of increasing international anarchy) that the specific reason for the founding of *city-states* was the securing of private property (*On Duties*, II, xxi, 73. xxii, 78). In his insistence on the absoluteness of the latter (later criticized by St Augustine), the general wrongness of theft even in dire need, and even from foreigners, and the non-commutability of debts (thereby treating negative sums, in contrast to Pythagorean tradition, sustained by Plato and Aristotle and paralleled by the Hebrew Bible, as if they were just as real as positive ones), Cicero comes across as proto-liberal and proto-capitalist (*On Duties*, II, xxiv, 94; III, vi, 28–33). His internationalism is already predicated upon a 'respect for person and property' that begins to equate the two. In this instance the practical translation of the deontological axis of his political thought, as later in the end with Kant, is the sacralization of private ownership – sacralization because political duty now refers to property as axiomatic *principium* instead of according property on just and principled lines as granted on certain conditions and in relation to the performance of certain responsibilities.

In this way the ethical character in Cicero seems to cede sway to the givenness of the mere individual and his 'own'. Nevertheless, Christian theology was able to adopt and borrow from Cicero (among other sources) his understanding of character as *persona*. As for Aristotle, Cicero sees 'personhood' as arising in part from universal human nature, in part from natural aptitudes, in part from accorded social role and in part from habitual personal effort (*On Duties*, I, xxx, 107; xxxii, 115).

In this respect *persona* in Cicero would seem to mediate between invisible and visible in a way that *dignitas* fails to do. It is therefore fascinating to realize that in some medieval texts these two terms become practically synonymous (Lebech 2004: 59–69). This implies that now 'axiomatic' value had been accorded to personhood. This is something quite different from the Ciceronian and modern liberal according of dignity to the rational human individual. For it presupposes a merging of universal natural birth with cultural and political birth. And for this in turn to have become possible, there had to emerge a political society that understood itself from the outset and intrinsically as cosmopolitan. For then universal citizenry ceases to be merely formal and abstract without thereby sinking back into the atavistically particular.

This new universal polity was, of course, the *ecclesia*, the Church: a city without earthly walls in which, in consequence, the network of friendship (agapeic-erotic) is truly open-ended and indeed infinite, even though membership is constituted by an always specific if dynamic and fluctuating (both horizontally and vertically) emplacement. Thus St Ambrose was able to rewrite and qualify Cicero's *De officiis* in newly ecclesiastical terms (Jordan 2005).

In consequence, citizenry is now personhood and personhood citizenry: at once cosmic, social and mystical-liturgical. The dignified status of human existence as such has become 'personal' because we play the role, wear the mask (the original meaning of *persona*) of God, who is himself personal and in whose image we are created. Thus Aquinas sustains the close new association of *dignitas* with *persona* and mediates the notion of dignity by treating the category of *persona* as itself something that analogically shifts between natural and social status – in a way that may seem slightly shocking to modern sensibilities. He declares that *persona* originally meant the mask of high-ranking persons in classical plays, then was transferred to mean high-ranking dignitaries in the Church and was finally applied to the high role played by all human beings as such. That this exalted status is nevertheless an assumed role is guaranteed by the fact that Aquinas thinks we may legitimately kill those who have effectively surrendered their humanity (*ST* I, q. 29 a. 3 ad 3 and aa 1–3; II.II q. 64 a.2 ad 3; q. 102 aa 1–3). As for Aristotle the ontological remains pragmatic: if we no longer perform human works, then we literally *are not* or are only vestigially human, at least as far the other human eye can discern.

Just because *persona* is a term that thereby shifts in its meaning and denotes a role whose performance is essential to the highest excellence as we know it, Aquinas thinks that it can be analogically extended to God, as in Trinitarian discourse. In this way personhood has been identified by him with the highest sublimity, dignity and *principium* of all.

So whereas liberal thought seeks to guarantee universality by reaching for a universal status behind any performed role, Aquinas prefers to run with original etymology by conceiving a universal and cosmic drama where the authentic remains the merely assumed. Even God is originally and exhaustively manifest in his interiority as a glorious interplay of a masked triplicity.

In his further understanding of *persona*, Aquinas blended Boethian 'rational substance' with Porretan and Victorine 'incommunicability'. But the two aspects tend to come together under the aspect of dignity: *hypostasis proprietate distincta ad dignitatem pertinent* (*ST* I. q. 29 a.3 ad 2). A person is someone who possesses elevated or dignified properties, such as reason, but in unique and diversified ways. Indeed, Cicero had already to a remarkable and almost Kierkegaardian degree insisted that one can only be ethical 'in one's own character' and not by trying to be someone else. Precisely like Kierkegaard he even defined the ethical goal as achieving 'consistency' (*constantia* and *equabilitas*) of character and thereby performing a stable social role (*On Duties*, I, xxxi, 110–115). This, for him, was the crucial heart of a decorous deployment of the convenient and of an honourable guiding of the decorous. To act consistently, therefore, was to possess social dignity. Aquinas now equates this with being a human person as such, since being a 'character' in relation to God trumps inwardness and even God is inwardly turned towards an interpersonal performance.

However, relationship to God as constitutive of the human person can seem to betoken another mode of refusal of outward dignity. If we are to honour humans as being in the image of God, then surely we are never honouring human beings as such, only God through human beings and maybe through their most interior aspect of reason. Protestant Christianity has often expressed this sort of idea. But Aquinas refuses it: just as sign to be a sign must also be something in itself, so also an image to be an image must be a reality in its own right. So if human beings are fit to be in the image of God, then they can be accorded honour for a dignity that they possess in a certain sense as properly their own (*ST* II.II. q. 101, a.3 ad 3).

The logic of the image, which we must first 'stay with' in order to 'pass through', therefore tends to integrate invisible and visible dignity. This suggests that without the notion of the *imago Dei*, such integration, with respect to dignity-talk, may be impossible for secularity to sustain. Moreover, the notion of iconicity that is here involved tends to disallow the disjunction of inward reason from outer corporeality through which character shines forth: each person in their face and body radiates a scintilla of the divine wisdom. Here a material presentation is valued as mediating a spiritual reality, while spirituality is only recognized along a specific visual trajectory or perspective.

In concrete terms this means that a messy, suffering human body can be in an evil-suffused world the most potent witness to human dignity or equally the dignity of the innocent, wondering, receptive child.[4]

The same personalist and iconic understanding of dignity implies that a person can remain fully dignified even when she performs a task assigned to her by another or even if she is forced to do something against her will. For in the first case she can act as a 'representative' which runs with and not against the drift of 'personhood', while in the second case she can bear representative witness through suffering to either the justice of her punishment or the inequity of her oppression.

This sense of personhood and dignity as the performing of a role, whether cosmic or cultural, lies at the heart of Pico della Mirandola's treatise that was posthumously entitled *Oration on the Dignity of Man* (della Mirandola 2012 [1486]). It is wholly erroneous to imagine that this work pre-announces a modern liberal constructivism, because its entire *topos* and conclusions are all anticipated in writings of the Church Fathers. Humanity is a *Proteus*: lacking any specific attribute of his own, his specificity is paradoxically to combine in himself, at the centre of the cosmos, the material, animate and spiritual, along with the ruling, knowing and loving functions of the three angelic orders of the Thrones, Cherubim and Seraphim. Between all these attributes he is free to choose. This is in part indeed a matter of creative construction with respect to the operation of natural magic, but herein our co-creation with God is as much a matter of discovery as invention, as we both shape and release hidden natural powers. This 'Renaissance' dimension of Pico's work is itself unfolded in wholly orthodox Catholic terms, but at the heart of human choice lies for him a more traditional selection of our destiny among pregiven locations. Our real dignity is our capacity to elect to be united in the love of the Cherubim to God. And while this is our highest destiny, it can in reality only be granted to us by God as an act of grace.

So for Pico human dignity lies finally in the divinely gracious gift. Dignity is something that we are granted, that we have borrowed. Since we do not possess dignity in ourselves or because of any inalienable property, it would seem questionable, for this outlook, to locate dignity in the conception of a human being as 'an end in itself' as does Kant. By contrast, for Christian tradition, human beings as divine images are more fundamentally means for other human beings to pass with them but also through them to God; nor are we ends to ourselves but rather destined for the contemplation of God, while the human race as a whole is a means first to display and then to restore the divine glory. Christianity agrees with Nietzsche (who was but distorting theological *topoi*) that humanity is 'a great bridge'.

As in the case of right divorced from status, it can seem that the Kantian conception is far more likely to secure human dignity than any notion which confines human beings to means, in however refined a way. Is not Kant ensuring that human beings can never be treated as commodities or instruments? But to the contrary, the idea of the human being as in himself a dignified *principium*, a first and final reality, is merely the reverse aspect of the reduction of everything, including human beings qua workers, to commodity-status. For the fungibility of *everything else* requires indeed that the owning subject be absolutely non-fungible, non-exchangeable, entirely free for the mere sake of freedom in order that his property-owning be freed of every condition, however honourable. The human subject who should not be treated as a means to an end that exceeds him (such as the glorification of God) is a subject that transcends all shared social purpose, but a subject that qua occupier of a social office can be (along with the commodified material earth) *all the more exploited* if ethics cannot be concerned with the discrimination of appropriate and inappropriate mediations which human beings can perform and be subject to.

To 'use' other human beings can sound odious to hypocritical non-reflection – since we do it and have to do it all the time. But actually, to treat oneself or another human being as an 'end', as the goal of an endeavour, is much more sinisterly objectifying. For an end is an objective full stop, without any personal characteristics – unless one is the infinite God – since these can only be displayed in dramatic and narrative terms which always involve still being on the way somewhere and still being a means to that end, employing other means. To see oneself or someone else as an end is to turn a person into a conclusion that is defined by the sublimely blank pages that follow it. Hence it is to seek to arrive at the ultimate, but ultimately empty capacity of the person for freedom in general as if this could function as an ultimate terminus. As the essence of subjectivity, this emptiness ensures that it dialectically coincides with 'objectivity' in the sense of a meaningless material thing that can be endlessly manipulated, just as absolute property owner and entirely alienable property are mutually co-established.

By contrast, from the writings of Aristotle, Cicero, Pico and Aquinas we have seen how dignity conceived of as transitory role strangely guarantees just distribution much better than dignity conceived of as an inalienably static property of possession. Moreover, the granting of dignity by grace suggests a final intensification of my interior versus exterior thematic.

For not only does this play out within dignity, it also plays in the contrast of dignity with grace. We have already seen this in the case of Cicero, since Friedrich Schiller in the late eighteenth century validly translated *venustas* as *Anmut* or 'grace' (Schiller 2005 [1793]). Even though both authors meant this in the aesthetic sense, the New Testament use of terms denoting grace involved a borrowing of the Hellenic term *charis* originally suggesting the divine bestowing of a supernatural, fantastic, aerial mode of beauty. And it is inaccurate to suggest that the New Testament and the Church Fathers abandoned rather than transfigured this connotation.

Hence a historical issue arises concerning the subordination of grace to dignity. Such a pagan, classical subordination is revived by Schiller, so that his immanent grace arises not as divine glory but as something merely fated or chanced, as opposed to the spiritual dignity of divinely dignified freedom, however much Schiller insisted in neo-Ciceronian terms against Kant that this freedom had to be decorously exercised.

We have seen how, in Cicero's case, an implicit self-deconstruction ensures on one reading that grace triumphs after all – but it does so in the interests of an impersonal, totalizing cosmos. What the biblical legacy, as appropriated by Christianity, suggests instead is the novel idea not of the dragging down of dignity to the level of charm or grace, but rather the elevation of grace to equality with dignity, of exteriority to equality with interiority, as in the case of the Trinity, as we have already seen. This means that grace or glory or honouring now goes 'all the way up' to the dignified divine height itself.

Such a reversal sustains and radicalizes the strange intellectual move authorized by Plato: beyond the highest height of reason itself lies a further height of divine grant and participation, the giving by the good 'beyond being' and reason, which yet establishes both being and reason. Dignity is supposed to be the reserved origin of the gift, but now we have the idea that gift and glory finally trump dignity itself: that the supplement is paradoxically prior to the origin. Thus if dignity is honourable display or *decus* before it is even itself or can be itself, no sundering of dignity from role, nor of rightful given status from working performance can ever be possible.

What is more, the elevation of grace is the metaphysical raising of a factor that has always been coded feminine. If the divine glory is God himself, then the divine personalizing essence is feminine 'wisdom', as the Bible suggests. And divine dignified 'restraint' depends upon a just, measured generosity whether in terms of the internal divine life or the 'economy' of his creation. Not the reverse, as paganism had at least initially taught.[5]

The implication of this reversal for actual gender relations is interesting. For once more in this instance it suggests that liberal equalization in terms of shared univocal dignity can turn out to be counter-intuitively oppressive.

Mary Wollstonecraft was undeniably right to insist that gender characteristics have absurdly tended to outweigh shared human ones through most of human history and also right to point out that the denial of dignity to women encourages them to indulge in the machinations of charms that tend to secure them the worst types of rakish men (Wollstonecraft 1996 [1790]). However, it is notable that in defining universal human dignity initially she seeks (just *like* the later work of her political opponent, Edmund Burke) a Ciceronian fusion of male dignity with feminine grace, yet finally abandons any incorporation of sexual difference in favour of a shared property of dignity as right and autonomy which effectively 'masculinizes' all human beings, since the reserve and autonomy of this mode of dignity is historically determined by natural and cultural male characteristics.

To adopt this strategy may be to forget how the realm of feminine grace and charm is implicitly elevated and de-trivialized by the Christian incursion, as witnessed by Dante's figure of Beatrice. For this incursion implies that a playfully abundant and gracious generosity, as summarized by Beatrice's elevating but gently mocking smile, takes ontological precedence over any 'male' pride in self-sufficiency. To accord women 'rights' mainly in terms of the latter can ensure that the generally different aspects of their nature, biology and needs are ignored, and that we pretend that naturally superior masculine physical strength and mental tendency to impose itself simply doesn't exist. In consequence, women are subjected to this inexpungable reality all the more, as we see with their now double exploitation in the workplace as well as at home and in the rising global tide of male violence against them.

Is it not better, in keeping with Christian tradition, to admit this masculine 'superiority' in one respect of 'strength', but then not just to temper but altogether to undercut it by insisting on a chivalric service of, and attention to, the grace-bestowing characteristics of the female sex that generally exceed those of the male?

In refusing this Burkean strategy it is by no means evident that Wollstonecraft is the more perceptive feminist, because – against Rosen – there is a remorselessly discerning and prophetic logic in Burke's contention that woman stripped of all symbolic mystique will thereby be reduced to a purely biological, animal status (Rosen 2012a: 69). He is here linking his defence of the civilizing centrality of feminine grace (in sharp rejection of his earlier adulation of the sublime as alone politically dignified, which could easily have led him to *support* Jacobin terror, as Wollstonecraft astutely noted) to a more general linking of cultural artifice to theological glory, in order to insist (against what theorists have now dubbed 'biopolitical' duality) that specific human nature is, paradoxically, a contingently cultural nature: 'All superadded ideas, which the heart owns, and the understanding ratifies, are necessary to cover the defects of our naked, shivering nature, and to raise it to dignity in our own estimate' (Burke 1969 [1790]: 108).

So here Burke makes dignity and grace coincide in a manner that would appear to be rigorously theological. Equally theologically discerning was his contention that Christian *chivalry* constituted the real political revolution in the history of the West – an observation which soon led Novalis in Germany, a youthful enthusiast for the French Revolution, to declare that Burke's anti-revolutionary book was nevertheless just as revolutionary as the revolution. This is because Burke realized, in the face of the terror, that the sheerly 'dignified' power of political will can never be adequately contained or resisted by a countervailing sublime will, which has an equal tendency to corruption. Hierarchical power can neither be abolished nor qualified as power by power, but only by something *other* to power which redirects it. This something other is Ciceronian *venustas*, feminine charm elevated by Christianity into the mediation of glory, tempering male violence with chivalric respect. Thus chivalry 'obliged sovereignty to submit to the soft collar of social esteem, compelled stern authority to submit to elegance' (Burke 1969 [1790]: 112). More generally, the real revolutionary achievement of Christianity was to entangle, beyond even classical aspiration, the political with the personal (exactly the aspiration of all truly radical feminism) and to mingle 'fealty' with legality (1969 [1790]: 170–171).

Nevertheless, Wollstonecraft was not altogether wrong to suspect that there is a false note in Burke, that this could all be something of a sham. For in her own more Ciceronian (or Shaftesbury-like) moments, she envisages affectionate love as ascending more clearly to the heavenly than it does in Burke (Wollstonecraft 1996 [1790]: 113). Unlike the real early romantics like Novalis and Coleridge soon to appear on the scene, Burke would indeed appear somewhat to aestheticize the religious, rather than truly combining them. Because, even in his later phase he remained wedded to a Whig contractualism as regards property and contract, one remains suspicious that his 'decent veil' is merely a superficial overlay upon a brutally masculine and 'sublime' reality: a matter of tradition grounded merely in human convention and not clearly in participation in the divine – even if there are some hints of this. This would mean that he after all sustained a gap between nature and culture and between naturally sublime dignity and the dignity of grace, elegance and charm.

Yet read in a truly theological and participatory manner, which would demand that 'chivalry' regulate even economic contract and exchange, Burke's diagnosis remains valid with respect to the nexus of dignity, grace, gender and justice.

But is not this diagnosis still wedded to the subordination of the female to the male and so of grace to dignity against supposed Christian intention? However, one can note here that while St Paul compares Bridegroom to Christ and Bride to the Church, both hierarchies are implicitly flattened by the circumstance that it is the Church which mediates the necessary response to Christ of the Holy Spirit who is divinely equal to the divine Son. The very work of deification itself would therefore seem to imply the historical elevation of women into equality with men as of the Church, including all the sons and daughters of God, into equality with Christ, the one Son of God who is the God-Man. This elevation is of a single metaphysical piece with the revelation that God is in himself the God of self-giving glory, eternally covered by the veil of feminine radiance.

Therefore to treat women as specifically women, but with regard to the progressively equal levelling upwards of grace with dignity, offers far more likelihood of women being raised to genuinely equal human status with men, just as the treatment of all human beings in terms of their specific talents and social roles in all their diversity and hierarchical inequality holds out a far greater prospect of democratization and equalization than either market capitalism or state socialism.

The liberal and Kantian notions of dignity do not so much offer us anything modern or progressive, but rather a lapse back into paganism and sophistry that divides internal from external dignity and unchivalrically elevates male dignity over feminine grace, thereby validating given arbitrary oligarchy and demanding that women turn themselves into somewhat more reliable versions of men.

(Though in reality an increasingly abstracted phallic patriarchal power continues to encourage them to exercise debased charms and oppressively regulative and psychologized 'maternal' power, to which many failing and indebted actual men are increasingly forced to become subordinate.)

In this way modern dignity by no means rejects hierarchy or status, but instead endorses the most dualistic and fixed sort of hierarchy which stockades the established reserve of subjectivity and endorses the arbitrary accumulations of property, money, male violence, female cunning and bureaucratic power by the most powerful subjective agents.

We have never abolished and could never abolish dignity as hierarchical status in favour of dignity as equal human worth based on right. To try to do so is instead to give more worth to the evermore worthless, as we see today. It remains a mystery to our media commentators and to many academics that Britain, since the 1950s, has become less deferential, yet more economically and socially unequal. They are unable to see the obvious: namely, that a collapse in deferential respect for the dignity of representative status and virtuous achievement *necessarily* results in increased inequality because *axia* will not tolerate a vacuum, where worth is no longer regarded, only money retains any value.

Instead, we can only acclaim human dignity as universal human talent and capacity for wisdom, love and grace and seek to elevate all in these respects, if we accord also more honour to those in whom these things are more expressed and realized, and diverse honours to the diverse but equally necessary modes of living dignified lives. To do so is the precondition for requiring that those so honoured go on giving to the community, in every sense, more than is expected from others.

Yet this requirement, which rests upon a valuation of the common good and so of the maximum possible flourishing of each and every one, reveals a final paradox that Christian tradition has always affirmed. Dignity indeed consists in virtue and therefore, though all humans are honoured as capable of virtue, more honour is accorded to the most virtuous. However, in the end the dignity of the human community and of all its members trumps even this height as the object of human virtue itself. The whole is more than the height, just as glory precedes dignity and the Triune God, at the highest dignified elevation, is an interplay of personal equality.

Notes

1   McCrudden points out that this mediation is also found in Paine and Wollstonecraft in England and in the Bolivarian tradition in Latin America.

2   *Summa Theologiae* = *ST*.

3   Robert Spaemann recognizes these two aspects while privileging the internal over the external in a way that may be too Kantian. Moreover, his invocation of the crucifixion rhetorically undercuts itself: 'The cross is the giant leap towards the internalising of the concept of dignity, towards the awareness of something in the phenomenon of dignity at once veiled and unveiled.' Precisely: the unveiling is crucial, otherwise Christ's dignity on the cross could not be iconically displayed. So no straightforward interiorization is involved here, but rather a new exposure of the secretly fundamental – Christ is most human because he is divine (Spaemann 2010: 49–72, 54). But there is much in this piece that is profoundly insightful and in accord with my own views.

4   It is extraordinary that Michael Rosen thinks that children do not possess dignity when their unselfconsciousness ensures they can possess it far more naturally than can adults (see Rosen 2012a: 77).

5   However, in contrast to Plotinus, the theurgic neo-Platonists like Iamblichus and Proclus (probably under unadmitted Judaic and Christian influence) tended to make divine reserve and divine outgoing, or the imparticipable and the participable, paradoxically coincide.

References

Burke, E. (1969 [1790]), *Reflections on the Revolution in France*, ed. C. C. O'Brien, Harmondsworth: Penguin.

Jordan, M. (2005), 'Cicero, Ambrose and Aquinas "On Duties", *or* the Limits of Genre in Morals', *The Journal of Religious Ethics*, 3 (3): 485–502.

Kant, I. (2012 [1785]), *Groundwork of the Metaphysics of Morals*, Cambridge: Cambridge University Press.

Lebech, M. (2004), 'What Is Human Dignity?' in M. Lebech (ed.), *Maynooth Philosophical Papers*, 59–69, Maynooth: Maynooth University Press.

McCrudden, C. (2008), 'Human Dignity and Judicial Interpretation of Human Rights', *The European Journal of International Law*, 19 (4): 655–724.

Michéa, J-C. (2007), *The Realm of Lesser Evil*, translated by David Fernbach, Cambridge: Polity Press.

Milbank, J. (1997), *The Word Made Strange: Theology, Language, Culture*, Oxford: Blackwell. (Chapter 'On Complex Space' 268–292).

Milbank, J., (2003), *Being Reconciled: Ontology and Pardon*, (London: Routledge).

Milbank, J. (2006), *Theology and Social Theory: Beyond Secular Reason*, Oxford: Blackwell.

Moyn, S. (2013), 'The Secret History of Constitutional Dignity', in C. McCrudden (ed.), *Understanding Human Dignity*, 93–111, Oxford: Oxford University Press.

Pico Della Mirandola, Giovanni (2012 [1486]), *Oration on the Dignity of Man*, trans. Francesco Borghesis et al., Cambridge: Cambridge University Press.

Rosen, M. (2012a), *Dignity: Its History and Meaning*, Cambridge, MA: Harvard University Press.

Rosen, M. (2012b), 'Dignity Past and Present', in J. Waldron (ed.), *Dignity, Rank and Rights*, 79–98, Oxford: Oxford University Press (article in response to the Berkely Tanner lectures given by J. Waldron).

Rosen, M. (2013), 'Dignity: The Case Against', in C. McCrudden (ed.), *Understanding Human Dignity*, 143–154, Oxford: Oxford University Press.

Schiller, F. (2005 [1793]), *On Grace and Dignity* in *Friedrich Schiller's "On Grace and Dignity" in Its Cultural Context*, trans. J. V. Curran and C. Fricker, London: Camden House.

Spaemann, R., (2010), *Essays in Anthropology: Variations on a Theme*, trans. G. Graaf. and J. Mumford, Eugene, OR: Cascade.

Wollstonecraft, M. (1996 [1790]), 'A Vindication of the Rights of Men 1790', in A. Ashfield and P. de Bolla (eds), *The Sublime: A Reader in Eighteenth Century Aesthetic Theory*, 294–299, Cambridge: Cambridge University Press.

10

Recovering Human Dignity: John Paul II's Personalist Philosophy

Miguel Acosta

Introduction

The philosophical ideas that I would like to analyse come from a man who lived through one of the worst horror-filled periods of history: the genocides of the Second World War. At just twenty-one years of age he had lost his whole family and, besides this, his country, Poland, suffered the Nazi invasion.

Karol Wojtyła was a philosopher and theologian who taught ethics at Lublin University in Poland from the 1950s to the 1970s. He was concerned not only about human interiority but also about all other facets of life, including the social aspects. We especially came to know him when he became Pope John Paul II in 1978.

I intend to show that his philosophical ideas about the roots of human dignity are linked to the concept of 'person' and also how these roots are closely related to the philosophical tradition of St Thomas Aquinas. The well-known principle in metaphysical realism of the essential substantial unity of the human being began with Aristotle and was highly developed by St Thomas Aquinas. This was also the point of departure of Wojtyła's conception of the human being.

This chapter aims to raise awareness of how Wojtyła restores the importance of human dignity through his personalist philosophy. It will explain the sources from three philosophical threads that allowed him to develop a new anthropological synthesis: Aquinas's metaphysics; Scheler's phenomenology; and twentieth-century personalism. It will then explore some fundamental connections between Aquinas's philosophy and Wojtyła's personalism, and concludes with some of the implications of his original synthesis.

At the same time, I will suggest a way to find clearer lines of communication within our relativistic and individualistic culture, which is full of false premises and fantastical explanations that come from science fiction, reductive ideologies and media manipulation.[1] Deeper exploration to find the strong roots of philosophy can help us rediscover the origins and foundations of reality which will allow us to face the challenges of our current civilization. We should never forget that *these* principles are what make our Western culture so important for the concept of human dignity, although they have often been overshadowed.

The roots of Wojtyła's philosophy: Phenomenology and anthropological philosophy

In 1954, Karol Wojtyła began teaching at the Catholic University of Lublin (*Katolicki Uniwersytet Lubelski*, KUL) and – with a group of lecturers – started a movement to:

1. think about the world in a different way, to confront both totalitarianism and individualism;
2. create contemporary proposals for rebuilding Western thought; and
3. disseminate the value of human beings recovering the importance of 'each individual's' dignity. This group was called the 'Lublin School of Philosophy'. (Zelić 2003: 5)

Stefan Swieżawski was considered the founder of the Lublin School of Philosophy (Zelić 2003: 7). Among other members of the Lublin School with different philosophical specializations, there were Jerzy Kalinowski (logic and philosophy of law), Mieczysław Krąpiec (metaphysics), Stanislaw Kamiński (epistemology or the theory of knowledge), Karol Wojtyła (ethics) (2003: 10–13).

Swieżawski explains that if metaphysics was the School of Philosophy of Lublin's first direct step, the second was the development of a philosophical anthropology. Both need to go hand in hand to establish a solid foundation, but that in turn must be complemented by a third: ethics.

> Philosophical realism presupposes a certain view of the Human being. Extreme spiritualistic dualism tends toward subjectivism, whereas the conception of the Human being as a psychophysical unity leads to objectivism. All four of us devoted significant attention to issues in philosophical anthropology, approaching it from various sides. (Swieżawski 1993: xii)

A person's acts are the centre of Wojtyła's philosophy. A good understanding of ethics requires deep comprehension about what a human being *is*. Only when we know this can we find the way to search for our self-fulfilment, according to our specific human nature. 'His own personal and pastoral experience taught him that even the best sermons and lectures do not automatically lead to real self-improvement' (Swieżawski 1993: xiv). In this sense, for Father Wojtyła, philosophy was the best way to pursue the ends of his vocation.

To explain the ethical dimension of Wojtyła's work in more detail would demand more space than is available here, so I will focus on the philosophical conditions of his ethics through the philosophy known as 'personalism'. I would also like to show that even with the importance that our author gives to Aquinas's philosophy, he also recognizes the necessity of looking for other philosophical resources to explain human subjectivity, and he believed that the twentieth-century concept of 'person' could help in this way.

The connection between anthropology and ethics is not only derived from Aristotle and Aquinas, although of course they have to be taken into account, but we must also engage with modern thinkers such as Hume, Kant, Stuart Mill, Moore and others. Their influence is great and permeates our contemporary culture and, according to Wojtyła, has not always been benign. The catastrophes of the two World Wars, which took place among the supposedly most advanced civilizations of the times, have had profound consequences to our current civilization, for example, in philosophy our mistrust on our capacity to find truth and the complete rejection of universal systems by nihilistic and postmodernist currents.

In this context, both phenomenology and personalism adopted a new approach and a set of resources to think about the interior concept of the 'human being'. Wojtyła always accepted and followed the core premises of metaphysical realism in Aristotelianism and Thomism. Even so, he had some criticisms of Aquinas's philosophy and looked for other understandings from, for example, Scheler's phenomenology or some aspects of Kant's ethics but under new perspectives. The theologian Modras elaborates two of these criticisms:

1. The Thomist explanation of human nature seems too *objective* and, studying the human person, personhood is understood in terms of the faculties of human nature more than the analysis of its subjectivity. 'Wojtyla sees Thomistic anthropology as open to enrichment with the concept of the human person offered by the philosophy of consciousness and phenomenology' (Modras 1980: 685).

2. Related to ethics, both Thomism and Aristotelianism are teleological and explain reality considering its ultimate purpose. But Kant was responsible for altering the formulation of the central problem of ethics not so much to point out the ultimate aim of moral behaviour but to identify the ultimate basis of moral norms. In other words, Aquinas's moral philosophy was teleological and naturalistic, whereas Wojtyła's proposed the stress on moral norms and a personalized approach.

Theory of human nature: Aquinas and Wojtyła

The influence of Aquinas's philosophy in Wojtyła's anthropology is clear. This influence is not accidental, but essential. Our author always considered the classical explanation of human nature, and in his writings Aquinas's metaphysical realism is completely respected. We cannot say that the concept of the human being is different between Aquinas and Wojtyła. The difference is more about the specific methodology that reveals some deeper aspects of the concept 'person' that medieval philosophy did not consider.

It is completely normal that each period of time looks for an explanation about God, Nature and Man according to its historical circumstances. Some of them respected philosophical tradition, while others offered new systems (e.g. Descartes, Hume, Kant or Hegel). In any case, along the time line there remain some common aspects that allow for what we call the *philosophia perennis*. Philosophy has a continuity in time, but we can also see new currents or systems, depending on the age and cultures.

We can understand that after the impact of nineteenth-century materialist philosophy, and with the terrible tragedy of two wars, some philosophers and thinkers needed to re-explain why each human being is important and not only in terms of pieces of organic machinery. In this context, there developed one of the new philosophical movements in our contemporary age called 'personalism'.

Personalism

The core of personalism is to recover the value of each human being as a member of a unique *human species*. This means a creature with rational faculties and a special richness and perfection that we must respect.

Personalism is not a monolithic philosophy. It has different modes of methodology and explanation, but with something that unifies all of them:

the focus on human inner life and existence. In this way, its approach is more existential than essential. There are several types of personalism: 'In 1947 Jacques Maritain could write that there are at least "a dozen personalist doctrines, which at times have nothing more in common than the word 'person'"' (Williams 2004; Williams and Benegtsson 2018). These different currents of personalism had special salience in Europe in the twentieth century. They were philosophical reflections prompted by social and moral disorientation, and attempted to recover the spiritual vision of men instead of the mere materialistic and individualistic point of view (Williams 2004; Williams and Benegtsson 2018).

The phenomenologist Roman Ingarden introduced both phenomenology and personalism to Poland in the early 1940s and encouraged the young priest Karol Wojtyła to read Max Scheler. 'Having previously received an Aristotelian-Thomistic formation, Wojtyła drew from his studies of the phenomenological method to develop a creative and original personalistic synthesis, complementing Thomistic metaphysics and anthropology with insights from phenomenology' (Williams 2004; Williams and Benegtsson 2018).

Personalists of all kinds thought that human exceptionalism was because they possessed inner lives or subjectivity. This exceptional value highlights the importance of human dignity. 'Whenever we say that man is a person, we mean that he is more than a mere parcel of matter, more than an individual element in nature, such as is an atom, a blade of grass, a fly or an elephant ... Man is an animal and an individual, but unlike other animals or individuals' (Maritain 2011: 66).[2] In this way, personalism is a clear reaction to 'the main forms of idealism, the materialism, and the determinism of the nineteenth century, but even to the objectivism of Aristotle' (Williams and Bengtsson 2018).

Thomist personalism

In the case of Wojtyła, his personalist philosophy is a synthesis of thomism and phenomenology. He uses metaphysical concepts of Aristotelian-Thomistic realism to explain the ontological basis of being human. But, as Williams points out:

> Wojtyla does not simply draw out a series of inchoate elements present in Aquinas's writings into a personalistic whole, or a sort of 'Personalism according to Aquinas'. Wojtyla also shows how some of the insights of twentieth-century Personalism can build on and complete Aquinas's thought regarding the human person, especially as regards the subjectivity of the person. (2004: 163–164)

And he adopts the phenomenological method to better understand the phenomenon of personal experience, which is otherwise too difficult to achieve from an objectivist and essentialist approach. The study and knowledge of our own subjectivity require a subjective approach to avoid reductionism and to describe, in an in-depth way, what we can examine within us. In this sense, contemporary phenomenology has been revealed as a strong method.

Using both Thomist metaphysics and phenomenological description, Wojtyła offers an original version of philosophical anthropology, putting together the essential and existential aspects of the person in his 'Thomist personalism'.

He understood the importance of the analysis of subjectivity through the lived experience, and he found in Scheler's phenomenology a good method to elucidate human insight. Besides this, he was also aware of the importance of connecting to reality to avoid the risk of idealism or even subjectivism, which was one of the problems in Scheler's approach to the study of values. Wojtyła accepts the objective aspects of reality – that is to say, the independent conditions of entities that can affect humans through their own subjectivity. The realist position is fundamental and Wojtyła wanted to show it clearly:

> I am convinced that *the line of demarcation between the subjectivistic (idealistic) and objectivistic (realistic) views in anthropology and ethics must break down and is in fact breaking down on the basis of the experience of the human being ...* With all the phenomenological analyses in the realm of that assumed subject (pure consciousness) now at our disposal, we can no longer go on treating the human being exclusively as an objective being, but we must also somehow treat the human being as a subject in the dimension in which the specifically human subjectivity of the human being is determined by consciousness. And that dimension would seem to be none other than personal subjectivity. (1993a: 210, emphasis in the text)[3]

All of these do not mean a rejection of phenomenology, except when the analysis of subjectivity drives into *subjectivism*. Wojtyła takes advantages from phenomenology, as he explains in his article 'Subjectivity and the Irreducible in the Human Being':

> The traditions of philosophical anthropology would have us believe that we can, so to speak, pass right over this dimension [the lived experience], that we can cognitively omit it by means of an abstraction that provides us with a species definition of the human being as a being, or, in other words, with a cosmological type of reduction (*homo = animal rationale*) ... The method of phenomenological analysis allows us to pause at lived experience as the irreducible ... [I]t also

contributes to a disclosure of the richness proper to human existence in the whole complex *compositum humanum*. (Wojtyła 1993a: 215–216, emphasis in the text)[4]

Talking about metaphysical realism, he admits the necessity of better clarifying some phenomena that are too hard to explain with the philosophy of being: for example, the notion of 'person' is the core idea of his philosophy and how we can understand why he chose the expression 'Thomistic personalism' and not 'phenomenological personalism'.

In addition, he was very sure that the point of departure, not only in cosmology and natural theology, but also in anthropology, should be the *actus essendi* (act of being).

> It is from this proclamation of being that the philosophy of St. Thomas derives its ability to grasp and to 'affirm' all that shows itself to the human intellect (what is given by experience, in the widest sense) as a determinate existing being in all the inexhaustible richness of its content; that it derives its ability, in particular, to grasp and to 'affirm' that 'being' which is able to know itself, to be filled with wonder in itself, and above all to decide for itself and to fashion its own unrepeatable history. (John Paul II 1979)

The core of this idea remains in the concept 'person' that Aquinas expresses clearly in the *Summa Theologiae*: '"Person" signifies what is most perfect in all nature – that is, a subsistent individual of a rational nature' (*Summa Theologiae* I, q. 29, a. 3).

Thomism and Wojtyła's philosophy

At this point, I would like to comment concisely on some links between Aquinas's and Wojtyła's philosophies.[5] We may begin to notice that our author not only respects the classical metaphysical concepts but also adopts a new and different approach which is to consider anthropology from the perspective of the 'person'. This idea revolves around the human person and his or her ontological dignity. No matter whether someone is lacking some capacities or suffers whatever illness, the ontological value remains consistent due to its spiritual foundation. This is something that transcends the natural level and goes deeper on a very intrinsic level that Wojtyła, following Aquinas, called *the human person*. But this does not mean a refusal of the body at all. To express not only the word 'person' but '*human* person' signifies the need to stress the two necessary and complementary principles, 'body and soul'.

Consciousness reveals human subjectivity

Consciousness is how we examine our own inner experiences, which is why it is fundamental to knowing not only ourselves, our subjectivity, but also our moral behaviour through the conscience. 'Consciousness reveals the reality of the concrete human being as subject who has experience of himself' (Wojtyla 2003: 33, n. 7; Acosta and Reimers 2016: 131).

Wojtyła follows the classical concept of consciousness, which comes from St Thomas and not from Husserl. In the first case, 'consciousness' is a type of cognitive act and is the real reference *in the present* to knowledge *of the real*. Husserl claims, to the contrary, that the object *is constituted* by means of consciousness. Wojtyła refuses this active function, the constitution of the object – and the elaboration of cognition – on the part of consciousness, just as he also does not accept that consciousness is a faculty or an independent and self-sufficient reality, the unique subject of its contents. In this case, we would be faced with *immanentism* (Acosta and Reimers 2016: 132). He argued that cognitive acts performed by man have three goals: to investigate a thing, to intentionally objectivize it and to understand it (Wojtyla 1979: 32).[6]

> Consciousness is, so to speak, the understanding of what has been constituted and comprehended. The purport of the preceding remarks is that the *intrinsic cognitive dynamism*, the *very operation of cognition, does not belong to consciousness*. If acts of cognition consist in constituting in a specific way the meanings referring to cognitive objects, then it is not consciousness that constitutes them, even if they are indubitably constituted also in consciousness. (Wojtyla 1979, emphasis in the text)

His position is clear; he denies that consciousness is an autonomous subject. He knows that recognizing consciousness as an independent subject could create the possibility of conceptualizing it in absolute terms and would therefore lead to idealism. This is to say, to take the consciousness as the sole subject of all the contents and admit that it is nothing but an expression of its own doing that follows the reductivist formula: *esse = percipi* (Wojtyla 1979: 33).[7]

Consciousness reveals subjectivity not in an objective way but subjectively.[8] 'We then discern clearly that it is one thing to *be* the subject, another to *be cognized* (that is, objectivised) as the subject, and a still different thing to *experience* one's self as the subject of one's own acts and experiences. (The last distinction we owe to the reflexive function of consciousness.)' (Wojtyla 1979: 44).

Realist intentionality against subjectivism

Closely related to consciousness is another *act* of intelligence that comes from medieval philosophy, the concept of intentionality, which is very important nowadays in the study of neuroscience.

Wojtyła could have had knowledge from thomism and phenomenology, but more probably from the latter, through Brentano and Max Scheler, as Husserl did not understand intentionality in the classical sense (Spiegelberg 1981: 12). In realist philosophy, *intentio* is the 'act of the intelligence' that makes the contact with objects of reality possible. Currently, this word has changed to 'intentionality' and, according to some philosophical currents, could have a realist or subjectivist sense.

A characteristic of Aristotelian-Thomistic realism consists of admitting that knowledge is 'the immaterial appropriation of the forms of things' that we call *objects* (known things). In realism, human knowledge is 'transobjectual'; it is not confined in consciousness, as occurs in immanentism, and this is thanks to the act of *intentio* (Acosta 2011: 93).

The experience of a human being does not result from the apprehension of sensations which will then be integrated by the intelligence (as in Hume's empiricism), nor from phenomena captured by the a priori forms of sensibility without having attained to the *noumenon* or reality in itself (as in Kant's phenomenalism). Experience results in knowing – with the apprehension of sensations – that there is a real immaterial contact with the object. It is also possible by means of 'cognitive intentionality' (in the Thomistic sense), which gives human intellect the possibility of entering into direct contact with the object and not to become trapped in subjective consciousness, as is characteristic of epistemological immanentism.

Again, in opposition to Hume, Wojtyła maintains that there is no reason to say that these objects of facts can be directly captured only through sensible acts. 'It seems, rather, that the understanding is engaged already in experience itself, and thanks to it establishes a relationship with the object, a relationship that is also direct, albeit in a different way' (Wojtyła 2011: 40).[9] The idea of intentionality in Wojtyła differs from that found in phenomenology and points towards Aquinas realism.

The last quotation is key, as it positions Wojtyła's philosophy clearly within the realist framework, overcoming the subjectivist frameworks we encounter, for example, in Scheler's phenomenology.[10] Wojtyła says that Scheler divests experience of its essential content, which shows itself in its natural foundation given by experience itself – the fact that the work is linked to the subject of work – that is, he separates the action from the agent of the act, who is a person (Styczen 2003: 121). 'The language which Wojtyła uses is that of phenomenology, but what he intends also has to do with Thomistic metaphysical knowledge' (Buttiglione 1997: 124). Even so, Wojtyła finds a point of coincidence between realism and phenomenology: in human experience there is a degree of comprehension of that which is experienced; and there exists a unity of the acts of human cognition (AP: 10).

To sum up this topic, I agree with Simpson who says:

> At all events the phenomenology that Wojtyła adopts in his investigations of the human person is realist phenomenology, a phenomenology that does not construct or constitute everything out of an absolute and free-standing consciousness, but that discovers in consciousness, or conscious experience, the objective reality or its intentional character, is experience of a real, external world, and is itself the act or experience of a real human subject. Wojtyła turns to phenomenology as a way to get at this subject from within, to grasp it in its interiority as a conscious self. But that this self is first a real being in the world, in direct contact with other beings in the world, is never matter for doubt (AP: 8–10, 19, 21). (Simpson 2001: 10)

Suppositum and the self

After his analysis of consciousness, Wojtyła had to solve another problem. The experience of the *self* is related to multiple objective experiences. But where does one sustain the unity of all their experiences that are given to their existence in order to comprehend their subjectivity in a fundamental manner?

Considering the history of philosophy, he reduced the possible answers to three different currents that each attempts to comprehend that subjectivity (Acosta and Reimers 2016: 138):

1. *Immanentism.* This considers that subjectivity is pure consciousness or the pure subject. We can see that there is a break between 'objectivity' and 'experience based in reality' and, actually, the experiences that we have from the real world and our interiority are what show us human subjectivity. Immanentism secludes the experience from outside that we get through the *intentio.*
2. Particular sciences and *Scientism.* Due to the remarkable advance of scientific knowledge, and thanks to the impressive results of its practical

consequences through technology, science tries to explain whole aspects of life, including subjectivity. There are confirmed data thanks to the scientific method which backs this comprehension of the person and their subjectivity. Regretfully, this comprehension is not enough; it is only a partial fragment of reality. The scientific method will always remain incomplete because there are more things that cannot be measured or fully explained with mathematics or statistics: one of them is subjectivity.

3.   *Phenomenology*. If we try to understand subjectivity by way of phenomenology, Wojtyła sees advantages in an analysis that allows a philosophical image of the person. The reservation here is that the experiences are resolved 'in consciousness' by performing an *epoché*. This presupposes another rupture with reality, as in immanentism, and to be valid, 'those "contents" should be transferred out of the consciousness level and integrated into the reality of the person. Wojtyła considers there to be an "almost" in phenomenology which turns out to be insufficient'. (Acosta and Reimers 2016: 138)

What could solve the problem of the unity of subjective experiences? The answer comes from another classical concept that focuses on the reality that enables us to link the concepts of experience and self-consciousness: the *suppositum*.

Wojtyła explains that *suppositum* is the transphenomenal expression of metaphysical subjectivity and the ultimate guarantee of the person's existing and acting. If there were not a *suppositum*, we could not speak of a subjective experience in existing and acting. And if the *suppositum* is the fundamental expression of man's experience, it ought to contain every particular experience of his 'self', facilitating the knowledge of the person's subjectivity.

Our author distinguishes the difference between *suppositum* and the 'self'.

Self is a broader concept than that of *suppositum*, because it always designates a concrete person, combining the moment of experienced subjectivity with that of ontic subjectivity; by contrast, *suppositum* refers only to the latter characteristic. *Suppositum* prescinds experiential characteristics and speaks of the individual being, inasmuch as he is the basis of existence and action. (Acosta and Reimers 2016: 139)

In this sense, *suppositum* is a metaphysical subjectivity or ontic substrate.

Wojtyła gives another meaning. The concept *suppositum* is no longer the subject in the metaphysical sense, but that which 'makes the human being an individual personal subject' (Wojtyla 1993a: 223).

We must, therefore, define more precisely the subjectivity proper to the human being. Namely, personal subjectivity, taking as our basis the whole of human dynamism [*operari*], but especially the dynamism that may properly be called the activity of the human being as a person: that is, the act. (Wojtyla 1993a: 224)[11]

To go deeper in a full significance of the human being's personal subjectivity, it is necessary to study that which the *suppositum humanum* contains, to enter through experience and consciousness into the person's deeper inner life.

Difference between act and operativity

In the title of his main philosophical work, *Osoba i czyn*, Wojtyła uses the Polish concept *czyn* and the translation of this word in both English and Spanish allows room for misconceptions. This term has a very specific connotation in the philosophy that we are analysing. The confusion arises because attempting to understand the concept of 'act' in an Aristotelian way is not enough to clarify what Wojtyła tries to explain. Nor does the concept 'action' that derives from the Greek *praxis*, which scholastics called *actus humanus*. Aquinas explains the difference between 'human acts' and 'acts of the man' by saying that the former are voluntary acts, whereas the latter are involuntary acts that the human being performs according to his nature without wilful action (e.g. blood circulation, digestion, etc.). Only human acts do we consider to have a moral aspect.

At this moment, it seems convenient to recall the difference between 'act' and 'action' with ordinary examples to clarify the philosophical context of these concepts. Reimers explains:

Normally 'act' implies operativity. An act connotes purposeful behavior. 'Action' is more impersonal. I perform the *action* of lighting a cigarette for the sake of signalling to my secret contact (I am a spy) that I have information to pass over. So my *act* is to signal another spy. We may speak of the 'action' of the pistons in the engine. A film with car-chases, explosions and gunfire is filled with *action*. Of course, these distinctions are not perfect, but in general 'act' connote 'operativity', but 'action' could also connote only movement.[12]

Besides this digression, the key to understanding the sense of the concept 'act' in Wojtyła is the word 'operativity' that which involves the dynamism of human acts under the perspective of the person. 'We are dealing with the ontological interpretation of the person through the act as act. By "ontological" interpretation we understand an interpretation that manifests what the reality of the person is' (PA, 63, n. 2).[13] For this reason, the concept of action will not simply be a human act – which is assumed – but the 'dynamization of the human being as a person'. The differentiating nuance lies in that the 'act' speaks of the action as a specific form of becoming according to the potentiality of the personal subject, placing the emphasis on the dynamism itself. The 'operativity' indicates the ontic structure of the person (*supossitum*) (Acosta and Reimers 2016: 142–145).

In this way, we can observe that the 'act' has a special moment called 'operativity'. This has the greatest importance in Wojtyła's anthropology, because through it the dynamization is converted into a person's act.

Integration of nature and person

The concept nature has several senses: the natural world, some attributes of beings or some specific property of a subject (that is, its essence). But there is also a difference between nature and essence. Whereas *essence* points to the ontological constitution that distinguishes one being from another, *nature* indicates the principle of a being's operation, that is, its form of dynamism. When we say 'human nature', the reference is to specific common features that make a being human. In this view, nature is the metaphysical explanation of the operative way of a being that has received the initial *esse*, the act of being. Once a being has the *esse*, it should act in a specific way due to their essence, obeying certain operative conditions. A human has to operate as human, not as a kangaroo. Therefore, nature is the operational principle of beings or, in Wojtyła's words, dynamization. That is, a synthesis of 'acting' and 'happening'.

The concept of nature is absolutely essential in distinguishing two structures in Wojtyła's personalist philosophy through experience: the structure of 'something happens to me' and the structure of 'a human being acts'. One points out the natural condition and the other the personal condition; both are complementary. Nature manifests itself in the moment of activation and the person in the moment of action.

Wojtyła explains that if we separate these two experiences too much and fail to seek integration between them, there will arise a relationship of opposition, as if there existed one world of the person and another world of nature. The synthesis of acting and happening is supported by the same ontic substrate, and a mutual complement is important between actions and activation, operativity and subjectivity. This requires the integration of person and nature (PA, 141. AP, 83–84). Of course, it is impossible to create a break between nature and person, since the nature of a human being *is* personal. Another issue is if the action of this human being, of the person, suffers a disintegration, e.g. in a psychological way. The unity of the human being-person in Wojtyła is clear:

> What happens under the form of various kinds of 'activation' is a property of my 'I'; what's more, it comes from it … The experience of the unity and identity of my own 'I' is objectively prior to and more basic than the experienced distinction between acting and happening-in, between the operativity and non-operativity of the 'I'. (PA, 137–138. See also AP, 81)

Self-determination as the core of personal morality

Probably one of the most powerful aspects of human dignity that comes from Wojtyła's personalism is his concept of liberty. He coined a new concept to express human liberty from the point of view of the person: 'self-determination'. This time, our author pays attention to will power, as there we can find the natural aspect of the dynamization of the human being.

The will is the other classical rational power for humans 'without whose participation no experience has full personal value or the gravity appropriate to the experiences of the human person' (Wojtyla 1993b: 117). The man-person fulfils himself freely throughout his life, this means self-determination.

First, Wojtyła acknowledges this capacity to be free (Acosta and Reimers 2016: 53–56):

> In virtue of his power to know the truth, the person is able to order himself through his acts to the good, independently of what happens in him … This does not mean that his freedom is a kind of causality separate and, as it were, detached from physical, material causality, as Kant suggests. Rather, knowledge enables the person to direct and govern his physical causality, to determine its practical finality here and now. (Reimers 2011: 176)

Then he adds the new perspective. From the point of view of the person, there is a special efficacy of the human act that reveals the person's transcendence in the action and trespasses the experience of 'I will' contained in the experience of 'I may but I need not' (PA, 167. AP, 105). This happens when both consciousness and self-determination are present. Self-determination is essential to the person and includes two moments: self-possession that is 'the capacity to form and govern one's behaviour according to the truth, according to an understanding that transcends the desires and urges that happen within' (Reimers 2011: 176). And self-governance that happens only when there is self-possession. Both are realized in an act of self-determination. In addition, self-governance is not the 'self-control' of colloquial speech; 'self-control' is used to apply to the functions of humans' dynamisms, to some powers or set of capacities and virtues. Self-governance implies the self-possession of the entire person by himself (PA, 168–169. AP, 106–107).

Here we can discover another intrinsic characteristic of the person. In *Love and Responsibility*, which was written before *Person and Act*, Wojtyła already had the intuition about transcendence through self-determination as a key point for human value.

> We speak of individual animals, looking upon them simply as single specimens of a particular animal species. And this definition suffices. But it is not enough to define a man as an individual of the species *Homo* (or even *Homo sapiens*). The term 'person' has been coined to signify that a man cannot be wholly contained within the concept 'individual member of the species', but that there is something more to him, a particular richness and perfection in the manner of his being, which can only be brought out by the use of the word 'person'. (1993b: 21–22)

We find the reason for our distinction among other living beings in Boethius's definition of person: an 'individual being of a rational nature'. This characteristic of our essence, that is, that 'rationality' shows our special 'intrinsic value', is the most fundamental basis of ethics.

Wojtyła points out two aspects of our rationality that distinguish us from even the most advanced animals: specific inner self and inner life. Another aspect that shows the intrinsic value of the person is:

> The incommunicable, the *inalienable*, in a person is intrinsic to that person's inner self, to the power of self-determination, (more than) free will. *No one else can want for me.* No one can substitute his act of will for mine. It does sometimes happen that someone very much wants me to want what he wants. (…) I may not want that which he wants me to want – and this is precisely why I am *incommunicabilis*. I am, and I must be, independent in my actions. (Wojtyła 1993b: 24 emphasis in the original)[14]

The term 'transcendence' denotes a consequence of self-determination. There is a *horizontal* transcendence that is 'transgressing the subject's limits in the direction of an (external) object' (AP, 119. See PA, 185) through the natural will power, but the other is the *vertical* transcendence as a result of self-determination of the person, and this one transcends or trespasses his structural thresholds through the capacity 'of being free in the process of *acting*, and not only in the intentional direction of will toward an external object' (Wojtyła 1993b). Reimers (2011: 73–95) explains:

Horizontal transcendence is a response to value, as well as an effort to realize a value in a particular situation. Vertical transcendence, on the other hand, questions the value in terms of some standard of good, because the values as presented immediately in consciousness do not, of themselves, validate their own goodness.

In this way, we reach the main point about the intrinsic value of 'each' human being. Nobody can act in a way unbefitting of a human person, even if one loses the normal use of one's reason, or is in a coma state, or dying; this does not mean a sort of depersonalization, in the sense of ceasing to be a person. A human being is a person because of their particular act of being; the rationality. This means that even at the beginning of life – from the conception of a human being – until the end, that person has an ontological dignity that deserves respect. This is impossible to understand if we misunderstand metaphysics and the immaterial aspects of reality, such as the spirituality of life.

Conclusions

The above is a general description of a new type of personalism that comes from Karol Wojtyła. I open the door a little to show just part of the whole panorama of his philosophy, which is an original way to explain the mystery of human beings.

We can see how, from the very beginning, Wojtyła's purpose was to better understand human behaviour in a metaphysical and phenomenological way, to look for the inner value of each being and discover a way to look at our inwardness.

The originality of his work cannot be denied. In my opinion, this is a new type of philosophy that we have to study from its own perspective. Only if we follow the logic of its concepts and the different argument relations, can one make a true judgement.

The first time that I tried to study *Person and Act*, I had to stop without finishing the first chapter. Later, I gave the author a second opportunity and, with patience and effort, I could understand more points of this remarkable book. I put in parenthesis my own prejudices and I discovered a different point of view, a brand new way to study philosophical anthropology.

I would like to transmit the idea that Wojtyła's philosophy gives us some solid arguments to admit the fundamental value of human dignity and to sustain the principles of ethics in our complex society.

Finally, I hope also that this text has shown a different way to deal with our inner self and to face life from the perspective of a good 'person'.

Notes

1   These affirmations require further explanation but this is not the place to do that. Some theoretical paradigms such as cyberculture, transhumanism and posthumanism have increased since last decades of the twentieth century. In certain aspects, they permeate our current culture and affect human dignity and education for good or evil. We can find several critiques of them, for example, C. S. Lewis, *The Abolition of Man* (1943); George Orwell, *1984* (1949); Martha Nussbaum, *Cultivating Humanity: A Classical Defense of Reform in Liberal Education* (1997); William Derensiewicz, *Excellent Sheep: The Miseducation of the American Elite & the Way to a Meaningful Life* (2014).

2   This idea does not go against the natural value of animals or other species of living beings, but only underlines how special human condition is.

3   Original source: 'Podmiotowości i "to, co nieredukowalne" w człowieku', *Ethos* 1, no 2–3 (1988): 21–28.

4   Wojtyła 1993a: 215–216 (emphasis of the source).

5   In this section, I discuss some of the main ideas found in Wojtyła's *Person & Act*. For a synthesis of the main principles in this philosophy, see Acosta and Reimers (2016: 115–124).

6   Wojtyła, Karol, *The Acting Person*, 1979 (henceforth AP). *The Acting Person* is the English translation of Wojtyła's *Osoba i czyn*.

7   As the sense of reality is dealing with a reality, it is transcendent in relation to cognition. 'If reality were identical with cognition, if *esse* were equivalent to *percipi* (as the idealists maintained), then the necessity of cognition to tend toward truth would be completely unintelligible... The truth of the fact of knowing would be exhaustively contained in each cognitive act (*percipi*). No necessity of tending toward truth would have a reason for being in this act, since *esse = percipi*... Cognition must go beyond itself because it is realized not through the truth of its own act (*percipi*) but through the truth of a transcendent object – something that exists (*esse*) with a real and objective existence independently of the act of knowing.' Wojtyła, Karol, 'The Problem of the Experience in Ethics', in PC, 116.

8   In his study of consciousness, Wojtyła explains two main functions of human action (besides the moral) adding new perspective to the classical explanation. (Acosta 2015: 66–67). The first is the *reflective* function, where consciousness acts like a mirror, reflecting what objectively appears to the intellect; and the second one is the *reflexive* function (different from the reflexion of intelligence in the

act of *reditio*). "[T]he reflexiveness of consciousness is something different from reflection as cognizing our own acts of thinking. Its turning to the subject is of a quiet different sort: it makes the subjetiveness of the experiencing ego appear, it directs everything back to the subject, and it makes the ego experience himself as the subject." (Półtawski 1978: 120).

9   Wojtyła, Karol, *Persona y Acción*, ed. José Manuel Burgos and Rafael Mora, trans. Rafael Mora (Madrid: Ediciones Palabra, 2011), 40 (henceforth PA).

10 '(Scheler) used the theoretical-cognitive premises of phenomenology in such a way that values are manifest, in particular moral values, only as the contents of an affective-cognitive perception... This essentialism runs hand in hand with the lack of appreciation for the causal relationship of the person with respect to ethical values... Scheler denies the being of the person as a substantial being who acts and substitutes being through a series of acts, that is, of experiences that are co-experienced in the experience of personal unity' (Wojtyla 1982: 208).

11 Translation revised by Adrian Reimers according to Wojtyła, Karol, '*Osoba: Podmiot i wspólnota*' [Person: Subject and Community], in *Osoba i czyn: oraz inne studia antropologiczne* [Person and Act: and other anthropological studies] [Lublin: Towarzystwo Naukowe KUL, 2000], 380.

12 Adrian J. Reimers and Miguel Acosta, personal email (11 April 2016).

13 PA, 63 n. 2 (Translation from Spanish *Persona y Acción* by Adrian J. Reimers). See AP, 303 n. 12.

14 The words in parenthesis distinguish the aspect of self-determination of the person from 'free will', which Wojtyła began to use later in *Person & Act*.

References

Acosta, Miguel (2011), 'La intentio como clave de la transobjetividad de la inteligencia en la filosofía realista', in Manuel Oriol (ed.), *Filosofía de la Inteligencia*, 79–102, Madrid: CEU Ediciones.

Acosta, Miguel (2015), 'La conciencia y la aporía de la objetividad de la subjetividad desde la onto-fenomenología de Millán-Puelles y Wojtyła', *Daimon. Revista Internacional de Filosofía*, 66: 55–69.

Acosta, Miguel and Adrian J. Reimers (2016), *Karol Wojtyła's Personalist Philosophy. Understanding Person & Act*, Washington, DC: The Catholic University of America Press.

Buttiglione, Rocco (1997), *Karol Wojtyła: The Thought of the Man Who Became Pope John Paul II*, translated by Paolo Guietti and Francesca Murphy, Cambridge: Eerdmans.

John Paul II (1979), 'Speech at Pontifical Athenaeum Angelicum', *L'Osservatore Romano*, English weekly edition, 17 December 1979, 7 (6): Available online: http://aquinasactusessendi.blogspot.com.es/2009/08/what-did-pope-john-paul-ii-say-about_10.html (accessed 10 July 2018).

Maritain, Jacques (2011), *Christianity and Democracy and the Rights of Man and Natural Law*, translated by Doris C. Anson, San Francisco, CA: Ignatius Press.

Modras, Ronald (1980), 'The Moral Philosophy of Pope John Paul II', *Theological Studies*, 41 (4): 683–697.

Półtawski, Andrzej (1978), 'Ethical Action and Consciousness', in A. T. Tymieniecka (ed.), *The Human Being in Action. The Irreducible Element in Man Part II*, Analecta Husserliana, vol. VII, Dordrecht-Holland/Boston-USA: D. Reidel Publishing Company.

Reimers, Adrian J. (2011), *Truth about the Good. Moral Norms in the Thought of John Paul II*, Florida: Sapientia Press of Ave Maria University.

Simpson, Peter (2001), *On Karol Wojtyła*, Belmont: Wadsworth.

Spiegelberg, Herbert (1981), *The Context of the Phenomenological Movement*, The Hague: Springer.

Styczen, Tadeusz (2003), 'Presentación. Karol Wojtyla: Filósofo-moralista', in Karol Wojtyla, *Mi visión del hombre. Hacia una nueva ética*, translated by Pilar Ferrer, 117–134, Madrid: Ediciones Palabra.

Swiezawski, Stefan (1993), 'Introduction. Karol Wojtyla at the Catholic University of Lublin', in Karol Wojtyła, *Person and Community. Selected Essays*, translated by Theresa Sandok, ix–xvi, New York: Peter Lang. Original source: Swieżawski, Stefan (1978), 'Karol Wojtyła w Katolickim Uniwersytecie Lubelski', in M. Filipiak and A. Szostek (eds), *Obecność: Karol Wojtyła w Katolickim Uniwersytecie Lubelskim*, 9–18, Lublin: Redakcja Wydawnictw KUL.

Williams, Thomas D. (2004), 'What Is Thomistic Personalism?', *Alpha Omega*, 7 (2): 163–197. Available online: http://www.uprait.org/archivio_pdf/ao42_williams1.pdf (accessed 10 July 2018).

Williams, Thomas D. and Jan Olof Bengtsson (2018), 'Personalism', in Edward N. Zalta (ed.), *Stanford Encyclopedia of Philosophy*, Summer Edition, Available online: https://plato.stanford.edu/archives/sum2018/entries/personalism/ (accessed 10 July 2018).

Wojtyła, Karol (1979), *The Acting Person*, Anna-Teresa Tymieniecka (ed.), translated by Andrzej Potocki, Boston, MA: D. Reidel.

Wojtyla, Karol (1982), *Max Scheler y la ética cristiana*, translated by Gonzalo Haya, Madrid: BAC.

Wojtyła, Karol (1993a), *Person and Community. Selected Essays*, translated by Theresa Sandok, New York: Peter Lang.

Wojtyła, Karol (1993b), *Love and Responsibility*, trans. H. T. Willetts, San Francisco, CA: Ignatius Press.

Wojtyla, Karol (2003), *El hombre y su destino. Ensayos de antropología*, translated by P. Ferrer, Madrid: Palabra.

Wojtyla, Karol (2011), *Persona y Acción*, José Manuel Burgos and Rafael Mora (eds), translated by Rafael Mora, Madrid: Ediciones Palabra.

Zelić, Ivan (2003), 'The Lublin School of Philosophy', Disputatio Philosophica, 5 (1): 5–21.

Abbreviations

AP   *The Acting Person*
PA   *Persona y Acción*
PC   *Person and Community*
LR   *Love and Responsibility*

11

Religious Freedom and Dignity

Roger Trigg

Religious belief and dignity

Why is religious freedom important? Many think that this question immediately begs several others. Does religion matter more than other ethical commitments? Is freedom itself so important when other demands, such as those of equality, fight for attention? One political theorist is not afraid to say very firmly that there is nothing special about religion (Laborde 2017: 28). More precisely, she says, religious beliefs and practices are not more ethically salient than the nonreligious commitments and conceptions (Laborde 2017: 32). Religion, therefore, must not claim privileges for itself. Yet this goes against a long-standing belief, not least in the United States, that religious freedom is the first freedom. Not only is it mentioned first in the First Amendment of the US Constitution, but many thinkers have long since realized that religious freedom is indivisible from other freedoms. If you cannot live by what you believe is most important (and that is by definition your religious belief or lack of it), you are not free. Democracy depends on the contribution by the citizens of their understanding of how life should be lived and what constitutes human flourishing. In pluralist societies, like those of the contemporary Western world, there is no consensus of basic beliefs.[1] Democracy becomes all the more important as a method of learning to live together even if we do not agree about everything. Freedom is the precondition of democracy, and freedom of religion is the precondition of all freedom. So it is often been thought.

Yet in the present age, many think that religion should not be allowed into the public square (Trigg 2007). A constant theme in current liberal political thought is that so-called public reason should rely on evidence that is accessible to everybody. We are told that 'some reasons are problematic in public justification because ... they are not accessible to common reason' (Laborde 2017: 120). It is claimed that religious reasons are problematic because of this. This view is often expressed. Brian Leiter, a writer on how law ought to treat religion, claims that 'the distinctively religious state of mind is that of *faith* – that is, believing something *notwithstanding the evidence and reasons* that fail to support it or even contradict it' (Leiter 2013: 39). Yet this seems immediately to weigh the scales against religious people. It assumes that they cannot provide arguments in the public square just because some people who reject them do not accept or even understand them. It appears that non-religious people are saying that they are not willing to listen to arguments that they do not already find cogent. Those we do not want to hear must be kept silent. Apart from the fact that this seems profoundly undemocratic, Leiter relies on the controversial belief that the only reasons that are valid are those that can be investigated scientifically. He explicitly appeals to 'evidence and reasons as these are understood in common sense and in science' (2013: 39). Something that is not susceptible of public verification or falsification is not counted as meaningful. Since physics itself is willing nowadays to entertain conceptions of realities that are far removed from our ability to observe, or reach experimentally, this is derived from an outmoded view of science (Trigg 2015).

The freedom not only to worship but to manifest one's religion in the public sphere cannot be taken for granted. It has to be justified and argued for. Doing so must bring us to the most basic questions of what it is to be human and why humans need not just freedom but also religious freedom. It has often been thought that reference to so-called human dignity can help resolve these matters. At the end of the Second World War, there was a considerable revulsion against the barbarity that had gone before. This was one of the motivating factors for the Universal Declaration of Human Rights promulgated by the United Nations in 1948. The Preamble set the scene by declaring that 'recognition of the inherent dignity and of the equal and inalienable rights of all members of the human family is the foundation of freedom, justice and peace and world'. Article 1 proclaims: 'All human beings are born free and equal in dignity and rights. They are endowed with reason and conscience and should act towards one another in a spirit of brotherhood.' Human dignity is thus linked with the idea of human rights. Freedom is linked with equality. Yet it is made clear that dignity and rights are not bestowed by the United Nations or any other body. They are objectively part of what it is to be human. They are not the result of human will, freedom or autonomy, but their precondition. They are inherent in us, and our true nature as human beings has to be recognized by political bodies as pre-existing. They are built into the very nature of things.

That is how the idea of human dignity is often seen. Recognition of it is the recognition that we all matter equally. Being human gives an inherent value and status. In recognizing that, we recognize a pre-existing fact. Rights are not political constructs but are naturally there. We have been endowed with our character as free and rational beings, and because of that we are able to recognize our common humanity and worth. The universal applicability of the Declaration of Human Rights did not depend on political agreement or the signatories to the declaration. They merely claimed to be recognizing truth. Yet why is it true? Tracing political consequences from the recognition of inherent dignity is easier than certainty of an inherent dignity in humanity in the first place. The *Declaration* wisely did not delve into such metaphysical or even theological questions but hoped to achieve agreement about what was true, even if people may not have agreed on why it was true. Yet it is undeniable that the language of the *Declaration* fits most happily into the Judaeo-Christian tradition. Reference to acting in a spirit of brotherhood immediately invokes the idea of the fatherhood of the one God, as Creator. Talk of 'inherent dignity' and being 'endowed with reason' further suggests such a background. We are all made in the image of the God Who created us, and in His sight we are equal. We should matter to each other precisely because we matter to Him.

This theological background gives ideas of human dignity, equality and freedom a particular salience. Yet what happens to the status of the *Declaration* if that background is not only ignored but positively rejected? That is the predicament we are in today. There is no longer any agreement about what constitutes human nature or whether there is such a thing. Some still think that the idea of human dignity can provide an anchor for ideas of rights and freedoms. The problem is that unless we all agree about the nature of humanity, and its dignity, the same words can be used to mean many different things to different people. So far from Christian principles grounding the idea of dignity, it can be combined with the language of human rights in such a way as to put into question our freedom to practice religion in general and Christianity in particular. The danger is that the idea of 'inherent dignity' becomes ambiguous, a mere placeholder for different philosophical conceptions of what is important about human beings.

The idea of human rights can even be made to appear to be at odds with religion. From concern about the activity of some religious 'extremists', particularly in the outer reaches of Islam, all religion, which is at odds with prevailing prejudice, can be regarded as extreme and an attack on human dignity. In 2007 the Council of Europe (which makes the judicial appointments to the European Court of Human Rights) issued a Recommendation on *State, Religion, Secularity and Human Rights*, which said: 'States must not allow the dissemination of religious principles which, if put into practice, would violate human rights.' It continues: 'If doubts exist in this respect, states must require religious leaders to take an unambiguous stand in favour of the precedence of human rights as set forth in the *European Convention on Human Rights* over any religious principle' (Council of Europe 2007: para. 17). More recently, the Council of Europe has moderated its tone and has seen the importance of some form of reasonable accommodation to deal with the sincere consciences of religious people. Nevertheless, its original statement exemplifies a growing attitude that human rights and religion are opposed to each other. Many now simply assume that that is the case.

Facts and values

Western nations have often been reluctant countries to champion religious freedom above other freedoms. This has merged into the more general fear that religious views oppose human rights and, in particular, the principles of non-discrimination and equality that various governments want to forward. With the growth of an aggressive secularism in many societies, religious views are forced more on the defensive. Distrust of Islam has reinforced suspicion of Christianity by some. Traditional religious views about marriage and sexuality are routinely attacked. The mere expression of them can bring opprobrium and even dismissal from some positions. A report by the United States Commission on Civil Rights, entitled 'Reconciling Non-Discrimination Principles with Civil Liberties', includes an attack by its chairman on the very ideas of religious liberty and religious freedom. He wrote that 'the phrases will stand for nothing except hypocrisy so long as they remain code words for discrimination, intolerance, racism, sexism, homophobia, Islamic, Christian supremacy or any form of intolerance' (2016: 29). Thus the expression of Christian moral principles in public debate becomes the target of abuse.

In the same report, one commissioner named Peter Kirsanow makes a minority report that analyses the situation as follows: 'Criticism of an individual's behaviour is considered an attack on the dignity of the person. This worldview is at odds with many aspects of traditional morality grounded in sexual restraint.' He suggests that the nub of the conflict between the proponents of non-discrimination norms and proponents of constitutionally protected liberty in the United States is a dispute about the status of moral standards, namely whether 'moral standards of behaviour are external to a person, not internal' (US Commission on Civil Rights 2016: 44). He thus illuminates an important issue in disputes about discrimination and liberty. A typical Christian view of moral principles is that although we are free to adopt or reject them, their nature is anchored in reality. Morality has to be about what is in fact good for human beings, what makes them flourish and what harms them.

Christianity with its doctrine of human nature teaches that because we all matter equally to God, and have an inherent dignity, it matters how we treat each other. We should care for each other and pursue each other's interests. Yet what those interests are is not the result of our own decision. What counts as good and bad, harm and benefit, suffering and happiness, is built into the way things are. It is a physical fact that smoking over a long period of time is likely to harm our lungs, even if we personally think it will not and continue smoking. Similarly, other forms of behaviour can harm ourselves and other people, whatever we think or want. Moral experience and tradition can help show us what is good and helpful, and what is not. The world is not our own construction. We have to confront it, and going against the grain of nature, particularly human nature as it should be, will always bring a cost.

This itself is traditional moral teaching, particularly Christian teaching. Yet in our modern age, it seems anathema to suggest that there are principles of conduct that should apply to everyone, because otherwise harm will result. Not only is there much controversy about what is good and bad, harmful or beneficial. Perhaps as a result of seemingly irresolvable disputes, many people relapse into the subjectivism that suggests that each person's opinion is as good as anybody else's. This quickly produces the view that any claim to moral truth implies criticism of other people's points of view. That is seen as both intolerance and a lack of respect for other people. Thus, any assertion of moral norms becomes an assault on the dignity of those who do not accept them. The idea of freedom becomes extended into a claim to total autonomy that suggests that we are free not only to decide how to act but to decide what standards of right and wrong there are for each of us as individuals. The autonomous self becomes sovereign, to be put in the place of God. We set our own standards, because, so it is said, we have a radical freedom that can reject the imposition of such standards by other people. This autonomy can easily itself become entwined with the idea of human dignity.

Criticism of another person's moral behaviour then becomes an assault on human dignity. Authenticity and sincerity become the salient virtues. Yet even

Hitler was presumably sincere and 'authentic'. That was precisely why he was so dangerous. People who pursue evil policies because they believe that they are the right ones are the true fanatics and are exceptionally dangerous. Sincerity is a necessary, but far from sufficient, condition for right behaviour. I am not infallible and should be willing to learn from others, as well as from moral tradition. Some would maintain that what counts as human depends on the society we live in, because human nature is socially constructed. In that case, however, there would be no standard against which we can judge the genuine effectiveness, let alone the truth or falsity, of morality. Majority opinion in my society then becomes automatically right, however fickle or fluctuating it may be.

The idea that causing offence is a major moral failing is the result of a belief in the lack of any objective anchor for morality. If morality is what I think it is, and you attack my moral beliefs, it follows that you are attacking my identity as a person. When there is no objective standard for right and wrong, my own beliefs largely constitute who I am. Even the most polite criticism of those beliefs seems an attack on my person. Everybody is then only answerable to themselves. Questioning my beliefs becomes tantamount to questioning my right to hold them, my freedom as an individual and my dignity as a human being. The growing reluctance to listen to views with which one does not agree, whether in religion, morality or elsewhere, suggests a lack of grasp of any idea of truth. Once that is removed from morality, and beyond, rational discussion becomes pointless, because there is nothing left to find out. When my first view is as good as my last view, why do I need to listen to other people in order to learn from them? My own dignity becomes identified with my freedom to believe what I want. Once the possibility of recognizing truth is removed, all attempts to persuade me that I am wrong become attacks on me and evidence of the intolerance and prejudice of other people.

This approach has become endemic in our culture. The idea that human dignity is linked with the exercise of a will that is so autonomous that it can brook no contradiction is persuasive because of the rhetorical force of appeals to dignity. They gesture at the roots of who we are. We value the expression of our own individuality. It is significant, too, how the language of values has become the vehicle of contemporary moral language. We no longer talk about principles and standards emanating from the very nature of things. Instead, reference to values removes our focus from the way things are, and our common human predicament, to how we may react individually to different situations. That provides our morality. Our reactions, it seems, constitute our morality without our being accountable to anything beyond ourselves.

Values are not the kinds of things that are true or false but are what people hold and help to define the kind of people they are. For anyone versed in the development of moral philosophy throughout the last century, this pervasive talk of values has a familiar ring. The so-called distinction between facts and values took on the character of a logical fallacy, so that it was understood that trying to deduce a value from a fact was a crass logical mistake, on a par with saying that black is white or that two and two is five. Facts, it seemed, could not be altered, while values could be adopted or rejected, whatever the facts.

This fitted well in the mid-twentieth century with the prevailing logical positivism that saw science as the sole standard of truth. What could not be verified by scientific means could not be true. Statements about metaphysics and other matters beyond the reach of science were crudely rejected as meaningless. This immediately put into question the status of all moral statements. Very often they were considered to be mere expressions of emotion, although in the end they were considered to be more a matter of subjective taste. I may not like bananas, whilst you may. My values may be very different from yours because of the logical gap between facts and values. Nothing I produce as evidence could rationally have relevance to any attempt to change your moral beliefs. Only science could tell us what that world was like and that itself could have no impact on values.

As we saw in discussion above of the views of Brian Leiter, this view has crept far beyond the philosophy of science. Science itself has moved beyond such crude ideas of empirical verification, and physicists now talk about worlds, and indeed even universes, that in principle are beyond our reach. It all seems suspiciously metaphysical (Trigg 2015). We could not do modern science without recognizing that references to realities beyond our immediate experience, or possibility of observation, may still have a claim to be real. Yet such realism, recognizing that reality is not constructed by the beliefs of individuals or societies, is as relevant for ethical theory as for scientific theory. However, in common parlance, facts still seem to have a universal application that values do not.

Subjectivism and relativism

Values express preferences. They are the product of individual choices, which can show great diversity. The current stress on values reflects an increasing scepticism about the very possibility of objective standards of morality or universal principles which can be accepted by all. Sometimes the matter is complicated by recognition that a society of individuals all pursuing conflicting values is no society at all. Social cohesion has been a major preoccupation of governments in recent years. Extreme individuality can destroy society. What is there to stop it becoming, in Hobbes's famous words, 'the war of all against all'? One answer is to retreat from an extreme subjectivism to a more modulated relativism. The difference is that while subjectivism stresses the individual as the source of autonomous choice, relativism recognizes that there must be some shared values, because we all have to live together. There has been concern in the United Kingdom in recent years about the nature of 'British values', with the question being how there can be a cohesive society when there is so much disagreement. One answer is that there must be some shared standards of civility and mutual respect, not to mention toleration. These then become fundamental values required for the existence of a society, but without any claim to be resting on truth.

In the case of subjectivism, human dignity becomes the right of every individual to live as he or she chooses according to whatever personal values happen to be held. The retreat to a relativism that looks to society implies that we have an obligation to worry about how we treat other people. The required values are the ones necessary for living together in a pluralist society, where there may be little common agreement about how to live. Subjectivism places stress on the inherent dignity of all individuals to choose their own way of life. Relativists realize that there must be limits on what each individual can choose if they are not to collide with others in their own society. In the case of subjectivism, once we can each choose our own values, respect for other people, together with toleration of their views, may not rank very high. Some can even relish using their power to impose their will on others. The more an autonomous will is glorified, the more the danger is that that it will impose itself on other people. Everything becomes an exercise in power.

The nuances of relativism can try to avoid this trap by recognizing that the right of each individual to make a choice is something that has to be respected within a society. If the autonomous will of each individual constitutes their dignity, there is still need for that dignity to be upheld by others, whatever they personally wish. Toleration then becomes the greatest virtue of all for that society. Yet the paradox is that because toleration has to be enforced, with moral criticism of other people's views frowned upon, moral criticism of intolerance is reinforced. An attack on the idea of any objective moral standards has to result in the upholding of toleration as one such standard, coupled with a particular objectivist view of human dignity. Similarly, the relativist society can try to make toleration its defining characteristic by becoming intolerant of any view opposed to the basic principle of relativism and pointing to moral truth. It can come very near to proclaiming that it is true there is no truth and also that we ought as a matter of objective fact to be intolerant of any claim to any objective moral standards. Relativism can become an instrument of oppression and power in a society, and the phrase 'the dictatorship of relativism' can become all too appropriate. Majority opinion can become oppressive. Yet the whole outlook rests on a mesh of inconsistencies.

The greatest irony of all in both the subjectivist and relativist versions of upholding values, as opposed to facts, is that they are each forced back into making an appeal to human dignity, to uphold the right of each of us to have freedom to decide how we live. We have, we are told, to respect it, because once we claim to be rationally challenging other people's values, we do not recognize the intrinsic dignity of individual autonomy. This appeal to dignity carries considerable rhetorical force, but it only works when it is seen as an appeal to an objective characteristic of human beings, a reference to the way things are. Once dignity becomes assimilated to our individual autonomy as human beings, its status as an objective characteristic becomes swallowed up in subjectivity. Freedom becomes assimilated to ideas of radical autonomy. If I am totally autonomous, my freedom constitutes that autonomy, and should not be restricted by anything outside myself, and my will. Yet unless I will my, and other people's, dignity, its status evaporates. The exercise of individual autonomy, and the arbitrary pursuit of personal values, can be all that there is.

This all causes confusion and contradiction. It seems logical that if I want to exercise an autonomous will, I should respect a similar exercise by other people. Yet why should I, if that gets in the way of my exercise of will? If I feel that my very identity is bound up with my choices and my status, why tolerate other people who wish to thwart me? Ideas of religious freedom cannot be rooted in subjective notions of the exercise of conscience or the imposition of will. People think that such freedom matters, because they wish to express, and act on, beliefs concerning what is true about the world. Their beliefs about what is beneficial and harmful must often be intimately bound up with a religious conception of the world and the place of people in it. Religious notions of freedom can respect reason, precisely because of a concern with issues about truth. Subjectivist notions allow no room for the exercise of rationality and resort instead to that of power. The same applies to relativism where the authority of a group or society is used to impose standards, and conventions, governed by majority opinion. There is nothing beyond that can be used to persuade those who disagree.

Autonomy and freedom

Just how crucial in practical terms these disputes can be is illustrated daily in the present-day courts of the Western world. Freedom of religion is protected in all human rights documents, but it is often given second place to liberal conceptions of autonomy. In the name of personal freedom, what is seen by many as the most important freedom of all is highly restricted. To take one instance, where arguments are likely to rage for many years, the Canadian Supreme Court ruled in 2015 that what it coyly described as 'physician-assisted dying' should be regarded as perfectly legal. This immediately raised ongoing issues in a nationally provided health system about the status of doctors, who do not wish to take part in such practices either directly or indirectly. With the imperative that such practices be available to everybody, that could result in the assumption that all doctors, and those entering the medical profession, must be prepared to offer that 'service'. A doctor with a profound religious belief in the sanctity of life will be put in an impossible position. Debates about the scope of religious freedom in such situations are echoed in many countries where the spread of secular 'values' puts the outworking of traditional religious beliefs at risk in many areas.

The concept of dignity comes to the fore in such disputes. No one doubts that the idea of dignity is important because of its link with our idea of the importance of each individual human being. Nevertheless, if freedom is reduced to individual autonomy, in the strong sense already discussed, dignity may be thought simply to be the ability to indulge such autonomy. That is far from a traditional understanding, and the word again becomes a mere rhetorical weapon. This became clear in the judgement of the Canadian Supreme Court. The justices pointed out that in some people's eyes the right to life protects quality of life, and therefore, as they say,[2] 'there is a right to die with dignity'. Others arguing for assisted suicide and euthanasia are also portrayed as arguing that the 'right of life protects personal autonomy and fundamental notions of self-determination and dignity, and therefore includes the right to determine whether to take one's own life'. The decision of the Court was that[3] 'an individual's response to a grievous and irredeemable medical condition is a matter critical to their dignity and autonomy'. We see here the deliberate linking of the idea of dignity with personal autonomy. Unresolved is the incoherence between an objectivist view of the nature of human beings, and their inherent dignity, and the subjectivist view of strong individual autonomy. Religious freedom itself drops out of sight.

The idea of individual autonomy has something right about it, which is why the concept is superficially attractive, particularly to liberals. If we believe in human freedom and rationality, then the right of each person to decide what is to be important for them is crucial. This should be rooted in an objective feature of human beings. All may recognize it, but it makes particular sense, given a religious understanding of the world of how humans have been created in the image of God. Autonomy without rationality is worthless and becomes a matter of arbitrary judgements, moulded by passing fashion and social influence. Freedom needs reason, and the idea of reason can be grounded in the idea of a rational God who made an ordered world with creatures like us in it capable of understanding it (Trigg 2015). Such religious freedom recognizes the foundations of our very nature as human beings. It allows us to discuss such issues with people who disagree and is a better guarantee of freedom than the ideals of liberal autonomy which pervade in the Western world.

One of the most influential declarations about religious freedom over the last century was made by the Second Vatican Council in 1965 in its declaration on religious freedom, *Dignitatis Humanae*. Its ringing declaration was 'the human person has a right to religious freedom' (Second Vatican Council 1965: para. 5). Furthermore, this right has its foundation 'in the very dignity of the human person'. Most significantly, however, it proclaims that 'the right to religious freedom has its foundation not on the subjective disposition of the person, but in his very nature'. It is not because we will it, or want it, but as a result of who we are. Dignity is inherent in the nature of the human being. The document begins by stressing the growing sense of the dignity of human person in the modern age. It says: 'The demand is increasingly made that men should act on their own judgement, enjoying and making use of a responsible freedom, not driven by coercion but motivated by a sense of duty.' This highlights the tension in much contemporary thought about the nature of freedom.

It should be an absolute principle in any democratic society that no one should be coerced into acting against their conscience. No one should be forced to believe what they do is wrong, in the way that medical professionals in nationally provided health services can often feel that they are being pressured. We should bear responsibility for our moral decisions and be free to make a stand on what we think is right. Yet this can easily slide into the view, as we have seen, that individual judgement creates standards of right and wrong, instead of enabling us to recognize what they are. The freedom that underlies moral responsibility can easily become a licence to do what we want. Assertions of religious truth can then be seen as assaults on individual liberty and personal moral identity.

Freedom, as the precondition of moral agency, can come to undermine its point when every decision and every action is as right as any other, if I have decided so.

The continuing paradox is that appeals to dignity are only persuasive, if we accept them as more than the result of subjective decision. Imputing dignity to others merely through my own judgement gives the concept an insubstantial base, and I cannot rationally expect other people to make the same decisions. If the recognition of human dignity is seen as a matter of sheer preference by individuals, they have no reason to take account of it when that becomes inconvenient or against the agent's interests.

Dignity can be a malleable concept, to be used to fit into whatever suits personal views, or the interests of a society and its current fashions. At the extreme, each individual becomes a law unto himself or herself. It is ironic that the idea of human rights, with its fundamental emphasis on rights derived from our common humanity, can itself produce an individualist vision of the world that loses sight of our place in the wider scheme of things. Human rights cannot be properly explained by a subjectivist account, because if they mean anything, we should hope that they are recognized by everyone universally. Even so, once they are moulded into support for liberal notions of absolute autonomy, they can, it seems, be used to deny our subjection to any truth beyond ourselves and undermine any vision of universal human dignity and freedom.

Dignity and moral norms

The Russian Orthodox Church in its *Basic Teaching* links human rights theory with human dignity 'as its fundamental notion' (Russian Orthodox Church n.d.: 1.1) and our God-given dignity with the voice of conscience within us. The stress by the Russian Orthodox Church is that in Eastern Christian tradition, the notion of dignity has first of all a moral meaning with ideas of what is dignified being bound up with the moral notions and actions of a person. Human sin can be an obstacle to the exercise of our God-given dignity. The preservation of this dignity is constituted by living in accordance with moral norms because such norms, we are told, exemplify 'an authentic human nature not darkened by sin' (n.d.: 1.5). The problem comes when the Church tries to steer clear of an excessively individualistic notion of morality. It recognizes that 'while every individual is endowed by God with dignity and freedom' (n.d.: III.1), the misuse of that freedom harms one's own dignity and that of others. It proclaims (with emphasis) that 'one's human rights cannot be set against the values and interests of one's homeland, community and family'. (n.d.: III.5) The exercise of human rights, we read, cannot be used to justify an encroachment on 'cultural values and the identity of a nation'.

While the besetting problem for Western liberal morality is a relapse of morality into subjectivism, this stress on culture and national identity can produce a lapse into relativism or even a totalitarian imposition of one view of what is true. The temptation can be to suppose that the traditional moral principles of a nation have some kind of transcendent value which cannot be questioned. Once it is assumed that the traditions of a nation constitute the truth about the dignity of human beings and how they should be treated, the consequence can be a remarkable intolerance of any alien institutions and principles seen as a threat to national tradition and identity merely because they are alien. The issue should not be what is authentically Russian but what is objectively right. The Russian Orthodox Church seems in danger of eliding the two, in a way that can promote a sense of certainty and infallibility about moral principles that result in intolerance, and a suspicion of any institutions and influences that have their source beyond Russia. It is indeed in this spirit that religious freedom is very limited in present-day Russia. Even such a mainstream Protestant denomination as the Methodist Church (with its origins in the eighteenth-century Church of England) is regarded with hostility, and faces legal restriction, because of perceived financial and other support from South Korea and the United States.

According to the Orthodox tradition, it is being claimed, human beings preserve their God-given dignity, and grow in it, only if they live in accordance with moral norms. Yet when these moral norms are equated with the social norms of a particular society, there are the seeds of trouble. Too great a stress on freedom can make morality seem arbitrary. Too great a stress on conventional moral norms can result in a restriction on freedom. In both cases part of the answer is to recognize that human nature, and the reality it is placed in, act as a constraint about what counts as beneficial and harmful. Freedom is an essential part of our dignity as human beings, but we are fallible beings who are free to make mistakes and have false beliefs, however sincerely held. Reality can all too often hit back.

Liberal political theory is right to see the central importance of individual freedom. Democracy is predicated on the exercise of that freedom by all citizens. According to Christian theology, such freedom is God-given. Its exercise expresses our basic human dignity and our nature as creatures of a God who has made us in His own image. Our ability to reason about, and even access, truth gives that freedom point and purpose. Otherwise, an absolute freedom that denies the ability to pursue and recognize truth becomes arbitrary. We then live in a nihilist universe where nothing matters. Without a distinction between what is and is not the case, reason and understanding become impossible.

There are clearly dangers in an extreme view of the autonomous will of an individual. We have to recognize common standards in order to live together. The Russian Orthodox view recognizes this, but its appeal to traditional morality links it too much to the interests and identity of one nation. Even so, religion has a corporate as well as an individual nature. It is an essential part of the recognition of the role of religious freedom to realize that we are all set in communities which teach and nurture us. We need churches and other forms of community in which we can associate with each other and learn from each other. They can nurture that respect for human dignity, which is vital for the proper functioning of any society.

Any notion of human dignity that involves the unbridled exercise of an autonomous will gives rise to obvious difficulties. Each individual is likely to collide with others. There has to be regulation and coordination to police exercise of different individual wills which are apparently not constrained by anything beyond themselves. As the influence of churches and other forms of community has been eroded, the individual is exposed and unprotected. The only body left that can step in to control people's self-willed, and indeed selfish, actions is the state. It is a paradox that the more that the importance and dignity of the individual has been stressed, the more liberalism, as a social theory, has turned to the state as the ultimate referee. The background to all this is a major pluralism of beliefs and attitudes, with no agreed procedure for settling them outside normal democratic procedures. Such pluralism can go very far down and infect the most basic beliefs about what constitutes human nature, human dignity and human good and harm.

A religious view of the world gives content to all these notions in markedly different ways to those derived from a secular, even anti-religious, viewpoint. The idea of a common human dignity has gained particular salience because of the Christian background the concept was nourished in. Reference to human dignity can still retain its rhetorical force in a post-Christian society, even when its rational underpinning has been removed. Yet eventually either we stop believing in it or, as seems to be happening, it can be implicitly redefined so that it means something radically different to different people. Instead of referring to the intrinsic importance of human beings as seen by God, human dignity can then mean my right to identify myself with whatever I prefer or desire, even to the extent of changing my biological sex if that is what I choose. The idea of the sanctity of life can then be understood in radically different ways. My right to life can become transformed, as it has in Canada, into my right to choose to die if I want to.

Appeals to ideas of dignity, and other common moral notions, can cloak rather than solve basic moral disagreements. Their use may reflect deep divergences in society. Yet we still have to live together. One way of doing that is to respect each other's sincerely held basic moral convictions and hope that people can be allowed to follow their consciences as much as possible. Unfortunately, much modern political theory dislikes the vacuum left by the lack of restraint on individuals because of the decline of intermediate institutions such as churches. Instead of being willing to respect such institutions and help them to survive, and nurture their members, many liberals see them as standing in the way of proper social progress. Liberalism all too often changes from a procedural method of resolving disputes in a pluralist society into a substantive moral view about how to create a better society, perhaps a more equal one. Where it gets its standards from, and whose criteria are to decide what is better or worse, is sometimes opaque. What is altogether too clear, however, is the assertion of the sovereignty of the state over religious institutions.

As the priority of the state and its intentions, however benevolent, are stressed more, a religious conscience will be challenged when it is out of step with fashionable mores. Those with such a conscience will feel obligations to an authority other than the state. They will see the state as itself subject to a greater power. Yet it is difficult for some governments to accept limitations on their own authority or what they see as a divided allegiance from their citizens. By definition, totalitarian states will be opposed to religion, because they will not accept alternative sources of power. However, even democratic societies depending on the combined autonomous will of its citizens can fail to respect an appeal to authority, and even truth, when it is outside their own control. A subjectivism, decrying objective truth, can then be transmuted into a relativism that places the source of authority not in the will of individuals but in the collective will of the majority. That will always be bad news for minorities. A strong sense of objective truth can constrain us to recognize that even people we disagree with may have insights that are important from which we can learn. If the will is paramount, whether individual or collective, there can, by definition, be nothing left to learn or find out. There are only others getting in the way of the exercise of power. Power has to replace reason, as indeed the nineteenth-century philosopher Nietzsche trenchantly taught.

This is illustrated when we are told by a political theorist that the priority of the state means that it must determine the limits of the role of religion. Cecile Laborde tells us that 'the liberal democratic state has the competence to decide the respective areas of competence of associations within it' (2017: 162). In other words, she says, 'citizenship trumps religious commitment' (2017: 163). Our duty as citizens must always be more important than any recognition of religious obligation. Liberalism, she says, 'is radical precisely because "it assumes state sovereignty"' (2017: 163). The state will decide what is harmful and what is beneficial to citizens and the limits of individual freedom. It will decide which rights are more important. It will decide whether freedom of religion must be limited if, in its view, the rights of others are being challenged. Its pursuit of various social issues, such as those of the non-discrimination of various groups, however defined, will take precedence over the views of individual religious believers, or of whole churches, about what is right and true. Laborde says explicitly that 'states define what constitutes *harmful* behaviour – a key notion in the regulation of religion, as it sets out the boundary of permissible religious activities' (2017: 166).

Conclusions

It is ironic that the strong belief in individual freedom, which presumably defines liberalism, seems to end up with the state controlling the exercise of religion in the interests of one social policy or another. Equality has loomed as large as freedom, but it is an equality which, in a pluralist society, is reluctant to treat one set of beliefs as better or more likely to be true than another. If people are equal, it seems their beliefs must be treated as such too (Trigg 2012). This is bound to be self-defeating. Human dignity may be partly constituted by our freedom to decide which beliefs to live by. It is nonsense, however, to suppose that dignity bestows the ability to rise above ingrained human fallibility. We are free to believe, but our dignity as human beings does not guarantee the rightness of our beliefs. The great challenge of a pluralist society is to recognize and respect our freedom to adopt which beliefs we choose to live by, while not succumbing to a subjectivism or relativism that reduces such freedom to a personal act of will or the conventions of a society. Truth must always be sought.

Giving the accolade of human dignity to a subjectivist or relativist position becomes incoherent. The notion carries the rhetorical weight it does because it appeals to the necessity of our realizing our true nature as human beings.

Yet, once we give the concept the importance it deserves, we have already taken sides in the argument about the status of the many competing beliefs of a pluralist society. We are talking of what is inherent in humans and are appealing to an objective morality. Referring to human dignity is not a way of settling arguments unless we first settle our basic conception of human nature and the constraints on it. Otherwise the different ways the concept can be used may simply mark deep divisions within society. One understanding of dignity can uphold the absolute sanctity of human life, but another can be used to justify euthanasia. Religious freedom is a precious part of the idea of human dignity for many people. Yet those who are suspicious of religion, and who wish to limit its manifestations, are also likely to object to the idea of special human importance and dignity that Christianity has given to the Western world. There is going to be no easy or quick way of resolving such deep disputes in a fractured society. We must continue to assume that truth is at stake for everyone and that is what gives those disputes their point. We must respect other people's views and perhaps learn from them. Unless, however, truth is the issue, everything collapses into meaninglessness.

Notes

1   For a discussion of the problems arising from religious pluralism, see Trigg (2014).
2   *Carter v Canada* 2015 SCC 5 #59.
3   #66.

References

Council of Europe (2007), Parliamentary Assembly, *State, Religion, Secularity and Human Rights*, Recommendation 1804.
Laborde, C. (2017), *Liberalism's Religion*, Cambridge, MA: Harvard University Press.
Leiter, B. (2013), *Why Tolerate Religion?* Princeton, NJ: Princeton University Press.
Russian Orthodox Church (n.d.), *Basic Teaching on Human Dignity, Freedom and Rights*, I. 1 mospat.ru/en/documents.
Second Vatican Council (1965), *Dignitatis Humanae*, December. www.vatican.va/archive.
Trigg, R. (2007), *Religion in Public Life*, Oxford: Oxford University Press.
Trigg, R. (2012), *Equality, Freedom and Religion*, Oxford: Oxford University Press.

Trigg, R. (2014), *Religious Diversity: Philosophical and Political Dimensions*, Cambridge: Cambridge University Press.

Trigg, R. (2015), *Beyond Matter: Why Science Needs Metaphysics*, West Conshohocken, PA: Templeton Press.

US Commission on Civil Rights (2016), *Peaceful Co-Existence: Reconciling Nondiscrimination Principles with Civil Liberties*, September.

12

Human Dignity in a Biotechnological Age

Michael Burdett

It is no secret that our world has become irrevocably transformed by technology. The face of the earth speaks of these vast changes. Indeed, an image taken from an orbiting spacecraft would likely reveal tiny sparkling lights that originate from our cities and even the Great Wall of China would be seen etching out parts of the landscape revealing the very sublime scale of our technological achievements. Furthermore, the global trend towards increasing urbanization shows we are at this moment, more than likely, in the company of more artificial objects than natural ones. Technology has moved from just a handful of useful objects that might make our lives easier to making up the central environment in which we dwell. It seems to be everywhere today.

What is more, technology seems to be transforming not only our world but ourselves as well. This is most visible in the field of medicine. Here, technology is primarily applied to the human body. We turn technology on ourselves directly and use prescription drugs and other technological therapies to intentionally change, alter and transform ourselves. Where would modern medicine be today without technology? Where would brain science be without magnetic resonance imaging (MRI)? Or diabetes without insulin pumps? Or the deaf without cochlear implants? The sheer sophistication of modern medicine is obviously attributable to the technologies which make possible the precision needed for it to thrive and heal the masses. Each member of the human race has the capacity to be healthier today than ever before because of these advances in medical technology.

This chapter is based on portions of an earlier work, Burdett 2014. For more information, see https://grovebooks.co.uk.

This level of biomedical transformation has reached a tipping point. Human beings are at an important stage in their evolutionary history. At no time in the past have we had such direct influence and impact on our environments and indeed on our own personal transformation. Advances in GRIN (genetics, robotics, informatics and nanotechnology) technologies in the last several decades have sparked a great deal of speculation about the possible personal, moral and special (that is, species-related) ramifications of applying them to the human body. For example, the new gene editing application everyone is raving about today, CRISPR-cas9,[1] was selected by the journal *Science* as its 2015 Breakthrough of the Year. Previous gene editing tools like TALENS (Transcription activator-like effector nucleases) and ZFNs (Zinc-finger nucleases), while giving us access to genomic change, were less reliable and much more expensive. CRISPR-cas9, on the other hand, is cheap (100 to 150 times cheaper than the others), more effective and universal. With such fine-grained access to the genome comes the ability to alter the phenotype and morphology of any biological organism – humans included. Altering the human genome can institute phenotypical changes that could alter capacities that shape personhood directly. Single-gene traits or single-gene genetic diseases are the lowest hanging fruit when it comes to gene editing for the simple reason that a change at one site on the genome will change the specific trait or disease. This could mean creating therapies for debilitating diseases like Huntington's, sickle-cell anaemia and cystic fibrosis. But others have speculated that changes on no more than ten sites on the human genome could lead to, e.g. bones that break surgical drills, a severe reduction in the risk of heart disease and Alzheimer's. In the long term, memory, behaviour and sociality are just some of the things that could be drastically affected by genetic engineering. These issues take on a new sense of urgency when GRIN technologies are applied for human enhancement purposes rather than just for therapeutic ones.

But with such far-ranging advances in medical technology come an equally difficult set of ethical issues that often impact human dignity. Just because we can create technologies that transform the human body doesn't mean we ought to in each instance. It is now possible to extract stem cells from human embryos for the sake of crafting very effective regenerative therapies. But should we do so knowing that it might damage or destroy this human embryo? Similarly, advancements in genetics have made it possible to change the expressed characteristics of our future progeny through human germline modification. But ought this biomedical procedure be available to everyone, even if it is used for non-therapeutic aims like changing height, hair colour or even intelligence?

These difficult ethical issues, and particularly the possibility of genetic engineering being used for enhancement, have led to an eruption of sophisticated ideologies. We can no longer content ourselves with the proximate ethics of bioengineering to understand what is at stake, for these biological changes have vast implications for the future of humanity as a whole and, hence, our common dignity. Indeed, we must also come to grips with the tacit pseudo-religion that seeks to go beyond genetic engineering and advocates the unfettered use of human enhancement: transhumanism – for the very dignity of the human being could be at stake.[2]

Human enhancement and transhumanism

On 21 February 2011 *Time* magazine had a rather provocative image emblazoned on its cover. The caption in bold letters read '2045: The Year Man Becomes Immortal'. On the cover you will find a picture of a powder white humanoid figure with some advanced electrical chord attached to the back of his head. A green LED is lit up as if to show that the electrical chord is transmitting some type of electrical signal to the humanoid figure. Perhaps something is being communicated to the humanoid or perhaps this electricity is vital to the actual functioning of the humanoid. Perhaps it isn't even a human in the sense we might normally think with an organic brain made up of flesh and blood. This humanoid may bear a greater similarity to an iPad or the mobile phone in your pocket. This image should not surprise us. We usually find this kind of image in the context of science fiction. Yet, here it is on the cover of *Time* magazine: a reputable publication not particularly known for venturing into the fictional like some crackpot independent publisher you might find at an anarchist bookstore trying to sell you the latest conspiracy theory. In fact, the journalist who was responsible for the main article associated with this image states: 'The difficult thing to keep sight of when you're talking about [transhumanism] is that even though it sounds like science fiction, it isn't, no more than a weather forecast is science fiction. It's not a fringe idea; it's a serious hypothesis about the future of life on Earth' (Grossman 2011).

This journalist's comment is instructive for us as well because we see people today intentionally retrofitting their bodies with technological apparatus for non-therapeutic purposes. Kevin Warwick, formerly professor of cybernetics at the University of Reading, is famous for championing the use of medical technology for human enhancement purposes. In 1998, Warwick implanted a computer chip in his arm that was used to operate doors, lights and other electronic devices in his proximity. In what has been called 'Project Cyborg', Warwick then took this electronic implantation to new levels. A more sophisticated device was linked to Warwick's nervous system and he was able to control a robotic arm in another country via the internet. And one of the most publicized events had Warwick's wife surgically insert a similar device and they were said to 'feel each others' sensations' that were captured from one of their nervous systems and transmitted directly to the other via these devices.

Warwick and others like him see vast potential in these transformative technologies and often speak about how they are changing the human species at the most fundamental level. Indeed, a growing group of activists have begun to call themselves transhumanists as a way to acknowledge and advocate for the enhancement of the human person/species through technology. Nick Bostrom, one of the lead philosophical gatekeepers of contemporary transhumanism, defines transhumanism in this way:

1. The intellectual and cultural movement that affirms the possibility and desirability of fundamentally improving the human condition through applied reason, especially by developing and making widely available technologies to eliminate ageing and to greatly enhance human intellectual, physical, and psychological capacities.

2. The study of the ramifications, promises, and potential dangers of technologies that will enable us to overcome fundamental human limitations, and the related study of the ethical matters involved in developing and using such technologies. (Bostrom 2003)

Transhumanism is related to humanism and shares many of the same values and convictions. Both are committed to human progress, rational thinking and the flourishing of the human species. Humanism seeks to improve the human condition through cultural means: education, art, politics. Transhumanism, however, applies technology directly to the human organism and radicalizes human transcendence and transformation. It advocates going 'beyond' the human. Transhumanism begins with an evolutionary account of the human being – recognizing the biological and cultural history that has led to modern human beings – but it is not content to allow these biological and social pressures dictate the future of the human race. Instead, it promotes the acceleration of human evolution through the intentional modification and enhancement of the human species by utilizing emergent technologies: nanotechnology, biotechnology and information technology. Transhumanism contends that human beings are in the process of becoming and are at a watershed moment: at no other time in history could we have such power over our own development and drastically affect the course of human history and each individual. Transhumanists say we ought to seize this opportunity, using any means necessary to enhance ourselves for the betterment of each individual, our societies and our species.

Why Christians ought to care about human enhancement and transhumanism

There are many reasons Christians ought to concern themselves with human enhancement and transhumanism. First, the issue of human enhancement is only becoming more pressing in our time with rapid advancements in biotechnology, nanotechnology and information technology. What we can do today in these fields would have seemed science fiction to our predecessors. These enhancements, which we didn't have the ability to initiate even half a century ago, should they be chosen, could be significant in unimagined ways. Second, society is inevitably starting to ask questions about where these advances should lead us – questions not just about our present actions but, more significantly perhaps, about our future identities. If Christians are to have an impact on society, then they must engage not simply with the decisions that are made in the present but also with the ideologies being sculpted for the future.

Transhumanism is a growing movement. The official international transhumanism organization that goes by the name 'Humanity+' (formerly called the World Transhumanist Association) is currently made up of approximately 6000 members from more than 100 countries. This number has doubled since 2005 when the last census was taken (Hughes 2005). But despite its relatively small number of official members, it is the ubiquity of its beliefs and its adherents in positions of power that make it a rapidly advancing force in the world today. For instance, Nick Bostrom sat on the President's Council for Bioethics in the United States and has consulted for the United Nations, the European Commission and the Central Intelligence Agency. He leads the Future of Humanity Institute at the University of Oxford and has been on several lists of top world leaders alongside notable figures such as Barack Obama, Bill Gates and Pope Benedict XVI. Transhumanism is anything but a fringe phenomenon.

But aside from advancing technologies and the growth of transhumanism as an ideological movement, it is also contemporary culture that has become preoccupied with human enhancement and transhumanism. Recent films such as *Her* (2013), *Transcendence* (2014) and *Gattaca* (1997) as well as the television show *Battlestar Galactica* (2004–2009) act as a barometer of the societal pulse. Christians need just to turn on the television to see the questions being posed and we had better have answers to them.

Transhumanism, human nature and the ends of humanity

It might seem that the most pressing issues for the future of human transformation are ethical in nature. Surely moral deliberation is needed, but so often in contemporary discourse on human enhancement, proximate ethical concerns are favoured at the expense of defining and characterizing the nascent and operating anthropologies – the nature and ends of humanity. These visions of the human are implied in arguments on either side of the ethics of human enhancement and play significant roles in the arguments even when not explicitly stated. For example, specifying a standard of health so as to differentiate it from enhancement implicitly appeals to a universal norm inherent in an image of the human being for a given stage of development. What is more, even certain ethical arguments against the use of human enhancement technologies have been made on the grounds that those technologies will irrevocably alter human nature and are, hence, an aberration not to be pursued. All of these reasons make further reflection on the inherent vision of being human important for any work on human enhancement and transhumanism. Indeed much of one's position depends on how the following questions are answered: What does it mean to be human? What is the ideal human and where are we going to achieve this?

Transhumanism and the human as mind and rationality

Aristotle famously defined the human being as a rational animal. The human being is a creature alongside other animals but distinct from them in its rationality and ability to reason. The Enlightenment and subsequently the modern period accentuated this Aristotelian maxim so that the human being was thought to be above the other animals precisely when it was utilizing its reasoning powers. Philosophical treatises by Leibniz, Spinoza and Kant sought to understand the primary purpose, function and limit of this supreme humanistic virtue: rationality. Transhumanism shares in this rationalist philosophy and, as its heir, locates what is distinctive about the human being in the mind and in its power of organization. It is the intellect that makes humanity great.

Transhumanism radicalizes this rationalist position and claims the only thing that is most essential to the human being exists in the patterns and make-up of each individual's brain. The mind is merely the manifestation of complex matter and the unique setup is housed in our neural networks. Our memories, our intellect and our personalities are solely products of interactions between neurons. Because of this, our embodied existences are only an historical and contingent coincidence. Of course, these ideas can be found among the neo-Platonists and the Gnostics so are not really that new. Many say the future of the human race is in uploading the mind: capturing the unique pattern of each person's neural network so that it can be transmitted to silicon-based hardware. Indeed, this is precisely what transhumanists recommend. Nick Bostrom notes we ought to abandon our bodies for more durable media because, he says, 'your body is a deathtrap' (Bostrom 2008: 3). For transhumanism, the human being is nothing less than the disembodied mind made up of complex calculations and logic.

Transhumanism and the human as information

When transhumanists claim that the essence of the human being, or what is really important for the human being, is captured in our brains and minds and easily transferred to whatever medium is necessary, they are really saying that the human being is nothing more than information. The human being can be reduced entirely to the representable where the reality of lived existence is reduced to the symbolic representation of that lived existence. Of course any contemporary treatise on human identity will take into consideration how our past experiences, history and memory play a significant role in who we are as individual persons. The content of that history and the unique experiences captured in our memories are important for understanding the identity of each person and what defines human being. Transhumanists, however, contend that the person is nothing but that which can be represented in information.

This basic anthropological tenet is manifest in two very concrete features of transhumanism. First, before mind uploading is technically feasible or possible, transhumanists advocate that human beings retrofit their current bodies with advanced computer hardware and utilize any and all enhancements to become, in the process, a veritable cyborg. In this move, we see one of their most central convictions regarding what it means to be human: the lack of distinction between that which is natural and given and that which is artificial and created. Transhumanists see no significant ontological distinction between the two. This conviction can be held because transhumanists adhere to an 'ontology of information': the idea that the essence of anything is to be found in its corresponding representation in information. Both the natural and the artificial can be reduced to a corresponding set of 0s and 1s. Therefore, because they see no difference between the human body and any other object – because everything is reducible to information – they not only have no problem with artificial retrofitting of the human body but they even advocate it. Transhumanism invokes an ontology of information where the virtual is more basic and primordial than the real.

The second feature which reveals this 'ontology of information' is related to their stance on artificial intelligence and the Turing Test. The Turing Test measures whether artificial intelligence can think.[3] Recent philosophical work on the Turing Test is interpreted by many transhumanists as a sign that thinking artificial intelligence is possible. This test paves the way for transhumanists to take the extra leap and to make room for purely artificial life forms that are self-directed and enjoy many of the privileges of other persons. Despite how strange this might sound, what it exposes is once again how transhumanism depends upon an ontology of information. If a human being is nothing but its neural network and corresponding intelligence where the medium does not matter, then why shouldn't a purely crafted and programmed artificial intelligence also fit the transhumanist standard for what constitutes a person? The human being is like everything else: primarily made up of information.

Transhumanism and the human as freedom and will

Transhumanism and certain appeals to human enhancement depend upon recognizing that freedom of choice is one of the supreme virtues in our modern age. Proponents of human enhancement, such as are found in transhumanist circles, rely upon the inherent virtue recognized in being able to decide the fate and course of action our individual lives ought to take. Our political systems valorize individual human choice and are set up precisely to safeguard our rights towards self-direction. Transhumanism celebrates this freedom and, indeed, extends it to self-transformation of all kinds.

Modernity has always been defined by a powerful subject that subdues its environment and takes control of its affairs. Since Francis Bacon, and with increasing vigour through Nietzsche to today's transhumanists, the will has been at the core of what defines a human being. This will to transform was first directed towards nature where the individual's dominion was a direct product of the will's influence. But with the arrival of Nietzsche and other existentialists came a turning of the will inwards as well as outwards. The very notion of personhood and identity became more flexible and fluid in postmodernity but with no less emphasis on the will as the inscrutable centre of humanity. For the postmodernist, the aim of life's game is constant transformation and reinvention of oneself. In this world the environment and the players never stand still. Transhumanism is but the extension of this crowning postmodernist philosophy built on modernist soil taken to new logical extremes.

It is important to note that many of these anthropological convictions are not only visible in transhumanism. Other germinal instantiations are invoked by contemporary society today and by more sober advocates of human enhancement. For instance, we understand today how important psychology is to human identity and how people's actions are dictated by the reasons they might give for those actions. People are assumed to be genuinely rational and self-directed. Furthermore, the increasing rights given to corporations as virtual persons in politics today shows we are willing to accept personhood as a continuum which can be bestowed on non-biological entities in the way that transhumanists do. The rise of identity fraud and arguments over intellectual property also reveals how closely we associate information about ourselves with who we are and that our information and the things we create are somehow part of us and not to be manipulated without our consent. And, we laud the likes of people who can overcome the odds of their upbringing to make something of themselves, showing how important resolve and a strong will are to being human. The claims of transhumanist anthropology bear many remarkable similarities to less zealous contemporary anthropologies.

Christianity and being human

What do Christians say about being human, and is it very different from the anthropology of transhumanism?

Human beings as creatures

First, Christians understand the human being to be a creature. As human beings we owe our existence to God who is the Creator of all that is. Our source of existence and life is completely derived from the utter gratuity and freedom of God to create abundantly. The entire concept of 'creature' evokes dependency upon a creator. We have been created contingent, limited and fragile. We need food, water and air to survive and, hence, our dependency extends not only and primarily to God but to the rest of creation as well. Indeed, we are not alone as creatures but in a much larger 'fellowship of creation'. The first two chapters of Genesis place human beings in this created order and, as such, we are *imago mundi*, in the image of the world.[4]

Human beings as imago Dei

Second, human beings are distinct from the rest of creation as *imago Dei*, in the image of God. The image of God first arises in Gen. 1:26-8 and the functional view of it largely stems from modern biblical criticism on this very passage and several others in the Hebrew Bible. It is clear from modern biblical scholarship that the Genesis passages are drawing upon the Ancient Near Eastern (ANE) context and, specifically, the notion that ANE rulers/kings reflected the image of the deity. The biblical text takes this notion and democratizes and universalizes it such that it is not just rulers that reflect God but the entirety of humanity. Indeed, the functional interpretation gets extended when the issue of dominion found in these passages is also placed in the ANE context. ANE rulers would often place statues of themselves in remote parts of their kingdom as a way of conveying their presence and power when they were physically absent. In other words, their image in this context signified their dominion: the image had the function of rulership. The Genesis texts co-opt this ANE practice and locate humanity as the divine image bearer whose responsibility is likewise that of dominion. The functional model is captured well in the following quotation by Gerhard von Rad (1961: 60):

> Just as powerful earthly kings, to indicate their claim to dominion, erect an image of themselves in the provinces of their empire where they do not personally appear, so man is placed upon earth in God's image as God's sovereign emblem. He is really only God's representative, summoned to maintain and enforce God's claim to dominion over the earth. The decisive thing about man's similarity to God, therefore, is his function in the non-human world.

The functional view claims that human beings reflect God's image in the world through their role as agents of God's dominion in His creation. Humanity's action in the world reflects God within it.

What is fascinating is that the functional interpretation of the image of God, despite its close following of the biblical text and critical biblical scholarship, is one of the most recent interpretations in the history of the doctrine itself. The structural view is the most common view and also the earliest in church history. The structural model claims the image of God refers to some quality or faculty that is inherent in the human being. It is something in human nature, something it possesses that makes it an image-bearer. As Stanley Grenz says (2001: 142), the structural view understands the image of God 'as referring to certain characteristics or capacities inherent in the structure of human nature. Because they resemble the corresponding qualities in God, their possession makes humans like God'. It is often also referred to as the 'substantive model' because 'it depicts something of substantial form in human nature, a faculty or a capacity that we humans possess over against animals' (Van Huyssteen 2006: 126). So, we might say that some quality or component of human nature is shared with God and that this is unique in both human beings and God relative to the rest of God's creation.

Turning from the structural approach to the relational means moving the weight of the image 'from noun to verb' (Grenz 2001: 162). Christian ethicist Paul Ramsey defines (1993: 255) the relational approach this way:

> The image of God is ... to be understood as a relationship *within which* man sometimes stands, whenever like a mirror he obediently reflects God's will in his life and actions ... The image of God, according to this view, consists of man's position before God, or, rather, the image of God is reflected in him because of his position before him.

Here the image of God is rooted in the divine address, in the very relationship God has to humanity. In other words, what makes humanity in the image of God is primarily the unique relationship humanity has with God and the fact that the human being is responsible to God in a special way. Secondarily, this view can sometimes assert that it is not just that our unique relationship to God makes us image bearers but also that, because we are relational, as God is relational in the Trinity, we too reflect God's image in the world. Human uniqueness in this model, then, is rooted in this special relationship with God and/or in human beings' unique relational abilities with other humans and creatures.

The dynamic view is sometimes referred to as the Christological or eschatological model and for good reason, because both terms help better define what makes it unique: its focus on both Christ and eschatology. In reference to the latter, Stanley Grenz explicitly links (2001: 177) the image of God to eschatology when he says this model 'sees the *imago dei* as humankind's divinely given goal or destiny, which lies in the eschatological future towards which humans are directed'. The dynamic view proposes that the image of God is not something entirely held or completed at the beginning of anthropological history, but is instead the *telos* or end of the human being to be completed in the future. Thus, instead of it being a protological concept (having to do with origins) it is actually an eschatological concept. Instead of the image of God originating in and being rooted in the first Adam, it actually has its centre of gravity in the second Adam, that is, Christ, and in the glorification of man in Christ. Thus, the image of God is also a Christological concept.

Christ, the imago Dei, and the rest of humanity

While different Christian traditions across history emphasize different aspects of each of these views, all agree that the fullest image of God, and indeed all interpretations of the *imago Dei*, ought to be grounded in the person of Christ. If we want to understand what it means to be human we need to look to Christ. Since Christ is God in human form we will find in the Incarnation the supreme image of God, the very thing which makes human beings unique. It is clear the New Testament bears witness to Christ being the fullest image of God and often links this explicitly (e.g. 2 Cor. 4:4-6). However, the concept of the *imago Dei* is also explicitly linked to God's glory where Christ is the very 'glory of God' (e.g. Jn 1:14). Pauline Christology and the Gospel of John constantly link Christ to the already established sister concepts of God's glory and image found in the Old Testament.

What is of grave import is how the rest of humanity, then, relates to Christ relative to this image. It is here we are told we are in the process of being conformed to the image of God in Christ (Rom. 8:29). We poorly reflect God's glory and image today but insofar as we live in relation to Christ and reflect His glory by following Him and reflecting the fruits of the spirit, we too reflect the glory of God with Christ. In this way, the image of God takes on a thoroughly dynamic and eschatological character where our adoption as 'children of God' in Christ takes on its most important significance. For our conformity to Christ also means we share in His glory and resurrection at the end of time. The *telos* of human being, as image bearer, is in a glorified Christ who reflects God's glory in a thoroughly redeemed creation.

Christian and transhumanist anthropology: Divergence or convergence?

How does a Christian understanding of human being cohere with the transhumanist vision? Several items look similar. Depending on one's interpretation of the *imago Dei*, both can share in the conviction that certain features such as rationality or volition are key to being human. Additionally, both contend that the human being is bound for better things and that we are in a process of transformation today. However, the overall vision and final aim of humanity is very different in the two approaches. Transhumanism is just 'the human writ large'. It is but an extension or logical conclusion of the human as mind, rational, information and will. While a contemporary Christian anthropology might acknowledge these aspects as integral to being human, they are not ends in themselves. They are only good insofar as they can be used to reflect God's glory as image bearers. What is more, that final ideal image is not some androgynous human prototype but Christ Himself. Christians believe that a true human being, what a human ought to be and is becoming, is only possible in relation to God in Christ. No amount of enhancement will be able to contend with the reality of sin that has destroyed and marred the human – only Christ can redeem and bring to fruition the 'real human'.[5]

While it is clear that the Christian account of the human being ultimately diverges from a robust transhumanist ideology because of the lack of a shared *telos* in Christ, what do we make of human enhancement issues more generally that do not necessarily presuppose a fully fledged transhumanist anthropology? In other words, do contemporary understandings of human plasticity and certain ethical imperatives to enhance human nature cohere with traditional conceptions of the image of God? This is a difficult question, and it will not be resolved fully in this chapter. However, allow me to offer some recent responses that have been made to it.

Structural accounts of the image of God, as we have seen, often depend upon the presence of a certain set of faculties or characteristics that is shared between God and humanity. Indeed, humans are said to be in the image of God because they are, for example, rational, self-aware, free or highly moral or creative. It is the presence of capacities like these that make the human being an image bearer. How might the use of human enhancements affect the structural account of the image of God? At first glance, human enhancements might seem to be very good news for those who hold the structural model, for it seems reasonable that some of the capacities that are the seat of the image of God might themselves be elevated or made more prominent because of a particular enhancement application. For example, suppose someone were to take the drug oxytocin for enhancement purposes which lead to greater altruistic feelings to those around them. One might say their moral sentiments were made better. Of course someone could argue that this temporary state of the individual surely should not be ascribed to their character, but what if someone could permanently alter the person's genome so that they were more altruistic and less aggressive and prone to violence? Wouldn't this be something adherents of the structural model might actually support? They could, but they might also worry that tampering with human capacities that are related to the image of God might actually lead to a dulling or even a complete loss of the image of God. These individuals might say that human beings *are* in the image of God and that any changes to the human being would risk a possible diminishment, since there is no way they can gain or elevate the image of God any more than they presently have it.[6] Therefore, the risk ought not be taken because no gain is possible, only a possible mismanaged enhancement that actually, in the end, leads to the diminishment of the image of God – in which case, the enhancement could not be defined as an enhancement anyway.

How might a relational account of the image of God accommodate or reject human enhancement? In this case, the very thing that might be elevated by the enhancement is more indirect than in the structural model because the seat of the image doesn't necessarily reside in the human being itself but in the relationship that God enacts and calls to be. Those in this position might say no amount of human enhancements will alter the relationship God has ordained between human beings and God because this relationship depends on God as initiator and creator of that relationship. Therefore, they might be entirely agnostic on whether human action, enhancements or otherwise, will actually do anything to influence the image of God. However, it is clear from our understanding of human relationality and the evolution of relational abilities that certain cognitive and cultural features are required as a presupposition to the kind of relationship valorized by those supporting this model (e.g. Dunbar 2010; Tomasello 2009; Tomasello 2016). Frankly, God and humans cannot have this kind of moral and spiritually rich relationship unless human beings possess the underlying capacities to have such relationships. Therefore, this model might be in the same position as the structural model where underlying capacities that give rise to relationships might be accessible to human enhancements. The capacities in question will obviously relate to human relationality so one can imagine enhancing things like theory of mind, heightening one's altruistic dispositions or even enhancing one's spiritual experiences.[7] In these cases where the underlying structures of the human being that give rise to relationality are enhanced, the same criticisms and hopes levelled with the structural model would apply here.[8]

Synthesizing the functional and dynamic models with human enhancement has many of the same issues as with the relational and structural model. If either is dependent on a relatively fixed anthropology or a very limited scope of human action to transform human nature and, hence, the image of God, then these models will be more hesitant or hostile towards human enhancement because of the presupposed malleability of human nature with human enhancement. However, both the functional model and the dynamic model have traditionally been the least tied to such a static view of human nature and human action.

Indeed, the functional view of the image of God highlights just how important human action in the world is to reflecting the image of God. By acting as God's representative in creation and bringing to fruition His intentions in it, we are said to be in God's image. Our human creativity in the world, one might say, is paramount to that image. This can go in one of two directions relative to human enhancement: (i) this action in creation can be extended to human transformation so that it is not just the non-human creation that is the object of human creativity but the human being itself; or (ii) this action on the human being will undermine the very creativity that acts as the divine reflection, for it signals an infraction of the natural and moral order and, in doing so, could forfeit divine reflection. There may seem to be little precedent for (i) in Christian history, and most Christian scholars tend to focus their efforts on (ii) above. Yet, a lack of precedent can be explained by the precise reason that such radical and basic physical change has never been possible up to this point. We just have not had to consider the radical physical and personal changes we can work on ourselves today. Therefore, the lack of precedent does not necessarily mean human action on the human being is anathema. However, extending the dominion image inherent in the functional view to include humanity itself and indeed its very nature does seem to go beyond the remit of what this action has entailed in the model. Further biblical and theological research would need to be done to test whether this expansion of remit was faithful to the tradition and Christian belief.[9]

The dynamic view of human nature is the most amenable to human enhancement because of its commitment to the present malleability of human nature. The dynamic view holds that human beings do not adequately reflect the image of God at present because of sin but when seen through the prism of Christ's redemption and the conformity of each individual to Christ, humans do reflect that image. Inherent in this dynamic view is that human beings are to be sanctified in Christ and that they grow in virtue, spirituality and faith. Hence, the Christian life is to be marked by this growth and presupposed in this growth and the dynamic view is a flexible human being. As Kathryn Tanner notes (2010):

With this loss of a primary preoccupation with human nature per se as the image of God comes an odd refocusing of what is of interest about human beings. Since human beings do not image God in and of themselves but only when radically reworked into the divine image through Christ, it is the plasticity of human nature that becomes important. Plasticity is the capacity that allows humans to image God.

Arguments, therefore, can be made that human enhancements can shape the human being towards entirely productive ends, that is towards conformity to Christ. Those in this camp will argue that the human being, as he or she is presently, should not be protected or safeguarded at all costs (for it is mired in sin and is not complete), but that instead what matters is the correct employment of Christ as the end and template of the human being. They might say human enhancements could have a role in shaping the human towards Christian ends.[10]

The repercussions of human enhancements for the image of God are anything but clear. Depending upon which model one holds, or indeed which combination of models, the acceptability of human enhancements is varied. The three major controlling questions that really dictate the level of acceptability in any model are: (i) How fixed is the human being in the model? (ii) How far can/ought human action on human nature go? and (iii) Do enhancements really contribute to man's bearing of the final image of God in Christ? Related to all of this, Ted Peters and Ronald Cole-Turner note, it is often our overall view of creation that will largely affect our stance on enhancement. If we only see creation as good we

> tend to overestimate our own goodness (e.g., our powers of reason and ability to know what God wants); or we find it hard to name defects in nature that should be corrected. However, if we see creation *only* as flawed or fallen, we then assume that it is open to any and all manipulations; and we fail to see that it has value independent of us. (Cole-Turner 1993: 71; Peters 2010: 235).

However Christians decide to respond to human enhancement and the image of God, serious reflection, study and discernment is called for because the challenges themselves will not be subsiding any time soon.

Conclusions

Research on theology, transhumanism and human enhancement is very much a work-in-progress today. Theological perspectives on transhumanism and human enhancement have slowly been forming the last several decades.[11] What is more, the impact of both human enhancement and the ideology of transhumanism on one area of Christian theology, the image of God, is at the very forefront of academic research in science and religion. Transhumanism is a growing ideological movement. Advancements in biotechnology, nanotechnology and information technology are provoking a great deal of speculation about the future of each individual human person and indeed humanity as a distinct species. Society is inevitably starting to ask questions of where these advances should lead us – questions not just about our present actions but, more significantly perhaps, about our future identities. If Christians are to have an impact on society then they must engage not simply with the immediate decisions regarding human enhancement that are made in the present but also with the ideologies being sculpted for the future. A robust Christian response requires both short-term proximate engagement with human enhancement and the longer-term goals found in contemporary transhumanist ideology.

I have argued here that, at least on the question of humanity, the ideology of transhumanism diverges from typical Christian anthropologies. There might be shared beliefs about the make-up of human beings – such as rationality or volition – and that the human being is bound for better things but the overall vision and final aim of humanity differs. Transhumanism is the extension of present definitions of the human as mind, rational, information and will but, for Christians, this is not what is most important – they aren't the goal or purpose of human existence. Instead, they are only good insofar as they can be used to reflect God's glory that has its most complete image of God in Christ. However, the Christian response to how human enhancements themselves might impact the image of God depends on the model or combination of models held: functional, structural, relational or dynamic. What seems to be the most relevant to the acceptability of human enhancement and its relation to the image of God is (i) prior belief in the plasticity of human nature, (ii) the acceptability of human action to transform itself and (iii) whether enhancements can actually contribute to the final image of God in Christ.

Notes

1   The full acronym refers to 'Clustered regularly interspaced short palindromic repeats, CRISPR associated protein 9'.

2   For an excellent treatment of how human dignity functions in bioethics and enhancement discourse, see President's Council on Bioethics (2008), Bennett (2016) and the December 2017 issue (Volume 23, Issue 3) of *Christian Bioethics*.

3   The Turing Test consists of a person and another person or artificial intelligence
     separated by a barrier where the only means of communication between them is
     through texts. The task of the person is to correspond with the other person or
     artificial intelligence and at the end of this correspondence to assess and judge
     whether the entity they are speaking to via text is a real human person or an
     artificial intelligence. The artificial intelligence passes the test if the human person
     concludes that the artificial intelligence is a human being. For more information on
     what the Turing Test does and does not prove, see Shieber (2004).
4   Indeed this is a central claim of Jürgen Moltmann in reference to creation
     (Moltmann 1985).
5   See the section entitled 'Real Man' in §44 of Barth 1960.
6   How does this relate to the apparent lack of conformity of present human beings to
     the full image of God in Christ? In the Christian tradition, from Irenaeus onwards,
     a distinction is introduced that is relevant here although it received great criticism
     during the Reformation. Certain scholars sought to distinguish between the
     'image' (*tselem* in Hebrew, *imago* in Latin) in the Genesis text from that of 'likeness'
     (*děmuth, similitudo*). These scholars claim that the 'image' of God is something
     that is universal in human beings; it is equated with both reason and the will and
     survives the fall of man. However, the 'likeness' (*similitudo*) to God is lost in the
     fall. Therefore, they can say that the image of God remains fixed in present human
     beings while also noting the moral and spiritual failings of human beings. For
     more, see Crouch (2010), Miller (1972).
7   For a fascinating article on enhancing spirituality, see Cole-Turner (2015).
8   For an interesting argument for enhancement within a structural and relational
     model of the image of God, see Miletić (2015).
9   For initial forays into this discussion, see Cole-Turner (2016), Deane-Drummond
     (2008), Peters (2010), Garner (2006), Russell (2003).
10   Scholars like Ted Peters, Jeanine Thweat, Ronald Cole-Turner, Stephen Garner and
     Tomislav Miletić argue, in some form, for this possibility.
11   Seminal texts which aim at large coverage of these issues include Cole-Turner, ed.,
     2011; Mercer and Trothen, eds., 2015.

References

Barth, Karl (1960), *The Church Dogmatics, Vol. III/2*, Edinburgh: T&T Clark.
Bennett, Gaymon (2016), *Technicians of Human Dignity: Bodies, Souls, and the Making
     of Intrinsic Worth*, New York: Fordham University Press.
Bostrom, Nick (2003), 'The Transhumanist FAQ: A General Introduction', World
     Transhumanist Organisation. Available online: https://nickbostrom.com/views/
     transhumanist.pdf (accessed 22 May 2009).

Bostrom, Nick (2008), 'Letter from Utopia', *Studies in Ethics, Law and Technology*, 2 (1): 1–7.

Burdett, Michael (2014), *Technology and the Rise of Transhumanism: Beyond Genetic Engineering*, Cambridge: Grove Books.

Cole-Turner, Ronald (1993), *The New Genesis: Theology and the Genetic Revolution*, Louisville, KY: Westminster John Knox Press.

Cole-Turner, Ronald, ed. (2011), *Transhumanism and Transcendence: Christian Hope in an Age of Technological Enhancement*, Washington, DC: Georgetown University Press.

Cole-Turner, Ronald (2015), 'Spiritual Enhancement', in Calvin Mercer and Tracy Trothen (eds), *Religion and Transhumanism: The Unknown Future of Human Enhancement*, 369–383, Santa Barbara, CA: Praeger.

Cole-Turner, Ronald (2016), 'Eschatology and the Technologies of Human Enhancement', *Interpretation: A Journal of Bible and Theology* 70 (1): 21–33.

Crouch, Carly (2010), 'Genesis 1: 26-7 as a Statement of Humanity's Divine Parentage', *Journal of Theological Studies*, 61 (1): 1–15.

Deane-Drummond, Celia (2008), 'Freedom, Conscience, and Virtue: Theological Perspectives on the Ethics of Inherited Genetic Modification', in Ronald Cole-Turner (ed.), *Design and Destiny: Jewish and Christian Perspectives on Human Germline Modification*, 167–200, Cambridge, MA: MIT Press.

Dunbar, Robin (2010), *How Many Friends Does One Person Need?: Dunbar's Number and Other Evolutionary Quirks*, Cambridge, MA: Harvard University Press.

Garner, Stephen (2006), *Transhumanism and the Imago Dei: Narratives of Apprehension and Hope*, Auckland: The University of Auckland.

Grenz, Stanley (2001), *The Social God and the Relational Self: A Trinitarian Theology of the Imago Dei*, Louisville, KY: Westminster John Knox Press.

Grossman, Lev (2011), '2045: The Year Man Becomes Immortal', *Time*, 21 February. Available online: http://content.time.com/time/magazine/article/0,9171,2048299,00.html (accessed 3 July 2018).

Hughes, James (2005), *Report on the 2005 Interests and Beliefs Survey of the Members of the World Transhumanist Association*, Willington, CT: World Transhumanist Association. Available online: https://www.academia.edu/1402638/Report_on_the_2005_Interests_and_Beliefs_Survey_of_the_Members_of_the_World_Transhumanist_Association (accessed 3 July 2018).

Human Dignity and Bioethics: Essays Commissioned by the President's Council on Bioethics (2008), Washington, DC: President's Council on Bioethics.

Mercer, Calvin and Tracy Trothen, eds (2015), *Religion and Transhumanism: The Unknown Future of Human Enhancement*, Santa Barbara, CA: Praeger.

Miletić, Tomislav (2015), 'Human Becoming: Cognitive and Moral Enhancement inside the Imago Dei Narrative', *Theology and Science*, 13 (4): 425–445.

Miller, J. Maxwell (1972), 'In the "Image" and "Likeness" of God', *Journal of Biblical Literature*, 91 (3): 289–304.

Moltmann, Jürgen (1985), *God in Creation: An Ecological Doctrine of Creation*, London: SCM Press.

Peters, Ted (2010), 'Can We Enhance the Imago Dei?', in Nancey C. Murphy and Christopher C. Knight (eds), *Human Identity at the Intersection of Science, Technology and Religion*, 215–238, Farnham: Ashgate.

President's Council on Bioethics (2008), *Human Dignity and Bioethics: Essays Commissioned by the President's Council on Bioethics*, Washington, DC: The President's Council on Bioethics.

Ramsey, Paul (1993), *Basic Christian Ethics*, Louisville, KY: Westminster John Knox Press.

Russell, Robert J. (2003), 'Five Attitudes towards Nature and Technology from a Christian Perspective', *Theology and Science*, 1 (2): 149–159.

Shieber, Stuart M., ed. (2004), *The Turing Test: Verbal Behavior as the Hallmark of Intelligence*, Cambridge, MA: MIT Press.

Tanner, Kathryn (2010), 'Grace without Nature', in David Albertson and Cabell King (eds), *Without Nature?: A New Condition for Theology*, 363–375, New York: Fordham University Press.

Tomasello, Michael (2009), *Why We Cooperate*, Cambridge, MA: MIT Press.

Tomasello, Michael (2016), *A Natural History of Human Morality*, Cambridge, MA: Harvard University Press.

van Huyssteen, J. Wentzel (2006), *Alone in the World?: Human Uniqueness in Science and Theology*, Grand Rapids, MI: Eerdmans.

von Rad, Gerhard (1961), *Genesis*, London: SCM Press.

13

Bioethics and the Secular Belief of Inherent Human Dignity

Calum MacKellar

Introduction

The *Oxford English Reference Dictionary* defines dignity as the 'state of being worthy of honour and respect' although the concept also includes aspects of 'value' and 'worth'.

Interpreting the concept of human dignity, however, remains a challenge for many commentators working in the field of bioethics since no clear or robust definition exists.

Some even maintain that human dignity is not a useful, meaningful or relevant concept in ethical discussions. For instance, British political theorist Alasdair Cochrane argues for a bioethics discourse where dignity does not play any role (2010: 234–41).

But others strongly disagree with this representation of human dignity, stating that the concept is crucial to understanding certain arguments in bioethics (Kraynak and Tinder 2003; Kirchhoofer 2013). In fact, a number of commentators affirm that such dignity is the only solid foundation to human ethics, human rights and bioethical legislation (Andorno 2009).

One of the reasons why the importance of the concept has been considered in such dissimilar ways, over the years, is that different forms of human dignity exist since it can be defined in diverse but complementary ways (Michael 2013). Accordingly, several authors have sought to characterize different categories of human dignity (see Sulmasy 2007: 9–18; Neal 2012: 177–200; Kirchhoffer 2013; Kirchhoffer and Dierickx 2011: 552–556; Thiel 2010: 51–62; Meilaender 2009). These can generally be divided into two main groups, namely (i) non-inherent (contingent) human dignity and (ii) inherent (absolute) human dignity.

Non-inherent human dignity

Non-inherent human dignity is usually considered as a state of being worthy of honour and respect, which can vary quite considerably between individuals and can even be gained or lost. Many different kinds of such dignity have been proposed. Sometimes it has been suggested to reflect the character, conduct, behaviour or personal qualities of a person (Nordenfeld 2004: 72; Mattson and Clark 2011: 303–319), such as the way certain individuals reflect a certain amount of grace, refinement and composure (Riley 2010: 119). This is what happens, for example, when a person does not respond to deliberate provocation.

At other times, non-inherent dignity has been defined as a kind of subjective dignity reflecting a personal and felt experience (Mattson and Clark 2011; Neal 2012). This is similar to using the term to express a sense of self-esteem and subjective feelings such as pride, shame, degradation or inferiority (Rendtorff 2002: 237).

A final example of how non-inherent dignity may be understood is when it is used to characterize an attributed respect which persons receive when they are seen to merit various honours or a certain amount of personal reverence such as a judge in a court of law.

Of course, the concept of non-inherent human dignity is very important in bioethics. When, for instance, patients are not being cared for in the way they find appropriate, one of the violations which they are experiencing is a disregard for their non-inherent human dignity.

But this kind of dignity cannot give any genuine value and worth to some human beings, such as neonates or those with severe intellectual disabilities. Moreover, since non-inherent dignity reflects characteristics that are not shared equally by all and which may even vary quite considerably between persons, it cannot be used to ground the concept of equality of worth and value in society. This means that another understanding of human dignity is necessary to ground the core values of bioethics.

Inherent human dignity

In contrast to the concept of non-inherent dignity, inherent human dignity reflects the value and worth of a person which is unconditional, permanent, immeasurable, inviolable,[1] inalienable and indivisible.[2] But, just as importantly, this kind of dignity refers to the inherent worth that is absolutely equal between all human beings (Rendtorff 2002). If one asks, for example, what the equality of human beings in civilized society is based upon, it must be on the equality of inherent dignity. As the US bioethicist Daniel Sulmasy (2007: 10) explains in the context of discussing what can be characterized as inherent dignity: 'Dignity is the answer to the more fundamental questions: "Why should I respect people's autonomy?" and "Why should I treat people with equity?" Dignity is the ground of rights, not synonymous for rights.'

As such, inherent human dignity is reflected in every person to an equal extent and can never be lost (in contrast to non-inherent dignity). It must be safeguarded and respected in all persons for a civilized society to survive. Indeed, it is because of this concept of dignity that societies continue to protect vulnerable individuals, such as those who do not have any rational or autonomous capacities.

At present, most people also accept that inherent human dignity is universal, whereby each and every person is expected to recognize this same dignity in everyone else. This is in accordance with the United Nations' 1948 Universal Declaration of Human Rights, which affirms in its preamble 'the inherent dignity and … the equal and inalienable rights of all members of the human family' as 'the foundation of freedom, justice and peace in the world'.

This text emphasizes the absolute nature of inherent human dignity while affirming the reality of a global community to which all human beings belong which is highlighted by the word 'all'. There are no exceptions. In other words, such a dignity cannot be destroyed or modified by an individual, an electoral majority or even a state. Moreover, it is not dependent upon any varying functional capacities such as intelligence, abstract reason, rational autonomy, language, creativity, ability to experience suffering, empathy, awareness, health or beauty and quality of life but reflects the immeasurable worth and value of everyone. It can be threatened, ignored, abused or hidden but never lost.

It is also worth noting that without the concept of inherent dignity, human beings would be open to being killed without restraint. Indeed, the only reason why the act of murder is totally inadmissible is because it is incompatible with the inherent worth and value of all human beings. This means that inherent human dignity is the very foundation of the rule of law in civilized society.

Accordingly, it must be acknowledged, firstly, to exist and, secondly, that it is reflected in all human beings enabling them to have a special and full moral status while regulating the manner human persons should treat each other. In this way, the human rights which are derived from the concept of inherent human dignity can be used to regulate and structure the relationships between people whose interests interact.

Furthermore, it should be emphasized that the concept of inherent dignity cannot be reduced to any physical science since it is impossible to demonstrate, logically, that any beings, even rational and autonomous adult human beings, reflect any inherent dignity, value or worth. From a purely scientific perspective, all life, including all human life, can just be considered as developing biochemical molecules which do not have any value whatsoever or reason to survive.

In other words, the question of the inherent worth of human life is deeply philosophical in nature, and science alone is incapable of providing any answers as to why human beings are morally valuable and equal.

On this account, and since inherent human dignity is something that cannot be completely defined (Andorno 2001: 151–168), any attempt to measure this concept constitutes a fundamental misunderstanding of its very meaning. This implies that inherent human dignity is simply something that is recognized or declared to exist and to be essential for a civilized society to survive as noted in the UN's 1948 Universal Declaration of Human Rights.[3]

In short, the concept of inherent and equal dignity is something in which all individuals in secular society must (or have a duty to) believe, meaning that it has normative implications.

To reject such a notion would be an extremely dangerous precedent in a world that has fought so hard to endow all persons with the same dignity in order to create a civilized society.

Network of inherent human dignity

It follows that if a civilized society and the rule of law are to survive, all human beings must believe that inherent human dignity exists and that it is reflected in themselves as well as in all others. In other words, the concept requires a secular belief in the notion of the absolute worth of all persons supported by a system whereby all individuals continually value and confer inherent dignity on everyone else while recognizing that everyone else has already conferred this dignity on all in society.

This also means that all persons in a civilized society must be prepared to accept the absolute value being given to them, as embodied persons, by everyone else – an absolute value they then permanently possess and which they can (if they are self-aware) pass on and bestow on others.

On this account, the concept of inherent human dignity in society necessitates a global network in which all who are aware should always believe that all who exist in the network reflect inherent equal worth in themselves and in others.

This further implies that when an individual deliberately refuses to value all others in the network, then from his or her own perspective, he or she cannot receive any value from these others since, in the eyes of this individual, these others have no worth to pass on. In other words, to refuse to take part in the mutually recognizing network of valuing all others is to refuse to be valued by others.

As the UK Supreme Court judge Baroness Brenda Hale indicated in 2009 while discussing what could be interpreted as inherent human dignity: 'Respect for the dignity of others is ... also respect for one's own dignity and essential humanity. Not to respect the dignity of others is also not to respect one's own dignity' (2009: 106).

But the reverse is also true in that if an individual believes that he or she does not have any inherent dignity, then he or she cannot value others.[4] That is to say, for an individual to refuse to recognize his or her own inherent worth is to refuse to take part in the mutually recognizing network of valuing others. In a way, such individuals take themselves out from the network.

The South African-British judge Lord Hubert Hoffmann developed such a position in 1993 when he indicated: 'The fact that the dignity of an individual is an intrinsic value is shown by the fact that we feel embarrassed and think it wrong when someone acts in a way which we think demeaning to himself, which does not show sufficient respect for himself as a person.'[5]

But the network of inherent human dignity demands that all who are self-aware and conscious should still continue to value and recognize the inherent worth of those persons who decide not to be part of the network. This is important for the network to remain robust even though any decision to leave the system weakens its strength.

Similarly, it is vital that all those who are self-aware in society continue to value individuals who cannot make any decisions such as infants or persons with very serious mental disabilities. These vulnerable individuals will then remain part of the network even though they are incapable of valuing anyone else.

Furthermore, in some situations, such as when solitary individuals are being tortured or abused, and where nobody else is recognizing the worth of these human beings, the only value-giving system that may remain for these individuals is for themselves to continue to acknowledge their own inherent human dignity.

Interestingly, for such an inherent human dignity network to begin to work (even if only very weakly at first), only one person needs to begin to recognize his or her inherent worth and that of others. A representation of such a system would, in a way, be like the electricity going through an electrical network. The current may be very small at first, if only one small source of electricity exists but it is still very present.[6] This means that for inherent human dignity to exist, there must be an originator who believes that inherent value exists while, at the same time, deciding to recognize this value in others.

The boundary of inherent human dignity

Significantly, the concept of equal inherent dignity is only protected if clear factors exist which can be used to determine boundaries between those beings who do and those who do not have this dignity. This was reflected by US bioethicist Leon Kass, a former chair of the US President's Council on Bioethics:

> All of the boundaries that have defined us as human beings, boundaries between a human being and an animal on one side and between a human being and a super human being or a god on the other. The boundaries of life, the boundaries of death. These are the questions of the 21st century, and nothing could be more important. (quoted in Smith 2005)

In other words, even though the concept of inherent human dignity is impossible to define completely, since it is a kind of secular belief, an entity with a moral status which straddles two sides of the boundary of this dignity is untenable. This is because the relevance of the whole concept could then be questioned.

As a result, it is now possible to understand how inherent human dignity may be undermined. This would happen, for example, if it became difficult to ascertain, with any amount of certainty, whether absolute, inalienable and inherent dignity should be recognized in, or conferred upon, certain living beings. In addition, if a being were denied the inherent dignity to which he or she is entitled, then the dignity of every individual in the whole global network may be undermined. This is because the whole network would no longer be consistent, coherent or reliable. It would also mean that the very basis, order and structure of society and its rule of law would be damaged and brought into question since a clear demarcation of inherent human dignity is essential for a civilized society to survive.

If, however, equal inherent human dignity is no longer recognized in certain individuals, this does not mean that civilized society will immediately collapse. But real risks exist and should not be ignored. No national community can ever take the moral high ground by affirming, either because of its geography or history, that it is immune from possible abuse or resistant to moral erosion. Such an attitude would reflect a significant lack of humility and sense of reality! It is, therefore, vital for each and everybody in society to be very careful when crossing the bright red line of acknowledging that any living human being can lose some or all of his or her worth and value.

Giving the benefit of the doubt

At this stage it is worth noting that a living being cannot have just a degree of this full inherent human dignity since there is no intermediate option.

Thus, those who questioned the inherent human dignity of certain human beings, such as black people throughout the slave trade, indigenous Amerindians (discussed in the Valladolid debate in the Catholic Church between 1550 and 1551), people with disabilities and a number of other minority groups in Nazi Germany, have all served to challenge the very network of inherent human dignity. In fact, it was this last horrendous violation of inherent human dignity by the Nazi regime that inspired the UN's General Assembly in 1948 to adopt and give expression to the concept in the Universal Declaration of Human Rights.

A key factor in these past controversies was the failure by society to accept and recognize the inherent human dignity of certain human beings. This is something that happened because a majority of the relevant society, at the time, believed that these human beings (Amerindians, Blacks, Jews) were not part of the inherent human dignity network. But since a significant minority disagreed very strongly with this view and had robust rational reasons for doing so, the majority should have given them the benefit of the doubt. A benefit that, if they were honest and consistent, they were also giving to themselves since the worth and value of all human beings is not a scientifically demonstrable concept but a rational secular belief.

Accordingly, when real and authentic questions exist in a society about the moral status of certain living beings, such as human–nonhuman interspecies beings, then these should be given the benefit of the doubt so that the strength of the network of human dignity is re-established. As a result, the new uncertain limits or frontiers of inherent human dignity are broadened to create a new larger, clearer and stronger border, which includes all the beings of uncertain moral status. In other words, it is crucial that the way some beings are considered should not bring about any perception of chaos or instability in society.

Inherent human dignity and autonomy

As already mentioned, a number of bioethical commentators have suggested that the very concept of inherent human dignity may be empty of meaning. For them, what really matters is the respect given to the autonomy of human beings who are seeking to make their lives meaningful and valuable – in other words, the ability for persons to be the author of their own lives (Bennett and Harris 2007: 201). This may then mean that an individual should only respect the autonomy of other persons because he or she wants them to respect his or her own autonomy. But such a form of social contract does not really give any strong or robust protection to those who have less or no autonomy. Those who are powerful with a strong sense of autonomy may, for example, begin to believe that they no longer need such a social contract for their autonomy to be respected. These powerful individuals may then impose their autonomy on the weak. Indeed, if a belief in inherent human dignity no longer exists, there is really no reason whatsoever for such abuse to be seen as wrong, in and of itself, even if these weak individuals retain full rational autonomy and are very much enjoying their lives.

Certainly, the advancement of autonomy, the reduction of suffering and the increase in flourishing of human persons are very important goals in any ethical appraisal. But these aims do not give any true value to human life. Inherent worth cannot be dependent on what individuals are able to do or feel or on the aims of their lives. Instead, it is based on what persons are and the absolute value that others confer on, and recognize in, themselves and all others. Moreover, if only autonomy or the lack of suffering were the basis of the value of a person, then every human being could be classified on a scale – classified as having a different worth making the very concept of an egalitarian and civilized society meaningless. Thus, inherent dignity must have priority over autonomy while also acknowledging that it is only because a person is recognized as having inherent dignity that his or her autonomy is even respected.

Inherent human dignity, euthanasia and assisted suicide

Those who are seeking to legalize euthanasia and assisted suicide are generally motivated by compassion in wanting to enable a person to end their lives in order to avoid any suffering. Compassion, in this context, would mean acknowledging that some persons may be in great distress because they cannot put an end to their lives which, they believe, have lost any meaning.

Advocates of euthanasia and assisted suicide, therefore, do so on the very strong themes of compassion and autonomy, a position that is extremely important in medical ethics. They also accept that what gives this life its worth is the person's ability to find value for himself or herself according to his or her own personal values, desires and relationships.

This would reflect what is believed to be certain standards of decency, autonomy and the quality of such a life. For example, it is sometimes suggested that euthanasia and assisted suicide should be accepted because the value of human life can be reduced by suffering or a dependence on others. This is how the concept of dignity is understood in the US state of Oregon with its 'Death with Dignity Act 1997' which legalized assisted suicide.

But if euthanasia and assisted suicide are decriminalized, it would mean that society has accepted that those who cannot find any value in their own lives lack lives of value and that the inherent value of all human beings is no longer universal and can actually be lost. Furthermore, it would indicate that some lives may no longer have any inherent worth and should be ended, including the life of the young man who wants to commit suicide or the very sick person who only has twenty-four hours to live. It would also mean that society, as whole, agrees that the value of some lives may be different because, for example, everyone suffers to a different extent.

In many ways, therefore, those who believe that euthanasia and assisted suicide should be accepted agree that their autonomy should have priority over their inherent dignity.

However, if a person decides that he or she no longer has any value or worth, and society agrees with him or her through its parliament, it is the whole of the network which is damaged. In a way, those who want to legalize euthanasia and assisted suicide are stating that an individual is entitled to refuse the inherent dignity that society is recognizing in him or her. They are asking the whole of civilized society to deny the universal equality of inherent value of all human beings on which it is built.

It would also give the message that the very value and meaning of a human life is merely based on subjective choices or decisions and whether a life meets certain quality standards. As a result, it would affect everyone in society and not just those contemplating euthanasia or assisted suicide. For example, such a society could no longer offer any robust arguments against ending the lives of people who may be considered as having an inferior or unworthy quality of life. The survival of a civilized society in which every life has inherent value and dignity would then be compromised.

On this account, vulnerable people need to know that they are valued and unconditionally accepted for who they are. They need to know that there is no shame in being dependent on others since that is what society is all about – a place where all members can help each other, where they are dependent on each other and where everybody recognizes the same value and worth in everyone else.

Inherent human dignity and the human embryo/foetus

Any discussion concerning the value of human life is generally associated to the question whether all living human beings have full, inherent dignity and thus deserve equal protection as soon as they are brought into existence. But, as already mentioned, this is usually grounded in essentially unprovable assumptions. Consequently, society is generally unable to reach a final consensus about the moral status of living beings such as human embryos or foetuses. This is especially the case when their use and destruction can be seen, in certain situations, as being useful or as a solution to a difficult problem (Banchoff 2011).

From this perspective, whether or not human embryos and foetuses are inside the boundary of the network of human dignity becomes the crucial question. An example of the kind of problems that may arise when clear boundaries relating to inherent dignity are not respected took place when the UK Human Fertilisation and Embryology Act 1990 was ratified. Legislators, at the time, were anxious not to recognize full inherent dignity to the early human embryo, but neither were they ready to completely deny this embryo any dignity. As a result, they decided only to give the human embryo a certain degree of this full human dignity reflecting what they suggested was its 'special status' as characterized in the UK's Warnock Report (1984). But eventually, with the passing of the years, the concept of a special moral status of the embryo was all but abandoned. Without any clear definition, and because it was seen as straddling the borderline of inherent human dignity, the concept was unintelligible and impracticable.

In December 2002, Baroness Warnock, admitted in the House of Lords[7]:

> I regret that in the original report that led up to the 1990 legislation we used words such as 'respect for the embryo' … I think that what we meant by the rather foolish expression 'respect' was that the early embryo should never be used frivolously for research purposes.

She added:

> You cannot respectfully pour something down the sink – which is the fate of the embryo after it has been used for research, or if it is not going to be used for research or for anything else.

Interestingly, when the 1990 Act was amended in 2008, hardly any discussion relating to the special status of the human embryo remained. The human embryo had, by then, gradually been reduced in societal discussions to 'a pile of cells'. But the destruction of human embryos is still considered as a form of state-sanctioned human sacrifice by a significant minority in UK society and as a practice which deeply challenges the very existence of civilized society.

This example demonstrates, once again, that when human beings such as embryos or foetuses are not given the benefit of the doubt as to their moral status and brought into the network of human dignity, it is this very network that may be undermined. Moreover, it is worth noting that any community which can no longer give any moral reasons to restrain human behaviour, especially in the way it considers vulnerable human beings, such as human foetuses, very much risks drifting into moral meaninglessness (Pullman 2010: 353–364).

Inherent human dignity and transhuman or posthuman beings

Until now, a great moral divide has always existed between human beings and other living beings. But this situation is now changing in the considerations of:

(1) Transhumans (defined as beings who have bodies which are recognizably human), such as:

-   Human–nonhuman interspecies combinations,
-   Human–computer cyborgs, and
-   Synthetic biological transhumans.

(2) Posthumans (defined as beings who no longer have bodies which are recognizably human), such as:

-   Virtual persons existing/living in cyberspace, and
-   Synthetic biological posthumans.

In this regard, the creation of human–nonhuman interspecies embryonic combinations in some countries, such as in the UK, at the beginning of the twenty-first century marks a significant milestone in human history.

Moreover, in the context of transhuman and posthuman entities, using the term 'inherent human dignity' may no longer be appropriate since many of these entities are only partly, or not at all, biologically human. In other words, it may be preferable to just use the term 'full inherent dignity' which is associated with having a full moral status. In this way, human dignity would only be one kind of full inherent dignity which is associated with the species *Homo sapiens*. Some transhuman and posthuman entities may then have a dignity which is not human but still have the same full moral, inviolable worth as human individuals with inherent human dignity (MacKellar and Jones 2012).

It is true that the moral classification and appreciation of some transhuman and posthuman combinations will be extremely difficult. This is because many new beings may not fit easily into the existing categories of either human or nonhuman beings with their respective rights. A certain amount of confusion and disorder may then arise. On this account, and following the previous discussion, the only appropriate way forward may be to consider some transhuman and posthuman living entities, whose moral status is uncertain, as reflecting the same moral value as other fully human beings. This uncertainty would probably continue even if, for example, an embryonic or foetal human–nonhuman combination was left to develop to term but, once born, remained unaware of its existence. But if the entity is brought into existence, then it should be given the benefit of the doubt and the same protection as any other person in society. This means that destroying transhuman or posthuman entities for research purposes could be considered as a form of murder and be ethically unacceptable (MacKellar and Jones 2012).

As already mentioned, if some transhuman or posthuman beings are not given the full inherent dignity to which they are entitled, nor given the benefit of the doubt, this would not only offend the beings themselves but would also undermine the whole community of individuals entitled to such a dignity (De Melo-Martín 2008: 331–346; Deutscher Ethikrat 2011: 61). In this manner, the global protective network arising from this dignity would become unstable, inconsistent and unclear while the whole concept of civilized society and its rule of law would be injured. For example, with human–nonhuman interspecies combinations, the relationship between human beings and other animals would have to be completely re-evaluated. As the German ethicists Gisela Badura-Lotter and Marcus Düwell indicated, 'it is hard to assume that we will be able to cope with the cataclysm that such a process would involve' (2011: 204).

In short, full inherent dignity is not only endangered because transhuman or posthuman beings may not be part of the *Homo sapiens* species as such. Instead, it is the whole concept of recognizing and conferring full inherent dignity to all individuals within the global community, without having to pass some test of acceptance, that would be endangered. As the North American ethical commentators Josephine Johnston and Christopher Eliot state: 'To intentionally create a creature that has human components or contains human biological material but does not have human rights ... could be an affront both to the creature itself and to our collective opinion of the worth of human beings' (2003: 7).

These considerations do not, of course, apply equally to all transhuman and posthuman entities. They do, however, imply that such entities should never be brought into existence unless they have a clear and uncontested moral status. If there is any uncertainty for a significant proportion of the general public, then they should not be brought into existence. Moreover, if these entities are unfortunately created with dubious moral status, then they should be given the benefit of the doubt as to their full inherent dignity (MacKellar and Jones 2012).

Inherent human dignity and the human body or its parts

The view that the body is less important than the mind reflects a number of ideas in the ancient world including those of the Greek philosopher Plato (428/427 BC–348/347 BC) and his theory of forms. This asserted that non-material abstract forms (or thoughts) enjoy the highest and most fundamental kind of reality in comparison to the material world which changes with time.

Subsequently, the French enlightenment philosopher René Descartes (1596–1650) presented a similar position by suggesting that the mind is a substance distinct from the body with a number of theories being developed by later commentators defending a dualism of human nature (1984 [1641]; 1991 [1637]). These maintained that the material body and the mind were totally separate in a person.[8]

From this perspective, persons could decide to distance themselves from their bodies, in a similar way to other objects, since these no longer had any part to play with the persons' 'real and genuine' selves.[9] In other words, it was possible to consider a human mind as being trapped in a material object, the body, which was part of, and belonged to, the human person but could not really contribute, in any significant way, to the inherent dignity of this person (see Garcia and Jochemsen 2005: 92).

But such a dualism, which considers the body as some kind of habitation for the real person, would presuppose the existence of non-bodily persons and non-personal living, integrated and whole bodies which is difficult to accept. Thus, an alternative understanding of the unity and integrity of the human person can be proposed. This does not just reduce the human body and mind to different parts of a whole, as in a *dualism*, but instead considers them as a *duality* whereby they both represent different complementary and interacting expressions of this whole. Accordingly, the body and mind of a person are never dissociated since this would, otherwise, reduce the person to something which he or she cannot be.

This also means that the way the human body is treated is related to the way the human person, as a whole, is treated since his or her body can be considered as a material manifestation of the whole person (Andrews 1986: 28–38; Kass 2002; Garcia and Jochemsen 2005: 93). When, for example, a person is tortured, it is the whole person, expressed in his or her body and volition of the mind, which is being violated from the perspective of human dignity. Furthermore, if a human being is sold (or sells himself or herself) into slavery for a price, it is not just his or her body that is sold but the whole person.[10] But this again would undermine the entire network of inherent human dignity because the integrity of the human body and every important volition of the mind of a person, which represent this person, have an immeasurable value which cannot, and should not, be measured financially. Consequently, it is necessary to reject any understanding of anthropological dualism in order to protect a genuine understanding of the inherent dignity of every human life.

What is more, since every part of a whole human person, including his or her body, is an intrinsic, interdependent, functional component of an overarching intergraded unity with inherent dignity, the moral value of the body's elements is similar to that of the whole body and cannot be measured financially. This means that if a whole body cannot have a price, then neither can any of its integrated elements making any possible sale of human organs for transplantation unethical (MacKellar 2014: 53–71).

In short, a person is a unified whole, a holism, and as such can be considered as a psychosomatic unity or an 'embodied mind' and an 'en-minded body'.

Inherent human dignity and the new eugenics

Reproductive eugenics can be defined as strategies or decisions aimed at affecting, in a manner which is considered to be positive, the genetic heritage of a child, a community or humanity in general (MacKellar and Bechtel 2014: 3). In this regard, it is worth noting that such procedures were comprehensively rejected after the Second World War as being completely unethical. But with their return into mainstream bioethics, another front has now opened up against the concept of inherent human dignity.

Of course, it is possible to ask what is ethically wrong in making sure that no children with short and very difficult lives of suffering are brought into existence. In response to such a question, however, it is important to recognize that it is difficult to see how parents can decide to only have certain kinds of children without making a value judgement that some children are less desirable. In other words, suggesting that choice should be available to make sure that certain kinds of children are not brought into existence may mean that there is such a thing as a 'life unworthy of life' in society[11] while indirectly agreeing that a hierarchical or unequal value can exist between human beings. As the Argentinean legal ethicist Roberto Andorno explains:

> In reality eugenic ideology presupposes stepping from a 'worthiness of life' culture to a 'quality of life' culture, in other words, to the idea that not every life is worthy of being lived, or to put it more bluntly, that there are some lives that do not have any worth. (2010: 139–140, my translation)

Of course, it is possible to argue, as does the 2017 US Academies report entitled *Human Genome Editing: Science, Ethics, and Governance*, that 'unconditional love for a disabled child once born and respect for all people who are born with or who develop disabilities are not incompatible with intervening to avert disease and disability prior to birth or conception' (2017: 97). But the report does not explain how or why any deliberate discrimination of possible future persons with a disability can be seen as acceptable before birth while suddenly becoming unacceptable after birth. Indeed, it is irrational to maintain that certain possible future persons should not exist while, at the same time, disagreeing that some persons, who exist at present, should not have been brought into existence. In a civilized society, all persons are considered to be equal in value and worth and nobody can say to anybody else that they should not have existed. With the new reproductive eugenic procedures, however, it would be possible to say that some presently existing individuals should not have existed which very much denies their equality in value and worth.

In a way, the US Academy report is projecting certain possible future lives into reality in order to make a decision about which ones should come into existence based solely on quality of life arguments and aspects of non-inherent dignity.

But it cannot then maintain, once the future has become a reality, that the lives of all existing persons should have existed. Moreover, those who are deciding between which possible future persons to bring into existence are basing such choices on their experiences and perceptions of similar persons who already exist. No real deliberate decision ever takes place without being informed by reality. Thus, as the Dutch ethicist Hans Reinders explains, it is more than likely that 'in any given case, the only reasonable answer to the question of why a disabled child should not be born is by reference to what one thinks about the lives of people living with the same disorder' (2000: 8).

It follows that when parents decide that only a certain kind of child should be brought into existence, based solely on genetics factors, this can only mean making a eugenic choice and preferring one possible future child over another. In this way, there is a very real sense that such a decision is based on the perceived quality of a life and not on the equal worthiness and inherent dignity of all lives. Moreover, the indirect message being given to persons, who have already been born with the same disorder, is that they should also not have existed.[12] This is clearly discriminatory and would undermine the inherent equality of all human persons in society regardless of their state of health. Indeed, many individuals who were brought into existence with a disability from the very beginning may consider this condition as an existential part of their very identity. This is in contrast to individuals who may have become disabled later in life and who may not associate their very existence with this condition. Indeed, from an ethical perspective, any use of a procedure seeking to treat a disorder in an already existing individual is completely different and would not undermine the network of inherent dignity.

In short, it is imperative for society to value equally each and every human individual without eugenic selection and preconditions. In the same way, it is the reason why a civilized society must welcome into existence all possible future persons independently of their biological or other characteristics such as their genetic qualities or disorders.

Of course, it is possible to challenge this statement by emphasizing that certain forms of prenatal eugenic selection, such as abortions for certain forms of disability, are already taking place without any perceived damage to the equality between persons with the same disability. But these procedures are in effect already sending the message that all persons are not equal in value and that some should not have been brought into existence. And the more the vulnerable edifice of equality in civilized society is undermined or eroded by decisions that weaken its very foundations, the more likely it is that this equality will eventually collapse.

Conclusions

Unfortunately, the secular belief in the concept of inherent human dignity in bioethics has come under intense criticism recently. At the same time, and as the above examples demonstrate, the very existence of the concept is being seriously undermined. This is because the important notion of the inherent value and worth of living beings is often overlooked or misunderstood when it competes against new procedures which are considered to be beneficial and/or able to increase autonomy (Beyleveld et al. 2009: 663). But a society which no longer believes in the full inherent dignity of persons cannot offer any real argument against the taking of life of those who do not have certain characteristics such as those who do not have the capacity for rational autonomy. It becomes a society that has lost its trust in the inherent value and meaning of life and cannot comprehend why it should be endured.

Looking at the state of the culture of American medicine in 1949, the US physician Leo Alexander (1905–1985) warned that there was a certain kind of inevitable progression to the disappearance of civilized behaviour. This begins by recognizing the pragmatic use of biomedical developments and then continues by discarding traditional moral values in its self-confidence of what can be achieved but always ends in a moral and ethical wasteland (Alexander 1949: 39–47).

Society then becomes a wilderness where the value of some human lives is purely subjective and relative. Where some can increasingly be considered as being of poor or even substandard quality and where it is possible to grade the worth of every human life to reflect its degree of usefulness and meaning. In this case, a society based on equal rights and equal worth of all individuals cannot exist. Indeed, there would be no reason to even seek to save the life of an individual if a society eventually undermined inherent dignity to such an extent that it no longer considered this life as having any real value.

But if inherent human dignity is constantly being undermined and even attacked, what other fundamental principle can civilized society be founded upon? Equality? But equality of what? The answer can only be inherent dignity, and it is this idea that is reflected in Article 1 of the UN's Universal Declaration of Human Rights which states: 'All human beings are born free and equal in dignity and rights.'

This means that a responsible benevolent and compassionate society must continue to affirm and defend the position that the lives of all its members have equal and full inherent dignity even though persons may be aged, dependent on others or may have lost their autonomy. This is also why the EU's Charter of Fundamental Rights insists so clearly in Article 1: 'Human dignity is inviolable. It must be respected and protected.'

Thus, it is vital in bioethics to believe that all individuals have the same full inherent dignity which enables a just and civilized society to exist in a spirit of solidarity – a responsible, civilized and value-giving society which continues to equally affirm and defend the worth, value, meaning and richness of the lives of all its members.

Notes

1   The concept of inviolability, here, is used in both a descriptive (it cannot) and normative (it should not) sense.

2   The concept of 'inherent' human dignity has sometimes been used alongside 'intrinsic' human dignity, although the meanings are slightly different. The concept of what is 'inherent' reflects a Latin verb meaning 'to stick in' or 'adhere to'. When something is inherent, it means that it is permanent and is an essential or characteristic attribute. It is reflected in concepts such as inherence which expresses a quality which is embedded and vested in a person or group or attached to the ownership of a property.
    On the other hand, what is 'intrinsic' reflects a Latin word meaning 'inwards'. It expresses a meaning of what belongs to the being or object 'from the inside' or from its interior. Thus, what is intrinsic belongs naturally to a being and is essential to it. In bioethical discourse, however, the concepts of 'inherent' and 'intrinsic' reflect very similar meanings. In the rest of this chapter, therefore, the term 'inherent human dignity' will be used since it is mentioned in the UN's Universal Declaration of Human Rights.

3   The concept of 'inherent human dignity' has been endorsed by a number of other legislative documents such as the German constitution (1949).

4   Inherent human dignity is relational and also self-relational. For example, in both the Hebrew Bible and the New Testament there is an emphasis on loving one's neighbour as oneself.

5   *Lord Hoffmann in Airedale NHS Trust v Bland* (1993) AC 689, 826. Quoted in Hale (2009: 106).

6   Of course, for all Abrahamic faiths, it is impossible for persons (considered as being piles of dust without God) to give value to themselves or others in any meaningful way. This is why, in these faiths, God's love for human beings is their only true and real source of value. Thus, God is the origin of inherent value, worth and dignity in human beings. And, here again, God's immeasurable love is like the source

of electricity passing through the network and making it come 'alive' with love between all the members of the network.

On this account, it is arguably the influence of Christianity in many countries supporting the equal and inalienable image of God, present in all human beings because he created them out of his love, that established the idea of the universal nature of inherent dignity. This is shared by all while, at the same time, needing to be respected by all.

7   *Lords Hansard*, 2002, Volume No. 641 Part No. 14, Column 1327.

8   Though body and mind worked independently, Descartes suggested a point of communion between the two in the pineal gland.

9   Similarly, the ancient belief of Manichaeism, present in the early Christian world between the third and the sixth centuries, taught an elaborate dualistic cosmology in which there was a good spiritual world of light and an evil material world of darkness.

10 Moreover, if a person is molested in the street, it is not just his or her body that is molested but the whole person. Similarly, the very fact that it is a person who consents to an operation on his or her arm means that this arm belongs to the whole person.

11 The phrase 'a life unworthy of life' (in German 'Lebensunwertes Leben') first occurred in the title of a book by German psychiatrist Alfred Hoche and lawyer Karl Binding, *Die Freigabe der Vernichtung Lebensunwerten Lebens*, Verlag von Felix Meiner in Leipzig, 1920.

12 For clear evidence of the feeling of offence being taken by persons with disability in such a situation, it is useful to refer to the disability witnesses in the prominent French court case of Nicolas Perruche. Public Hearings of the French Senate on the 18th of December 2001 relating to the jurisprudence of the 'Perruche' case.

References

Alexander, L. (1949), 'Medical Science under Dictatorship', *New England Journal of Medicine*, 241 (2): 39–47.

Andorno, R. (2001), 'The Paradoxical Notion of Human Dignity', *Rivista Internazionale di filosofia del diritto*, 78: 151–168.

Andorno, R. (2009), 'Human Dignity and Human Rights as a Common Ground for a Global Bioethics', *Journal of Medicine and Philosophy*, 34 (2009): 223–240.

Andorno, R. (2010), 'Fondements philosophiques et culturels de l'eugénisme sélectif', in J. Laffitte and I. Carrasco de Paula (eds), *La génétique, au risque de l'eugénisme?* 129–141, Paris: Edifa-Mame.

Andrews, L. (1986), 'My Body, My Property', *Hastings Center Report*, 16 (5): 28–38.

Badura-Lotter, G. and M. Düwell (2011), 'Chimeras and Hybrids – How to Approach Multifaceted Research?', in K. Hug and G. Hermerén (eds), *Translational Stem Cell Research*, 193–209, Totowa, NJ: Humana Press.

Banchoff, T. (2011), *Embryo Politics*, Ithaca, NY: Cornell University Press.

Bennett, R. and J. Harris (2007), 'Reproductive Choice', in R. Rhodes, L. P. Francis and A. Silver (eds), *The Blackwell Guide to Medical Ethics*, 201–219, Oxford: Blackwell Publishing.

Beyleveld, D., T. Finnegan and S. D. Pattinson (2009), 'The Regulation of Hybrids and Chimeras in the UK', in J. Taupitz, and M. Weschka (eds), *CHIMBRIDS: Chimeras and Hybrids in Comparative European and International Research*, 645–666, Berlin: Springer.

Cochrane, A. (2010), 'Undignified Bioethics', *Bioethics*, 24 (5): 234–241.

De Melo-Martín, I. (2008), 'Chimeras and Human Dignity', *Kennedy Institute of Ethics Journal*, 18 (4): 331–346.

Descartes, R. (1984 [1641]), 'Meditations on First Philosophy (1641)', in *The Philosophical Writings of René Descartes*, vol. 2, trans. J. Cottingham, R. Stoothoff and D. Murdoch, 1–62, Cambridge: Cambridge University Press.

Descartes, R. (1991[1637]), 'Discourse on the Method', in *Descartes: Selected Philosophical Writings*, trans. J. Cottingham, R. Stoothoff and D. Murdoch, New York: Cambridge University Press.

Ethikrat, Deutscher (2011), *Mensch-Tier-Mischwesen in der Forschung: Stellungnahme*, Berlin: Deutscher Ethikrat.

Garcia, E. and H. Jochemsen (2005), 'Ethics of Stem Cell Research', in H. Jochemsen (ed.), *Human Stem Cells*, 63–125, Jerusalem: Prof. Dr. Lindenboom Institute and Business Ethics Center of Jerusalem.

Hale, B. (2009), 'Dignity', *Journal of Social Welfare & Family Law*, 31 (2): 101–108.

Johnston, J. and C. Eliot (2003), 'Chimeras and "Human Dignity"', *The American Journal of Bioethics*, 3 (3): 6–8.

Kass, L. R. (2002), *Life, Liberty and the Defense of Dignity: The Challenge for Bioethics*, New York: Encounter Books.

Kirchhoffer, D. G. (2013), *Human Dignity in Contemporary Ethics*, London, Amherst, NY: Teneo Press.

Kirchhoffer, D. G. and K. Dierickx (2011), 'Human Dignity and Human Tissue: A Meaningful Ethical Relationship?', *Journal of Medical Ethics*, 37: 552–556.

Kraynak, R. P. and G. Tinder eds (2003), *In Defense of Human Dignity: Essays for Our Times*, Notre Dame, IN: University of Notre Dame Press.

MacKellar, C. (2014), 'Human Organ Markets and Inherent Human Dignity', *The New Bioethics*, 20 (1): 53–71.

MacKellar, C. and C. Bechtel, eds (2014), *The Ethics of the New Eugenics*, New York, Oxford: Berghahn Books.

MacKellar, C. and D. A. Jones, eds (2012), *Chimera's Children*, London: Continuum.

Mattson, D. and S. Clark (2011), 'Human Dignity in Concept and Practice', *Policy Sciences*, 44: 303–319.

Meilaender, G. (2009), *Neither Beast nor God: The Dignity of the Human Person*, Encounter Broadsides, New York: Encounter Books.

Michael, L. (2013), *Defining Dignity: What Is Dignity and Does It Matter?*, Dissertation for an MA in Bioethics, (Regnum: 124499), Twickenham: St Mary's University.

Neal, M. (2012), 'Not Gods But Animals: Human Dignity and Vulnerable Subjecthood', *Liverpool Law Review*, 23 (3): 177–200.

Nordenfeld, L. (2004), 'The Varieties of Dignity', *Health Care Analysis*, 12 (2): 69–81.

Pullman, D. (2010), 'Human Non-persons, Feticide, and the Erosion of Dignity', *Bioethical Inquiry*, 7: 353–364.

Reinders, H. S. (2000), *The Future of the Disabled in Liberal Society*, Notre Dame, IN: University of Notre Dame Press.

Rendtorff, J. D. (2002), 'Basic Ethical Principles in European Bioethics and Biolaw: Autonomy, Dignity, Integrity and Vulnerability – Towards a Foundation of Bioethics and Biolaw', *Medicine, Health Care and Philosophy*, 5: 235–244.

Riley, S. (2010), 'Human Dignity: Comparative and Conceptual Debates', *International Journal of Law in Context*, 6 (2): 1167–1138.

Smith, W. J. (2005), 'Is the World Ready for a Superboy? – or a Dogboy?', *Dallas Morning News*, 13 November.

Sulmasy, D. P. (2007), 'Human Dignity and Human Worth', in J. Malpas and N. Lickiss (eds), *Perspectives on Human Dignity: A Conversation*, 9–18, Dordrecht, The Netherlands: Springer.

Thiel, M-J. (2010), 'Human Dignity: Intrinsic or Relative Value?', *International Journal of Bioethics*, 21 (3): 51–62.

US National Academy of Sciences and National Academy of Medicine (2017), *Human Genome Editing: Science, Ethics, and Governance*, Washington, DC: The National Academies Press.

Warnock Report (1984), *Report of the Committee of Enquiry into Human Fertilisation and Embryology*, London: Her Majesty's Stationery Office.

Index